Ecology and German Realism

Studies in German Literature, Linguistics, and Culture

Ecology and German Realism

Poetics, Politics, and the Conquest of Nature

Alexander Robert Phillips

Rochester, New York

Copyright © 2025 Alexander Robert Phillips

All Rights Reserved. Except as permitted under current legislation, no part of this work may be photocopied, stored in a retrieval system, published, performed in public, adapted, broadcast, transmitted, recorded, or reproduced in any form or by any means, without the prior permission of the copyright owner.

First published 2025
by Camden House

Camden House is an imprint of Boydell & Brewer Inc.
668 Mt. Hope Avenue, Rochester, NY 14620, USA
and of Boydell & Brewer Limited
PO Box 9, Woodbridge, Suffolk IP12 3DF, UK
www.boydellandbrewer.com

Our Authorised Representative for product safety in the EU is
Easy Access System Europe - Mustamäe tee 50, 10621 Tallinn,
Estonia, gpsr.requests@easproject.com

ISBN-13: 978-1-64014-201-5

Library of Congress Cataloging-in-Publication Data
Names: Phillips, Alexander Robert, author.
Title: Ecology and German realism : poetics, politics, and the conquest of
    nature / Alexander Robert Phillips.
Description: Rochester, NY : Camden House, 2025. | Series: Studies in
    German literature, linguistics, and culture ; 251 | Includes bibliographical
    references and index.
Identifiers: LCCN 2024045681 (print) | LCCN 2024045682 (ebook) |
    ISBN 9781640142015 (hardback) | ISBN 9781805436065 (pdf) | ISBN
    9781805436072 (epub)
Subjects: LCSH: German literature—19th century—History and criticism. |
    Ecology in literature. | Realism in literature. | LCGFT: Literary criticism.
Classification: LCC PT134.E315 P45 2025 (print) | LCC PT134.E315
    (ebook) | DDC 831/.70936—dc23/eng/20250101
LC record available at https://lccn.loc.gov/2024045681
LC ebook record available at https://lccn.loc.gov/2024045682

The publisher has no responsibility for the continued existence
or accuracy of URLs for external or third-party internet websites
referred to in this book, and does not guarantee that any content
on such websites is, or will remain, accurate or appropriate.

In Memory of My Father,
Benjamin Wright Phillips III

Contents

List of Illustrations	ix
Acknowledgments	xi
List of Abbreviations	xiii
Introduction: Industrialization, Environmental Degradation, and the Aesthetics of Realism	1
1: Environmental Counterfictions: The Ethical Domination of Nature in Adalbert Stifter	33
2: The Styx Flows through Arcadia: Environmental Depredation and Aesthetic Reflection in Wilhelm Raabe's Late Fiction	72
3: Hydrologic Engineering, Social Change, and the Persistence of the Fantastic in Theodor Storm's *Der Schimmelreiter*	103
4: The Poetics of an Emerging Anthropocene: Theodor Fontane's *Der Stechlin*	128
Conclusion: The Nature of Realism	152
Bibliography	159
Index	173

List of Illustrations

1   Map of Cologne, 1807/08, from "Topographical Survey of the Rhineland," also known as the "Tranchot Map" (compiled 1801–28).   13

2   Map of Cologne, 1850, from "Preliminary Prussian Land Survey" (compiled 1836–50).   14

3   Cologne, 1893, from "New Prussian Land Survey" (compiled 1891–1912).   14

Acknowledgments

THREE WEEKS TO the day after I matriculated in graduate school, Lehman Brothers collapsed, triggering the 2008 financial crisis. While I did not know it at the time, the chain of events it set off would take me to Europe and ultimately India, where I was finally able to escape the cycle of precarity and find a position secure enough to complete this book. To my colleagues in the Department of English at Ashoka University, धन्यवाद : This book has benefited in ways large and small from the many conversations that I have had with everyone in the department over the years. Alexandra Verini, Johannes Burgers, Aparna Chaudhuri, Mandakini Dubey, Mali Skotheim, and Saikat Majumdar all read and provided valuable feedback on parts of this manuscript. Jonathan Gil Harris opened a door when I needed it most and expected it least. This book has benefited from other opportunities he has created for me. Thank you also to the many students I had the pleasure of working with at Ashoka, not in the least for giving me my groove back. Working as an American Germanist at an English Department in India has helped me to see my work well beyond its Germanophone contexts, which in turn has shaped this book. I am grateful to everyone at Ashoka for helping me to broaden my horizons.

At Camden House, I am grateful to Jim Walker for his astute feedback and enthusiasm for the book. Thank you also to the reviewers who read the manuscript and gave such helpful guidance. The faith that Anette Schwarz, Paul Fleming, and Patrizia McBride at Cornell University had gave me the faith to pursue this project in the first place. Beyond that, their guidance continues to reverberate in my writing and my teaching. Financial support for the initial research came from the David R. Atkinson Center for a Sustainable Future at Cornell, the Cornell Society for the Humanities, and the Cornell Graduate School. Their support made possible work in the Stadtarchiv Braunschweig, the Theodor-Fontane-Archiv in Potsdam, the Stadtmuseum Berlin, and a very memorable visit to the Raabe-Haus: Literaturzentrum. I am also grateful to the staff at those institutions for their help and for the work they do generally to advance knowledge and appreciation of these authors in the broader community. I had the opportunity to share some of these ideas with faculty and students at the Linnéuniversitetet in Växjö, Sweden, in January 2023. Thank you especially to Eleonor Marcussen for the invitation and the work that made that visit possible. Sections of chapter 1 were published in the volume *German Ecocriticism in the Anthropocene* and an earlier version of chapter 2 appeared in the journal *Interdisciplinary Studies in Literature and Environment* 24, no. 4 (2017).

The work on this book about environmental degradation took place against the backdrop of landscapes that had been shaped by processes similar to those discussed in this book, and as such, they also deserve acknowledgment. The final phase of work took place in Delhi. The blanket of smog that descends on us after the monsoon rains end and the winds die down is very real, but so is the work that people here do for a healthier and more just urban environment. The middle phase happened in Düsseldorf, steps from the Rhine, and it began while I was living in Ithaca and later Norwich, New York. During a set he performed at Cornell in October 2011, comedian Jon Stewart charmingly quipped: "On the way up I didn't pass anything I couldn't milk." But Ithaca is a city whose idyllic, small-town appearance belies the toxic legacies of its industrial history. Ithaca and Norwich are also situated in the homelands of the Cayuga and the Oneida people of the Haudenosaunee Confederacy, whose ongoing histories determine the landscapes that had such presence as I was first thinking about environmental history and ecoaesthetics.

The middle phase of writing this book coincided with several difficult years in the academic precariat under management openly hostile to faculty labor. I was nevertheless fortunate to find friends who supported and guided me, especially Ronald Schlundt and Amy Peaceman, Barbara Gayle and Ray Price, Andrew Sola, and Chizoba Udeorji. In the late phase of writing this book, I got by with more than a little help from my friends. Alexandra Verini (again) and Aagman Baury deserve special acknowledgment here. A very big thank you goes to Anwesh Pokkuluri. My feline companions, Bhuta, Rübezahl, and Sakkhi enliven everything.

Finally, the work on this book coincided with a period of loss in my life: my grandparents William and Eugenie Austermann, as well as Cynthia and (albeit more distantly) Robert Pile. I said farewell to both Ingeborg and Babette, who accompanied me from the beginning. And, most painfully of all, I lost my father, Benjamin Wright Phillips III. I may have the credentials, but he was the Germanophile, and I deeply wish I could have shown him this book. It is dedicated with love to his memory instead.

Ithaca—Düsseldorf—New Delhi

List of Abbreviations

BA	Wilhelm Raabe, *Sämtliche Werke: Braunschweiger Ausgabe*. Edited by Karl Hoppe. 26 vols. Göttingen: Vandenhoek und Ruprecht, 1966–94.
GBA	Theodor Fontane, *Große Brandenburger Ausgabe*. Edited by Gotthard Erler, Gabriele Radecke, and Heinrich Detering. 44 vols. in 12 parts. Berlin: Aufbau Verlag, 1994–.
HFA	Theodor Fontane, *Werke, Schriften und Briefe*. Edited by Walter Keitel and Helmuth Nürnberger. 22 vols. in 4 parts. Munich: Carl Hanser, 1975 (Hanser Fontane Ausgabe).
HKG	Adalbert Stifter, *Werke und Briefe: Historsich-kritische Gesamtausgabe*. Edited by Alfred Doppler, Wolfgang Frühwald, Hartmut Laufhütte, et al. 40 vols. in 10 parts. Stuttgart: Kohlhammer, 1978–.
ISLE	*Interdisciplinary Studies in Literature and Environment*
VASILO	*Vierteljahresschrift des Adalbert-Stifter-Instituts des Landes Oberösterreich.*

Introduction: Industrialization, Environmental Degradation, and the Aesthetics of Realism

SOUTH OF BONN at the western edge of the Siebengebirge range, the Drachenfels entices the tourist with a panoramic view of the Lower Middle Rhine Valley. Looking south from the modern viewing platform one can see the Laach Lake volcano, the eruption of which in the transition from the Pleistocene to the Holocene caused massive ecological disruption throughout the Rhine basin. Above loom the ruins of the twelfth-century Castle Drachenfels, while below barges ply their way up and down the Rhine, Europe's busiest waterway. And to the north, beyond the neogothic Schloss Drachenburg, the Lower Rhine conurbation fans out into the distance.

In addition to the view, an aura of legend draws tourists to the Drachenfels. According to tradition, it was here that Siegfried slew the dragon Fafnir and bathed in his blood, becoming all but invincible save for the spot on his back where an errant linden leaf fatefully landed. As with so many traditions, the association of Siegfried with the Drachenfels is of relatively modern provenance, having been first documented in 1818.[1] Those early decades of the nineteenth century were a time when the site captured the European Romantic imagination. J. M. W. Turner depicted it in his 1817 painting "Rolandseck, Nonnenwerth, and Drachenfels," and it is the subject of Lord Byron's 1816 poem "The Castled Crag of Drachenfels." But by the time the century was out, the Drachenfels—"Dragon Rock" in English—had been transformed by a

---

1   See Elmar Scheuren, "The Rhine as a Symbol: Aspects, Meanings and Functionalization of a Memory Landscape," in *The Rhine: National Tensions, Romantic Visions*, ed. Manfred Beller and Joep Leerssen (Leiden: Brill, 2017), 137–38. The association with Siegfried is described on the castle's webpage at "Drachenfels," Der Drachenfels: Ein Sagenhafter Ort, accessed December 23, 2020, https://www.der-drachenfels.de/der-drachenfels. The Nibelungenhalle, an art nouveau structure from 1913, also stands at the site and celebrates Richard Wagner's treatment of the Siegfried legend in *Der Ring des Nibelungen*. For a timeline of the Drachenfels Railway see "Geschichte: Die lange Historie der ältesten Zahnradbahn Deutschlands – der Drachenfelsbahn," Drachenfelsbahn Königswinter, accessed September 9, 2024, https://www.drachenfelsbahn.de/bahngeschichte.

technology with a salamandrine nature to match its name. On July 17, 1883, the Drachenfels Railway commenced operations. Twenty-three thousand cubic meters of earth were removed to make way for a coal-burning machine that could ferry tourists up and down the slope, obviating the need to make the ascent by animal power or one's own two legs.

Today, the opening of the Drachenfels Railway might seem like a minor event in the history of the fossil fuel economy. But for Ernst Rudorff, it was a sign of all that had gone wrong in the human relationship to nature in the era of German industrialization. Three years before its grand opening, Rudorff singled out the plans for the Drachenfels Railway in the opening of his essay "Über das Verhältnis des modernen Lebens zur Natur" (On the Relation of Modern Life to Nature, 1880), a jeremiad against the toll industrial modernity was taking on German land- and cityscapes. Rudorff, who went on to found the Bund Heimatschutz (League for Homeland Protection) in 1904, decried the fact that a railway tunnel now punctured the iconic Loreley rock upriver from the Drachenfels, that real estate speculation had led to the destruction of Nuremberg's historic city walls, and that throughout Germany creeks were redirected into straight channels, while landscapes had been divided into grids of forests and fields.[2] And yet, he argued, it was at this moment of destruction that a new aesthetic sensibility for nature was emerging, one that, in his view, was itself a factor in further destruction inasmuch as it was embodied by that most dreadful figure of modern travel: the tourist, whose search for "alle möglichen Schönheiten und Merkwürdigkeiten" (anything beautiful and interesting) leaves a "fatale Beigeschmack der Geschäftsmäßigkeit im Genießen" (dreadful aftertaste of commercialism in enjoyment).[3]

Rudorff's attack on modern tourism is only one dimension of what is ultimately a larger ecoaesthetic argument. The fact that Rudorff focuses on the aesthetic in no way trivializes the environmental politics. When it comes to ecology, nothing is "merely" aesthetic. For one thing, it is through aesthetics that objective facts become meaningful relative to embodied human experience. To say, for instance, that the Drachenfels is "degraded" once a part of it has been cut away so that a machine belching particulate matter and carbon dioxide can course its way up and down the hillside is to pronounce on the site's beauty, harmony, and balance, that is, its aesthetic integrity. For Rudorff, the larger ecoaesthetic problem was not limited to aesthetics in terms of perception and judgment, but also posed a problem for literary production.

---

2   Ernst Rudorff, "Über das Verhältnis des modernen Lebens zur Natur," *Preußische Jahrbücher* 45 (1880): 261–62.
3   Rudorff, "Über das Verhältnis des modernen Lebens zur Natur," 263. All translations are mine unless otherwise indicated.

Im Plauenschen Grund bei Dresden, dessen Lieblichkeit einst Wilhelm Müller zu seinen reizenden Frühlingsgedichten begeisterte, ist im Lauf der Jahre ein Wald von Fabrikschornsteinen aus dem Bodem emporgewachsen, die mit ihrem Qualm allen Duft der Poesie längst hinweggeräuchert haben, deren garstige, himmelhoch hinausgereckte Geradlinigkeit allem Malerischen Hohn spricht.

[In the Plauen Valley near Dresden, whose charm once inspired Wilhelm Müller to write his loveliest spring poetry, a forest of factory smokestacks has sprouted out of the ground, the fumes of which have long since smoked out any scent of poesy, and whose horrible, sky-scraping linearity makes a mockery of the picturesque.[4]]

Industrial sprawl is an aesthetic affront through and through for Rudorff. The artificial straightness of the smokestacks mocks the picturesque by resembling the trees that once stood there, but also denying the visual pleasure trees with their natural twists and curves might give. But while the smokestacks destroy a source of visual pleasure, the olfactory might be the graver offense. That is because "poesy," which Rudorff imagines here as an atmospheric quality, is both a feeling the place evokes as well as a material quality of the air that the stench of modern industry has driven off, making, in turn, actual verse poetry impossible. "Das Maschinenwesen in Verse zu bringen, wird Niemandem beifallen; wenigstens würden die Verse keine Poesie ergeben" (Nobody would think to put the world of machines into verse, at the very least such verses would not amount to poesy), Rudorff claimed.[5] His answer to the challenge "the world of machines" poses is to fall back on *völkisch* mythologizing: "In dem innigen und tiefen Gefühl für die Natur liegen recht eigentlich die Wurzeln des germanischen Wesens" (The roots of Germanic being lie in the deep and innermost feeling for nature), a feeling that is, according to Rudorff, at the heart of both German music and German literary history from the myths of Wodan down to the poetry of Joseph von Eichendorff.[6] This turn in the argument connects the aesthetic back to the political, insofar as the "feeling for nature" distinguishes "Germanic being" from other kinds of ethnic "being." Such arguments reflect Rudorff's reactionary tendencies, and while it would be far too facile to draw a straight line between 1880s conservative conservationism and 1930s National Socialist "blood and soil" rhetoric, it is a reminder that environmentalism never was an inherently liberatory politics.[7]

4   Rudorff, "Über das Verhältnis des modernen Lebens zur Natur," 261.
5   Rudorff, "Über das Verhältnis des modernen Lebens zur Natur," 269.
6   Rudorff, "Über das Verhältnis des modernen Lebens zur Natur," 276.
7   For an evaluation of the continuities and the case for emphasizing the discontinuities between the Wilhelmine-era Heimatschutz movement and National

4 ♦ Introduction

Rudorff's essay raises the very problems of environmental politics and aesthetics that are the subject of this book. The transformations of the landscape he lists, from railway construction to river "correction" to the cultivation of forests, are instances of the production of social nature. Social nature is nature that is "defined, delimited, and even physically reconstituted by different societies, often in order to serve specific, and usually dominant social interests."[8] The natures we encounter in the works of Adalbert Stifter, Wilhelm Raabe, Theodor Storm, and Theodor Fontane—canonical authors of German realism who will be the focus of this study—all have some sort of social character, having been transformed by human labor and the production process. The cultivation of fields, forests, and gardens in Stifter's stories serves to establish and maintain social hierarchies. In the works of Wilhelm Raabe, pollution and urban sprawl are the primary ways in which industrial capital transforms nature in its own image. The "reclaiming" of arable land from the sea in Theodor Storm's *Der Schimmelreiter* (The Rider on the White Horse, 1888) is connected to the ascendency of the bourgeoisie, while the telegraph wires, glassworks, and exotic plants that appear in and around Lake Stechlin in Theodor Fontane's *Der Stechlin* (The Stechlin, 1898), are all manifestations of global capitalist networks. In none of these examples is the production of nature a benign process. David Blackbourn, who

---

Socialist ideology, see William Rollins, *A Greener Vision of Home: Cultural Politics and Environmental Reform in the German Heimatschutz Movement, 1904–1918* (Ann Arbor: University of Michigan Press, 1997), 14–19; and Franz-Josef Brüggemeier, Mark Cioc, and Thomas Zeller, "Introduction," in *How Green Were the Nazis? Nature, Environment, and Nation in the Third Reich*, ed. Franz-Josef Brüggemeier, Mark Cioc, and Thomas Zeller (Athens: Ohio University Press, 2005), 5–11. For a discussion of Rudorff's politics specifically, see Rollins, *A Greener Vision of Home*, 74–79.

8   Noel Castree, "Socializing Nature: Theory, Practice, and Politics," in *Social Nature: Theory, Practice, and Politics*, ed. Noel Castree and Bruce Braun (Malden: Blackwell, 2001), 3. "Social nature" can be "historical nature," that is, actual ecosystems as they exist on Earth at given points in time, or abstract nature, that is, as Jason Moore defines it, "the family of processes through which states and capitalists map, identify, quantify, measure, and code human and extra-human natures in service to capital accumulation." Historical natures "are cause, consequence, and unfolding condition of successive long centuries of accumulation." Jason W. Moore, *Capitalism in the Web of Life: Ecology and the Accumulation of Capital* (London: Verso, 2015), 198. The observation that "social space is a social product" is developed most forcefully in Henri Lefebvre, *The Production of Space*, trans. Donald Nicholson-Smith (Malden: Blackwell, 1991), 1–67, here 26. Lefebvre observes that when it comes to nature, even as the social character becomes visible "this typical quality of visibility does not, however, imply decipherability of the inherent social relations. On the contrary, the analysis of these relations has become harder and more paradoxical." Lefebvre, *The Production of Space*, 83.

refs to the second half of the nineteenth century as the "golden age" of "the conquest of nature" in the German-speaking countries, axiomatically observes that "the human domination of nature has a lot to tell us about the nature of human domination."[9] These authors may not have been "environmentalists" in the ways in which we understand the term today, but in their representations of social nature they take up the core problem of environmental politics: who has what claim to what nature.

In connecting the social production of nature to the conditions of possibility for literary production, Rudorff was channeling a significant problem in literary discourse in Germany in the latter half of the nineteenth century, that is, how, or indeed whether, modern industrial capitalism could lend itself to aesthetic representation. In mid-nineteenth-century discourses on realism, this problem often appears in terms of intangible social and political relations. Borrowing from Georg Wilhelm Friedrich Hegel, Friedrich Theodor Vischer, in his influential treatise *Aesthetik, oder Wissenschaft des Schönen* (Aesthetics, or the Study of the Beautiful, 1846–57) lists the alienation of the state from the individual, bureaucratization, and mechanization as the developments that make up a modern "prosaic" reality from which the novel form must wrest "the poetic."[10] Such abstract processes, however, inscribe themselves in very material ways on the environment. To borrow Rudorff's examples, smokestacks embody mechanization, while grid-like landscapes can be traced back to bureaucratization. From this perspective, industrialization and its environmental consequences have simply destroyed the conditions of possibility for "Poesie" (poesy). For Stifter, Raabe, Storm, and Fontane, by contrast, the challenge environmental degradation poses

---

9   David Blackbourn, *The Conquest of Nature: Water, Landscape, and the Making of Modern Germany* (New York: Norton, 2006), 7.

10   Friedrich Theodor Vischer, *Aesthetik, oder Wissenschaft des Schönen* (Stuttgart: Carl Mäckes, 1846), 1304–5. More recently, Sabine Becker's history of German realism places the accent on the movement as reflecting a specifically bourgeois consciousness: "Es handelt sich um eine Bewegung für die sozialhistorische und soziokulturelle Kriterien ebenso bedeutsam waren wie ästhetische. Sie ist das Produkt der gesellschaftspolitischen Konstellationen, ist das Resultat einer bürgerlichen Gesellschaft, wie sie sich in der zweiten Hälfte des 19. Jahrhunderts entwickelt und präsentiert hat" (We are dealing with a movement for which socio-historical and socio-cultural criteria were just as important as aesthetic criteria. It is the product of socio-political constellations, the result of a bourgeois society as it had developed and presented itself in the second half of the nineteenth century). Sabine Becker, *Bürgerlicher Realismus: Literatur und Kultur im bürgerlichen Zeitalter 1848–1900* (Tübingen: A. Francke, 2003), 17. The material environment, by contrast, does factor explicitly into Gerhard Plumpe's history of German realism. See Gerhard Plumpe, "Einleitung," in *Bürgerlicher Realismus und Gründerzeit: 1848–1890*, ed. Edward McInnes and Gerhard Plumpe (Munich: Hanser, 1996), 23–24.

6 ♦ Introduction

turns out to be more generative. The argument of this book is that for each of these authors, environmental transformation becomes the very condition for their reflections on the aesthetic representation of reality, and as such constitutes a line of ecoaesthetic theorization developed in and through the fiction. The core conflict of German realism arises out of the fact that environmental degradation enters the worlds of the texts by virtue of realism's claim to mimesis, that is, to depict a world that is plausible by the standards of our own experiential reality. But literary realism also makes a claim to aesthetic status, to render that experiential reality "artistically" or "poetically" in a way that distinguishes literary realism from other realisms, such as that of the newspaper or the photograph.[11] Lilian Furst, for instance, sees the realist novel as being defined more by its truth claim, which inevitably privileges observation and experience over art.[12] But when observation introduces the signs of environmental degradation, they become, to borrow Mary Douglas's famous definition of pollution, "matter out of place" relative to literary realism's aesthetic claims.[13] Smog is ugly, polluted water smells bad, and urban sprawl paves over the very nature that Rudorff saw as the source of poetry.

The sheer pervasiveness of pollution, however, points to a different perspective than the normative one that sees pollution as too much of something in the wrong place.[14] As Heather Sullivan points out, "Pollution has no place but rather is everyplace" constituting a "dirty traffic" through bodies and ecosystems.[15] Pollution and anthropogenic environmental transformation more broadly function in an analogous way for Stifter, Raabe, Storm, and Fontane: "out of place," but also everyplace, constitutive of each text and its particular realism, and thus ultimately aesthetically generative. Viewed from such a perspective, German realist aesthetics appears largely as an ecoaesthetics, a dimension that drives the dynamism and open-ended theoretical reflection on ecology and the status of artistic representation broadly within the literary texts. The contradictions the environmental thematic introduces do not necessarily mean that German realism is characterized by its "ideology and paradoxes," a "normed discourse that excludes otherness," as Robert Holub

11 See also Sabine Becker's discussion of the distinction between realism and naturalism and her discussion of the realist concept of art in *Bürgerlicher Realismus*, 117–23.

12 Lilian R. Furst, *All Is True: The Claims and Strategies of Realist Fiction* (Durham, NC: Duke University Press, 1995), 6.

13 Mary Douglas, *Purity and Danger: An Analysis of the Concepts of Pollution and Taboo* (London and New York: Routledge, 1992), 36.

14 See also Greg Garrard, *Ecocriticism*, 2nd ed (Abingdon: Routledge, 2012), 6.

15 Heather Sullivan, "Dirty Traffic and the Dark Pastoral in the Anthropocene: Narrating Refugees, Deforestation, and Melting Ice," *Literatur für Leser* 37, no. 2 (2014): 83.

argues.[16] We might consider, for instance, the position of Ebert Pfister, the narrator of Wilhelm Raabe's *Pfisters Mühle* (Pfister's Mill, 1884), who recounts how water pollution brought his family mill to financial ruin. At the opening of the novel he addresses the difficulty of writing literature in a world thoroughly marked by human environmental transformation when he observes that, unlike Christoph Martin Wieland a hundred years earlier, he could never set a fantastic epic in the Middle East because the region has since been covered in railways and telegraph wires. The obvious fact that *Pfisters Mühle* does get written and that its confrontation with the reality of nineteenth-century pollution, in this case, produces a work that Wieland could not have, points to the fact that the contradiction between environmental degradation and aesthetic status does not produce a story of failure. Nor is it a story of cynicism, of a bad faith will to the aesthetic in spite of the presence of the ugly, the smelly, or the toxic. Instead, the apparent paradoxes surrounding ecology and aesthetics within the realist texts are "part of the texts' own intrinsic strategies, of their own double, conflictual nature," as Eric Downing characterizes German realism.[17] In contrast to Downing's psychoanalytic account of a pattern of repetition that defines realism's conflictual nature, this book returns to the state of the material environments that the texts depict, but it shares with Downing the view that in so doing we can see "the self-conscious, somewhat self-deconstructive dimension that is intrinsic to realism, and almost inseparable from what we value as *literary* realism."[18]

Understanding the poetic reflections in each text as ecoaesthetic reflections means re-thinking the relation between the fiction and the historical realities of urban and industrial sprawl. At a superficial level German realism stands out for an almost studied avoidance of urban and industrial realities compared to other European realisms. Dickens had London, Flaubert Paris, Dostoevsky St. Petersburg. By contrast, Stifter had mountains and forests, Storm the Frisian coast, Raabe the lost idyllic garden hosting an "alternative community" of outsiders,[19] and Fontane an increasingly anachronistic aristocracy. Scholarship on German realism has a long history of taking this circumstance at face value. Erich Auerbach famously argued in his 1946 study *Mimesis* that the dearth of scenes depicting urban and industrial modernity was a result of the fact that German life "was much more provincial,

---

16   Robert C. Holub, *Reflections of Realism: Paradox, Norm, and Ideology in Nineteenth-Century German Prose* (Detroit: Wayne State University Press, 1991), 17.

17   Eric Downing, *Double Exposures: Repetition and Realism in Nineteenth-Century German Fiction* (Stanford, CA: Stanford University Press, 2000), 12.

18   Downing, *Double Exposures*, 13.

19   The term "alternative community" is Jeffrey Sammons's. See Jeffrey Sammons, *Wilhelm Raabe: The Fiction of the Alternative Community* (Princeton, NJ: Princeton University Press, 1987), 200–210, esp. 209–10.

8 ♦ Introduction

much more old-fashioned, much less 'contemporary.'"[20] The notion that German realism was a provincial realism borne out of a provincial reality persisted in scholarship in varying forms into the twenty-first century.[21] The argument has a corollary in German historiography. Here the thesis is that the German states were places of "relative backwardness" because economic growth was hindered by a lack of political unity, poor infrastructure, and a largely agrarian economy, circumstances that only began to be overcome with the formation of the Zollverein, or customs union, in 1834 and accelerated with the establishment of a politically centralized German Empire in 1871.

German historians in recent decades have complicated the "relative backwardness" thesis by pointing to growth trends in urbanization and sectors of the economy not connected to agriculture going back into the eighteenth century.[22] In German literary studies, likewise, more recent scholarship has challenged the notion that German realism was a provincial realism. Postcolonial critics have demonstrated the extent to which nineteenth-century global realities appear even in the most rural German

---

20 Erich Auerbach, *Mimesis: The Representation of Reality in Western Literature*, trans. Willard Trask (Princeton, NJ: Princeton University Press, 2003), 516.

21 See Auerbach, *Mimesis*, 516–19. The persistence of Auerbach's judgment is attested to more recently in Sabine Becker's overview of German realism: "In Analogie zu bürgerlichen Ideologemen reagiert [die Literatur] mit dem Rückzug in die familiär-private Sphäre, in die Vergangenheit oder in vorkapitalistische Naturräume—zu denken wäre etwa an Fontanes Junkerwelt, an Raabes vorindustrielle Biedermeierwelten oder Stifters ästhetizistische Scheinwelten; und dies ungeachtet der Forderung nach dem Realitätsbezug von Literatur, nach der programmatischen Verpflichtung, literarisches Geschehen in einen realistischen, also einen plausiblen, für die zeitgenössische Leserschaft wieder erkennbaren Lebenszusammenhang einzubinden" (Analogously to bourgeois ideologemes, [the literature] reacts by retreating into the familiar-private sphere, into the past, or pre-capitalist spaces of nature—we might think of Fontane's world of the Junker class, of Raabe's pre-industrial Biedermeier worlds, or Stifter's aestheticist world of appearances; and this in spite of the of the imperative that literature have a relation to reality, according to the programmatic obligation that what takes place in literature should be folded into realist, and thus plausible, life circumstances that a contemporary readership would recognize). Becker, *Bürgerlicher Realismus*, 42.

22 For a discussion of this thesis and critiques thereof see Robert Lee, "'Relative Backwardness' and Long-Run Development: Economic, Demographic and Social Changes," in *Nineteenth-Century Germany: Politics, Culture and Society 1780–1918*, ed. John Breuilly (London: Edward Arnold, 2001), 66–67. On problems of periodizing German industrialization see Friedrich-Wilhelm Henning, *Die Industrialisierung in Deutschland 1800–1914* (Paderborn: Ferdinand Schöningh, 1973).

settings.[23] Arguing against a related thesis that sees German realism as focusing on human interiority at the expense of larger historical change, John Walker's *The Truth of Realism* makes the case that it is precisely in the representation of the characters' consciousnesses that we see social forces at work.[24] Looking back to the external world, John Lyon's *Out of Place* explores the experience of displacement in modernity and demonstrates how German realism was, in fact, pioneering in anticipating debates over place versus abstract space that continue today.[25] The analytic of "place," of course, has also been a central concern of much ecocriticism and environmental politics more generally, and it figures in this study in important ways.[26] While Lyon's book focuses on historical changes in the cityscapes in the German-speaking countries, the relations that produced those changes also affected places that did not experience a rise in population density or an increasing concentration of industrial production.

My own case against the argument that German realism was a provincial realism has to do with its very premises. It assumes that cities are the exclusive sites of modernity and progress, taking at face value the concentration of economic and political power in such places. It reifies cities as islands where historical development happens in opposition to the timeless rural life beyond the city limits. Distinctions between "the city" and "the country" were always ideological, but they become especially difficult to sustain in the nineteenth century, a time when city walls were coming down and suburbs coming up. Indeed, far from being "cosmopolitan," the conflation of "the rural" with "the provincial" is a perspective that reinscribes the very division of city and country that, as Karl Marx argues in *The German Ideology*, formed a key ideological basis for industrial production in the first place.[27] As we will see in the works included in this study, the social and economic relations of "modernity" shine through the veil of even the most seemingly idyllic Arcadianism. Privileging the urban likewise precludes the possibility of what Raymond Williams calls a "retrospective radicalism" that "is often made to do service as a critique of

---

23 For a discussion of the literary texts of the period and an overview of the postcolonial scholarship on them see Dirk Göttsche, Axel Dunker, and Gabriele Dürbeck, eds., *Handbuch Postkolonialismus und Literatur* (Stuttgart: Metzler, 2017), 250–59.

24 John Walker, *The Truth of Realism: A Reassessment of the German Novel 1830–1900* (London: Legenda, 2011), 1–16, esp. 2–3.

25 John B. Lyon, *Out of Place: German Realism, Displacement, and Modernity* (New York: Bloomsbury Academic, 2013), 3–4.

26 See especially Ursula K. Heise's critique of the analytic of place in her *Sense of Place and Sense of Planet: The Environmental Imagination of the Global* (Oxford: Oxford University Press, 2008).

27 Karl Marx and Friedrich Engels, *The German Ideology*, ed. C. J. Arthur (London: Lawrence Wishart, 1974), 68–69.

the capitalism of our own day: to carry humane feelings and yet ordinarily to attach them to a pre-capitalist and therefore irrecoverable world."[28] Of course, such "retrospective radicalism" might animate conservative critique as much as much as leftist critique, and can, as Williams points out, "leave the land to become the charter of explicit social reaction: in the defence of traditional property settlements, or in the offensive against democracy in the name of blood and soil."[29] Finally, the provincial realism thesis assumes that depicting the reality of modernity at least begins with picking cities and factories as subjects. But, as Bertolt Brecht once observed, "a photograph of the Krupp or AEG factories reveals practically nothing about these institutions."[30] There is no reason to think that if the authors of the period had only depicted more large cities and fewer small villages, more factories and fewer gardens, their works would have shown some greater truth about modernity.

The term "ecology" refers to the sets of relationships that structure natural systems, and thinking about German realist fiction in ecological terms, likewise, allows for a more holistic account of how the literature imagines industrialization as a socio-ecological reality. In the landscape transformations in the Hungarian Steppe in Stifter's *Brigitta* (1843, revised 1847), the exploitation of rivers and streams as industrial drainage pipes in Raabe's *Pfisters Mühle*, the socio-economic changes brought by the dike in Storm's *Der Schimmelreiter*, and the glass factories in the vicinity of Lake Stechlin in Fontane's *Der Stechlin*, we see places where capitalism arises out of the encounter between a shifting set of socio-economic relations on the one hand and given environments on the other. These supposedly remote places are, if anything, what Jason Moore labels "commodity frontiers," sites of appropriation that are actually central to the evolution of capitalism as a system that both produces and is produced in, through, and by the web of life.[31] To imagine that Stifter, Raabe, Storm, and Fontane occluded the realities of industrial production is to reduce the reality of industrialization to a phenomenon spatially contained within the factory or the industrial suburb. Such thinking was always reductive, but appears especially so today, when for instance the climate crisis confronts us with the global consequences of the local burning of fossil fuels.

In addition to being one of the primary ways through which Stifter, Raabe, Storm, and Fontane imagine the socio-ecological realities of their

---

28 Raymond Williams, *The Country and the City* (New York: Oxford University Press, 1973), 35–36.

29 Williams, *The Country and the City*, 36.

30 Bertolt Brecht, *Werke: Große kommentierte Berliner und Frankfurter Ausgabe*, ed. Werner Hecht (Frankfurt am Main: Suhrkamp, 1988–2000), vol. 21, 469.

31 Moore, *Capitalism in the Web of Life*, 53–54, 33–49.

times, the environmental thematic places them in a transnational and transhistorical genealogy of environmental aesthetics and politics. They lived at a time when "environmentalism" may not yet have existed as a concept, but in which key strands of contemporary environmental thought and politics were coming together: the publication of *On the Origin of Species* in 1859, Ernst Haeckel's coining of the term "Ökologie" in 1866 (from which the English word "ecology" derives), and Svante Arrhenius's discovery of the greenhouse effect in 1896 are just a few of the milestones of the period. Likewise the foundational problem of literary realism that their texts confront, the tension between the claims to mimetic truth and aesthetic status, is brought into focus when it comes to the representation of nature, a point of reflection they share with some of the major works of anglophone nature writing, for instance, and one that has also been an important point of debate in ecocritical theory.

Industrialization, Environmental Degradation, and the Concept of Nature

The German-speaking countries may have been much more than sites of "relative backwardness," but it remains true that between the time Adalbert Stifter was born in 1806 and the appearance of Theodor Fontane's last finished novel *Der Stechlin* in 1898, industrial and urban expansion fundamentally transformed their economies and ecologies. At the beginning of the nineteenth century, the territory that would become the German Empire (not including Alsace-Lorraine) had a population of twenty-three million, of which 90 percent lived in villages or towns with fewer than five thousand inhabitants.[32] Of 10.5 million German workers in 1800, 62 percent were employed in the agricultural sector, 21 percent in manufacturing, and 17 percent in the service economy. A hundred years later, with 25.5 million workers, 38 percent were employed in agriculture, 37 percent in manufacturing, and 25 percent in services.[33] During this period the German states also took increasing measures to intervene in environmental matters. In Prussia the *Allgemeine Landrecht* (Civil Code) of 1794 gave the state power to determine whether and where a factory could be built. While the law obligated the state to protect concessions once issued, it did allow for government intervention in cases where such privileges were

---

32   See Henning, *Die Industrialisierung in Deutschland 1800–1914*, 17; Hans-Werner Hahn, *Die industrielle Revolution in Deutschland*, 3rd ed., Enzyklopädie deutscher Geschichte 49 (Munich: Oldenbourg Wissenschaftsverlag GmbH, 2011), 5.

33   Henning, *Die Industrialisierung in Deutschland 1800–1914*, 20.

12 ♦ Introduction

abused or the factory was deemed to be doing something harmful.[34] The Prussian *Dampfkessel-Verordnung* (Steam Boilers Ordinance) of 1831 regulated technical aspects of steam boilers, and while its primary goal was to mitigate the danger of explosions, it also contained language requiring that smokestacks be at least sixty Prussian feet high (c. 18.8 meters) so that the smoke might dissipate in the higher air instead of bothering the neighbors down on the ground.[35] After unification in 1871, the problem of industrial effluent in the waterways sparked a number of so-called "Wasserprozesse" (water trials), one of which inspired Wilhelm Raabe's *Pfisters Mühle*.[36] Political and economic concerns, rather than the integrity of the natural environment, were the motivating factors in all of these cases, but nevertheless they are instances in which state institutions made decisions that ultimately affected air and water quality, often in ways that favored some people and places over others. The upshot is that in practice, by 1900 Germany could look back on an established history of environmental politics that matched its history of industrialization.

The transformations industrialization brought to the German-speaking regions were, to be sure, uneven. For one, the fact that in terms of percentage agriculture went from being the dominant employment sector to one still on par with manufacturing points to its continued strength at the end of the nineteenth century. Furthermore, the landscapes that industrialization had most obviously marked were concentrated in such areas as the Ruhr River region, the Kingdom of Saxony, the mining regions of Silesia, and the Saar.[37] But industrialization is more than a matter of what types of constructions stand where and how many people are doing what kind of work. It entails a more fundamental shift in socio-ecological relations, producing also more abstract transformations such as a changed perception of time and space with new modes of transportation and communication, giving rise ultimately to its own historically contingent concepts of nature.

The changes to Cologne and its environs over the course of the nineteenth century effectively encapsulate the new ecological realities industrialization created, to which the authors included in this study were

34 Franz-Josef Brüggemeier, *Das unendliche Meer der Lüfte: Luftverschmutzung, Industrialisierung und Risikodebatten im 19. Jahrhundert* (Essen: Klartext, 1996), 83–84.

35 Brüggemeier, *Das unendliche Meer der Lüfte*, 110–14.

36 Franz-Josef Brüggemeier, *Schranken der Natur: Umwelt, Gesellschaft, Experimente 1750 bis heute* (Essen: Klartext, 2014), 120–21. For an example of a court decision in one water trial decided by the Royal Provincial Court in Bielefeld, see "Der 'Wasserprozeß' gegen Hoffmanns Stärkefabriken (1890)," in *Quellentexte zur Geschichte der Umwelt von der Antike bis heute*, ed. Günter Bayerl and Ulrich Troitzsch (Göttingen: Muster-Schmidt, 1998), 356–59.

37 Hahn, *Die industrielle Revolution in Deutschland*, 38–39.

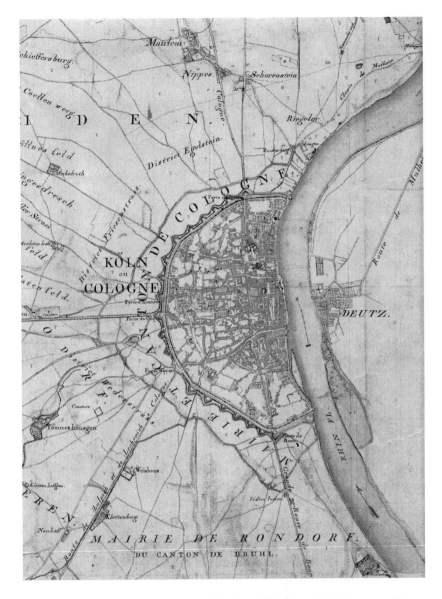

Figure 1. Map of Cologne, 1807/08, from "Topographical Survey of the Rhineland", also known as the "Tranchot Map" (compiled 1801–28).

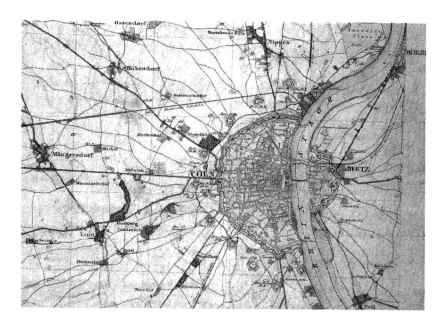

Figure 2. Map of Cologne, 1850, from "Preliminary Prussian Land Survey" (compiled 1836–50).

Figure 3. Cologne, 1893, from "New Prussian Land Survey" (compiled 1891–1912).

responding. Three maps, the Tranchot map of 1807 (fig. 1), the Prussian land survey map of 1850 (fig. 2), and its revision in 1893 (fig. 3), illustrate the diffuse environmental realities.

Between the map of 1807/08 and the map of 1850, Cologne's built area did not expand beyond its historic city walls, nor had it much since the twelfth century. The most obvious signs of historical change between the two maps are the fortifications around Cologne and Deutz that Prussia had constructed after its acquisition of the Rhine Province with the Congress of Vienna (1814–15). The 1850 map, however, does show signs of how industrialization and the fossil fuel economy would later transform the cityscape. We see the Rhenisch Railway skirting north of the historic center on the left bank, the Cologne-Mindener Railway entering Deutz on the right, and the Cologne Railway approaching the city from the south. The 1850 map also indicates a planned steam ferry line between the train station in Deutz and Cologne proper, spanning the river where now stands the city's Hohenzollern Bridge—an icon of modern iron construction (a type it shares with the roof of the adjacent cathedral, completed in 1880).

The arrival of the railroad heralds the far more dramatic changes that show up between the 1850 map and the revised Prussian land survey map of 1893. In a roughly equivalent span of time, the 1893 map depicts a radically altered landscape. Urban development has spread well beyond Cologne's medieval limits, as dense new neighborhoods stretch to envelope the smaller settlements beyond the historic perimeter, now occupied by a rail line running where the medieval city walls once stood. The Cathedral Bridge, predecessor to today's Hohenzollern Bridge, already stretches across the Rhine, and the railway line it supports cuts through the northern part of the old city. Artificial harbors have appeared on both banks, one of the many transformations of the Rhine in the course of the nineteenth century that made it into a major commercial waterway. All of these substantial changes had occurred within the living memory of the area's residents.

The physical reconstitution of the natural environment these maps showcase does not just alter natural systems, but also effects transformations in the concept of nature itself. Raymond Williams famously observed that "the idea of nature contains, though often unnoticed, an extraordinary amount of human history."[38] That history, Williams points out in the same essay, is one of labor congealed in the natural landscape itself, "and it matters very much whether we suppress that fact of labour or acknowledge it."[39] To miss this fact is to become subject to the

---

38 Raymond Williams, "Ideas of Nature," in *Culture and Materialism: Selected Essays* (London: Verso, 1980), 67.

39 Williams, "Ideas of Nature," 78.

16 ♦ Introduction

kind of critique Karl Marx leveled against Ludwig Feuerbach, who "in Manchester ... sees only factories and machines, where a hundred years ago only spinning-wheels and weaving-looms were to be seen, or in the Campagna of Rome he finds only pasture lands and swamps, where in the time of Augustus he would have found nothing but the vineyards and villas of Roman capitalists."[40] Feuerbach, in Marx's eyes, misses the social character of European landscapes, perceiving them only in binary terms: Manchester as an industrial landscape, "brown" in modern environmental parlance; the Campagna as pastoral, "green," and thus at a historical standstill. Marx's critique of Feuerbach is a reminder that the social character of nature is always a matter of degree and reflective of historical conditions rather than fixed, discrete categories of "green" versus "brown."

We might read in the three maps of Cologne a story of loss or alienation from nature as the built environment sprawls into the surrounding countryside. If we accept, for the sake of argument, the notion that German realism was a provincial realism, then the texts' focus on rural and marginal places, on threatened or lost natural idylls, either follows the alienation narrative, or at least responds to it through a focus on such places and subjects at the expense of the urban and industrial realities that threaten them. German theoreticians of realism in the mid-nineteenth century saw the focus on rural life as one way for literary texts to find "the poetic" in a prosaic world. While I see something more complicated at work, narratives of alienation have purchase in many strains of environmental thought and politics down to the present. In "The Historical Roots of our Ecologic Crisis," for instance, Lynn White argues that contemporary environmental stress begins with the technological subjugation of nature coupled with an ideology of dominion derived from Genesis.[41] Even as White critiques Latin Christianity, his account follows a lapsarian archetype, with the invention of the moldboard plow effecting the fall.[42] Rhetoric of human intervention "degrading" or "despoiling" nature also attunes here with Martin Heidegger's account of the technical domination of nature. Writing in 1954, at the height of Germany's post-war reindustrialization, Heidegger argues in his essay "The Question Concerning Technology" that the key difference between pre-modern and modern technology in their relation to nature is the manner in which modern technology "sets upon" (*stellt*) nature in such a way that it is a "challenging" (*Herausfordern*), altering the ontological status of the

40 Marx and Engels, *The German Ideology*, 63.

41 Lynn White, "The Historical Roots of Our Ecologic Crisis," in *The Ecocriticism Reader: Landmarks in Literary Ecology*, ed. Cheryll Glotfelty and Harold Fromm (Athens, GA: The University of Georgia Press, 1996), 3–14.

42 White, "The Historical Roots of Our Ecologic Crisis," 8.

natural phenomenon itself.[43] A hydroelectric plant on the Rhine, for instance, changes what the river is, so that "what the river is now, namely, a water-power supplier, derives from the essence of the power station."[44] Heidegger contrasts the hydropower station with a wooden bridge, a pre-modern technology that brings forth essential qualities of the river's being because the banks of the river only become banks when they are joined by the human structure. Even though the dam and the bridge are both technological interventions in the landscape, the dam constitutes a relation of dominance that is different from that which came before in the history of technology.

Many contemporary environmentalists would agree with the argument that technological intervention has caused an ontological change in nature itself. Bill McKibben's book *The End of Nature* (1989, re-issued 2003) is one influential example. Like Heidegger, McKibben understands the problem as one of a set of relations between humans, their technologies, and the non-human. "In the past, we spoiled and polluted parts of that nature, inflicted environmental 'damage.' But that was like stabbing a man with toothpicks: though it hurt, annoyed, degraded, it did not touch vital organs, block the path of the lymph or blood," McKibben writes.[45] The murder imagery here is one aspect of McKibben's deployment of apocalyptic rhetoric, but his apocalypticism is also not tantamount to a belief in total annihilation:

> By the end of nature I do not mean the end of the world. The rain will still fall and the sun shine, though differently than before. When I say "nature," I mean a certain set of human ideas about the world and our place in it. But the death of those ideas begins with concrete changes in the reality around us—changes that scientists can measure and enumerate. More and more frequently, these changes will clash with our perceptions, until, finally, our sense of nature as eternal and separate is washed away, and we will see all too clearly what we have done.[46]

One of the features of the apocalypticism in this passage is the extent to which McKibben evacuates it of its "end of the world" implications, while still retaining the meaning of apocalypse as a revelation, a moment where we finally dispense with illusion and see the truth of nature and all that

---

43 Martin Heidegger, "The Question Concerning Technology," in *Basic Writings*, ed. David Krell, trans. William Lovitt, 2nd ed. (New York: HarperCollins, 1993), 320.

44 Heidegger, "The Question Concerning Technology," 321.

45 Bill McKibben, *The End of Nature*, 2nd ed. (London: Bloomsbury, 2003), 48.

46 McKibben, *The End of Nature*, 7.

18 ◆ Introduction

we have visited upon it. McKibben's move here is, at least partly, a tactical one: apocalyptic rhetoric, for all the currency it has in environmentalist discourse, can distort environmental realities and lose its political force if it turns out to be a collection of failed prophecies.[47] Instead, the "end of nature" is a problem of "thinkability": for McKibben, global warming removes the possibility of imagining nature as something "other" to Homo sapiens, as that which is beyond human history.

By asking about the social character of the natural environments that appear in the text, this book regards nature largely in "constructionist" terms, or more specifically in materialist constructionist terms. Since its emergence in the 1980s and 1990s, much ecocritical theory has centered around a debate over whether nature is something at least partly culturally and historically constituted versus a position that ecocritical analysis should begin from a recognition of the independence and integrity of the non-human.[48] Such positions, of course, need not be absolute and mutually exclusive, and even as this book asks about social nature it also takes seriously the ecocritical challenge "to keep one eye on the ways in which 'nature' is always in some ways culturally constructed, and the other on the fact that nature really exists, both the object and, albeit distantly, the origin of our discourse."[49] Even so, critics of the constructionist position might raise the objection that it is fundamentally anti-environmentalist to premise a study such as this one on the argument that nature as a concept and a historical reality is contingent upon the very industrial relations that would threaten it. Glen Love argues as much when he attacks the "constructionist" position as one that holds "that nature constantly changes, that it has changed to the point where there is nothing 'natural' left, and so—spoken or unspoken conclusion—there is no reason to consider nature as anything but another venue for doing what we do: control it, change it, use it up."[50] I would argue that that is not the case: the mere

47 See Garrard, *Ecocriticism*, 93–166, esp. 113–16.

48 For glosses of this debate and the relevant positions, see Garrard, *Ecocriticism*, 9–11; Kate Soper, *What Is Nature?: Culture, Politics and the Non-Human* (Oxford: Blackwell, 1995), 8; and David Demeritt, "Being Constructive About Nature," in *Social Nature: Theory, Practice, and Politics*, ed. Noel Castree and Bruce Braun (Malden, MA: Blackwell, 2001), 26.

49 Garrard, *Ecocriticism*, 10.

50 Glen Love, *Practical Ecocriticism: Literature, Biology, and the Environment* (Charlottesville: University of Virginia Press, 2003), 21. Love is not the only one who worries that "constructionism" lends rhetorical fodder to agents of environmental destruction. S. K. Robisch makes the point in his polemic against postmodern theory when he writes that it "promotes the fiction of ecosystems being only humanly imagined and constructed—and so promotes those systems' exploitation." S. K. Robisch, "The Woodshed: A Response to 'Ecocriticism and Ecophobia,'" *ISLE* 16, no. 4 (2009): 704.

recognition that nature changes and that we can find the traces of human activity from the depths of the Mariana Trench to the heights of Mt. Everest and everywhere in between in no way means that environmental ethics are null and void and therefore anything goes. I also share the conviction of many literature-and-environment scholars since the 1990s that a robust ecocritical theory should be able to treat urban, industrial, or, in this case, "man-made" landscapes just as seriously as "wilderness."[51]

Still, Love's objection that a "constructionist" view enables environmental destruction is not baseless either, as another moment in nineteenth-century German environmental politics illustrates. In 1890, ten years after the publication of Ernst Rudorff's jeremiad, Dr. Konrad Jurisch, a chemist by profession, published *Die Verunreinigung der Gewässer* (The Pollution of the Waters), a "Denkschrift" (memorandum) written on behalf of the Verein zur Wahrung der Interessen der chemischen Industrie Deutschlands (Organization for the Upholding of the Interests of the German Chemical Industry). The interests against which Jurisch was defending the chemical industry were those of freshwater fishermen, who were under threat because Jurisch's patrons in the chemical industry were releasing pollution that was depleting fish stocks. In order to advance the chemical industry's claims on the water, Jurisch invoked the already social character of Germany's waterways, deploying an argument that strategically collapsed the difference between industry and non-human nature. "Haben sich an einem kleinen Flusse, wie z.B. Wupper, Emsche, Bode und anderen so viele Fabriken angesiedelt, daß die Fischzucht in denselben gestört wird, so muß man dieselbe preisgeben. Die Flüsse dienen dann als die wohlthätigen, natürlichen Ableiter der Industriewässer nach dem Meere" (If so many factories have established themselves on small rivers such as the Wupper, Emsche, Bode, etc., that they disrupt the fish harvest, then one must sacrifice the latter. The rivers thus serve as the beneficent, natural drains for industrial water to the ocean), he wrote.[52] In cases where industrial effluent was undeniably disrupting the ecosystem, in Jurisch's view that disruption was the price of progress, not just in economic terms but in political terms, as he cast industrialization as critical for the development of the newly unified German state. He envisioned industrial production transforming sparsely populated areas that otherwise had "an den Forstschritten der Civilisation nur geringen Antheil" (only a small part in the advancements

---

51 For an overview of this theoretical turn, see Lawrence Buell, *The Future of Environmental Criticism: Environmental Crisis and Literary Imagination* (Malden, MA: Blackwell, 2005), 22–25.

52 Konrad Jurisch, *Die Verunreinigung der Gewässer: Eine Denkschrift* (Berlin: R. Gaertner's Verlagsbuchhandlung, 1890), 103. For a history of debates about water pollution in the period, see Brüggemeier, *Schranken der Natur*, 114–22.

of civilization) into economic and cultural centers with new workers, centers of education, and transportation networks that would put the locals "in Berührung mit dem kräftig pulsirenden Leben der Nation" (in touch with the mightily pulsing life of the nation) allowing them to rise to a "höhere Stufe der Kultur" (higher level of culture).[53] If the claims of pre-industrial fishermen and those of industry on the rivers could not be reconciled, then the fishermen would simply need to get out of the way for the sake of progress. That the fish population should be preserved for its own sake does not factor into his argument, and as for the ocean, into which those "beneficent, natural drains" discharge their water, Jurisch appeared to regard it as a bottomless pit.

From an environmentalist perspective, Jurisch's argument is outrageous. Apart from its clear partisanship for polluters, part of what makes it outrageous is its appropriation of the concept of "nature" in its most normative sense. After all, if we accept Jurisch's argument, then there is no sense in opposing the practice of factories using rivers as waste disposal systems, because that is what rivers "naturally" are. The fact that his argument was calculated to serve economic interests does not change the fundamental fact that when used as systems for waste disposal rivers do become de facto extensions of the factory. And by the end of the nineteenth century entire rivers like the Wupper, the Emscher, and the Bode had already become sacrifice zones to the demands of industry.[54] Jurisch's argument, then, raises a number of implications for understanding how historical realities of environmental degradation determine concepts of nature and its others, concepts that will inform the environmental thematic at work in the texts this book investigates. While many environmentalists would rightly resist reducing rivers, forests, or other natural phenomena to a specific purpose, as Jurisch does, capitalist ideology does so all the time. Sometimes it does so explicitly, as when economists quantify the "ecosystem services" natural phenomena provide,[55] but more often implicitly through the appropriation of nature as resource at one end of the production process and waste disposal site at the other. This reduction of nature to resource on one end and dump at the other marks it with the very "prosaic" qualities that were a key theoretical concern for German realism as a movement both in criticism and in fiction.

53 Jurisch, *Die Verunreinigung der Gewässer*, 103.

54 Brüggemeier, *Schranken der Natur*, 121.

55 This problem connects to the question of natural conditions and the "value" of external nature. See James O'Connor, *Natural Causes: Essays in Ecological Marxism* (New York: The Guilford Press, 1998), 146–47.

Ecology and the Aesthetics of Realism

Aesthetics are inseparable from concepts of nature, and concepts of nature both arise out of and feed into material environmental conditions and the political contests surrounding them. The very title of Jurisch's memorandum is an example: "Verunreinigung" means pollution, but the root "(un)rein" connotes aesthetic judgments of purity versus impurity, cleanliness versus dirtiness, which are not objective scientific descriptors. Rudorff's complaint that nobody could write poetry about the Plauen Valley since a forest of smokestacks replaced a forest of trees is one example of how environmental aesthetics in the sense of the perception and judgment of a given environment was also perceived to have stakes for art in a general sense. And for many of the critics and theoreticians of German realism, environmental degradation did not square with realism's poetic imperatives. In his essay "Unsere lyrische und epische Poesie seit 1848" (Our Lyric and Epic Poetry since 1848), Theodor Fontane excludes the ugly sides of lived experience from his definition of literary realism. "Vor allen Dingen verstehen wir *nicht* darunter das nackte Wiedergeben alltäglichen Lebens, am wenigsten seines Elends und Schattenseiten" (Above all things we do not understand [under realism] the naked representation of everyday life, least of all its misery and its dark sides).[56] To represent the darker sides of everyday life would be a kind of realism, but would not be "poesy." "Poesy" in this context does not necessarily refer to poetry as a literary form, but instead to an aesthetic character that realist literature has and other realist forms, such as newspaper articles or essays, do not. What exactly that character is for the German critical discourse of the period is difficult to define, but what matters here is less the meaning of the concept than the insistence on the difference between "poetic" and other modes of realism.

The distinction between "naked representation" and poetic realism matters because German theoreticians perceived realism as an ethos that encompassed the literary movement. "Was unsere Zeit nach allen Seiten hin charakterisiert, das ist ihr *Realismus*" (What characterizes our time in all its aspects is its *realism*), wrote Theodor Fontane in "Unsere lyrische und epische Poesie seit 1848."[57] The year 1848 marks for mid-century German critics the failure of a pre-revolutionary "idealism" that, in their minds, got in the way of a sense for the practical that might have allowed them to realize the goal of establishing a unified liberal bourgeois state.[58] "Realpolitik" in the post-1848 critical discourse is likewise a manifestation of a realist ethos, but that also raises the problem of separating out

---

56 Theodor Fontane, *Sämtliche Werke*, ed. Edgar Groß, 24 vols. (Munich: Nymphenburger Verlagshandlung, 1963), vol. 21.1, 12.

57 Fontane, *Sämtliche Werke*, 21.1: 7.

58 See especially Plumpe, "Einleitung," 30–41.

a specifically "poetic" realism from politics, yet another everyday thing that lays claim on the concept. For "realism," then as now, was routinely invoked as a rhetorical cudgel against idealism, utopianism, or the speculative. Today we might think of those who claim that ending fossil fuel consumption would be "unrealistic" in light of the world's energy needs, an argument that forecloses on a critical step to addressing global warming and imagining a more sustainable future.

The term "realism" also functioned as a cudgel for liberal critics like Fontane looking back on intellectual and artistic developments in Germany from Romanticism through the revolution. The critic Julian Schmidt, liberal editor of the journal *Die Grenzboten* and one of the leading realist literary critics, argued that the task of realist literature was to find the ideal within reality, breaking from what he considered the intellectually and aesthetically misguided premises of both Romanticism and Idealism.

> Abgesehen von vielen andern Pardoxien der Romantiker, die kamen und gingen wie die Luft, z.B. Gespenster sind die Hauptsache, die beste Regierungsform ist der Despotismus, die katholische Kirche ist sehr tiefsinnig, die Rosen singen die gescheidteste Philosophie u.s.w., gab es ein Stichwort, auf das sie immer zurückkamen: das wirkliche Leben mit seinem ganzen Inhalt, mit seinem Glauben, Hoffen und Lieben ist ekel, schaal und unersprießlich. Wo sie das Ideal suchten, ob in Indien, oder im Mittelalter, oder in der spanischen Inquisitionszeit, oder wo sonst, war daneben gleichgiltig.[59]

> [Aside from many other paradoxes of the Romantics that changed with the wind, for instance ghosts are of utmost importance, despotism is the best form of government, the Catholic church is profound, roses sing the most elegant philosophy, etc., there was one point they always returned to: real life with all of its contents, with its beliefs, hopes, and loves is disgusting, empty, and useless. In comparison, whether they sought out the Ideal in India, or the Middle Ages, or in the period of the Spanish Inquisition, was all the same.]

Everything that was wrong with Romanticism, then, begins with its antirealism, but insisting on a return to "reality" does not dispense with the aesthetic problems that reality presents. For mid-nineteenth-century critics, working in the wake of Hegel and other "end of art" discourses, the question of the conditions of possibility for literature persisted as an epistemological problem in which realist literature must confront a historical reality that did not meet its own aesthetic premises. At least, not yet. As

---

59 Julian Schmidt, "Neue Romane," *Die Grenzboten: Zeitschrift für Politik und Literatur* 19, no. 4 (1860): 483.

Ulf Eisele points out, the ideological negation of the difference between the object itself and the knowledge of it produced a paradoxical agreement between Hegel and the mid-century literary theorists: for both, the conditions of "true" literature were not currently present, but whereas for the former such a literature was no longer possible, for the latter it was *not yet* possible.[60] In the words of Julian Schmidt, "Der Glaube der vergangenen Zeit war: das Ideal sei der Wirklichkeit Feind und hebe sie auf; unser Glaube dagegen ist, daß die Idee sich in der Wirklichkeit realisirt, und diesen Glauben halten wir für das Princip der Zukunft" (The belief of the past was: the ideal is the enemy of reality and suspends it; our belief on the other hand is that the idea realizes itself in reality, and we consider this belief to be the principle of the future).[61]

Schmidt's claim that realism is a future-oriented aesthetic is one that is shared by authors such as Adalbert Stifter and Theodor Fontane. Fontane's own essay, "Unsere lyrische und epische Poesie seit 1848," proclaimed realism as a normative mode of art, and that contemporary art was moving towards a future in which it would overcome the aesthetic and intellectual misguidedness of the past: "Der Realismus in der Kunst ist so alt als die Kunst selbst, ja, noch mehr, *er ist die Kunst.* Unsere moderne Richtung ist nichts als die Rückkehr auf den einzigen richtigen Weg, die Wiedergenesung eines Kranken, die nicht ausbleiben konnte, solange sein Organismus noch überhaupt ein lebensfähiger war" (realism in art is as old as art itself, but more than that: *it is art.* Our modern direction is nothing but the return to the one true path, the recovery of a sick man that could not be held at bay as long as the organism was capable of life).[62] The program of recovering the ideal within reality in German realist theory of the mid-nineteenth century is condensed in the famous "Verklärungspostulat" (transfiguration postulate). "Verklärung" designates a loosely defined mode of poesis, one that imagines the production of the work of realist art in Christological terms of redemption and rebirth.[63] The nineteenth-century critic Robert Prutz, for instance, defined it by way of a rhetorical question when he asked: "was ist alle Kunst selbst anders als die ideale Verklärung des Realen, die Aufnahme und Wiedergeburt der Wirklichkeit in dem ewig unvergänglichen Reiche des Schönen?" (what is all art but the ideal transfiguration of the real, the

---

60   Eisele, *Realismus und Ideologie,* 40.

61   Julian Schmidt, *Bilder aus dem geistigen Leben unserer Zeit* (Leipzig: Duncker und Humblot, 1870), 34.

62   Fontane, *Sämtliche Werke,* 21.1: 9.

63   Claus-Michael Ort, "Was ist Realismus?," in *Realismus: Epoche—Autoren—Werke,* ed. Christian Begemann (Darmstadt: Wissenschaftliche Buchgesellschaft, 2007), 21–22.

24 ♦ INTRODUCTION

assumption and rebirth of reality in the eternal realm of the beautiful?).[64] Fontane, on the other hand, seized on the connotation of "klären" (clearing) at the root of "Ver*klär*ung" when he described the process as one of "Läuterung" (purification), a process that distinguishes artistic representation from mere mimetic representation. Mimetic representation is "der nackte, prosaische Realismus, dem noch durchaus die poetische Verklärung fehlt" (naked, prosaic realism that is thoroughly missing poetic transfiguration).[65] Stifter used the term "Verklärung" in a similar fashion when he wrote in "Über Stand und Würde des Schriftstellers" (On the Status and Worth of the Writer), an essay that appeared in April 1848, shortly after the outbreak of revolution, that talent only produces "Schwulst und Redensarten, wenn ihr nicht [der Begabung] zugeartete Stoff gegeben wird, daß sie ihn erfasse und durch ihre inwohnende Kraft geläutert und verklärt die Welt wieder gebe" (bombast and clichés, if the material becoming of talent is not presented [to talent] in such a way that it can take it up and, by virtue of its own inner force, represent the world purified and transfigured).[66]

These statements on "poetic realism" are clearer on what realism is not than on what it is. Smog, effluent, and ugly industrial hulks would all seem to fall under the "dark sides" of everyday life that resist "transfiguration." But the importance of nature for realist representation does not stem from its degradation. Rather, the two are connected because these texts are also part of, or at least respond to, a tradition that holds that the representation of nature demands a kind of realism. That notion is neatly distilled in the famous "weather conversation" in Adalbert Stifter's *Der Nachsommer (Indian Summer*, 1857). The narrator, Heinrich Drendorf, insists that a set of gathering clouds portend a storm, but Freiherr von Risach tells him they do not. Risach explains that he felt moved to correct Heinrich because he cannot abide a false statement about nature, because "in Sachen der Natur muß auf Wahrheit gesehen werden" (in matters of nature one must look towards the truth).[67] The same belief in the importance of seeing the "truth" of the natural environment occurs in the last novel included in this study, *Der Stechlin*, when Dubslav von Stechlin reveals that he had the colored glass removed from the viewing tower in the forest because he found the glass artificially coloring the outside world

---

64 Robert Prutz, *Die deutsche Literatur der Gegenwart: 1848 bis 1858.*, 2nd ed., vol. 1 (Leipzig: Ernst Julius Günther, 1870), 58–59.

65 Fontane, *Sämtliche Werke*, 21.1: 12, 8.

66 Adalbert Stifter, *Werke und Briefe: Historisch-Kritische Gesamtausgabe*, ed. Alfred Doppler, Wolfgang Frühwald, Hartmut Laufhütte, et al., 40 vols. in 10 parts (Stuttgart: Kohlhammer, 1978–) [=*HKG*], vol. 8,1, 36.

67 Stifter, *HKG*, 4,1: 51.

to be a "Naturbeleidigung" (insult to nature).[68] The idea that nature demands truth also in artistic representation appears in another canonical novel of this period, Gottfried Keller's *Der grüne Heinrich* (Green Henry, 1855, revised 1879). In one episode the protagonist, Heinrich Lee, having been expelled from school goes to live with his uncle, who guides him in the development of his art. But when Lee begins depicting rock formations that do not exist in nature, or forests with only one species of tree, his uncle notices and criticizes him.[69] Being not a true representation of nature, Lee's is a false realism and thus, in the eyes of his uncle-teacher, bad art.

These are not isolated examples of a belief that nature is represented best when it is represented realistically, but rather are part of a pattern that we can trace beyond Germany from the nineteenth century to the present. In Herman Melville's *Moby-Dick* (1851), the truthful representation of nature is a frequent point of digression, addressed explicitly in the chapters "Of the Monstrous Pictures of Whales" and "Of the Less Erroneous Pictures of Whales."[70] Artistic license versus a claim to represent the natural world in a truthful way was the crux of the so-called "Nature Fakers" debate in the United States in the first decade of the twentieth century. The debate began when the naturalist John Burroughs polemicized in *The Atlantic Monthly* against writers such as Ernest Thompson Seton and William J. Long for their sentimentalized and anthropomorphized depictions of animals, depictions that for Burroughs amounted to a "sham natural history."[71]

The relation between the mimetic and aesthetic representation of nature is one that courses through subsequent American nature writing. In his foreword to *A Sand County Almanac*, for instance, Aldo Leopold proclaims himself part of a minority that rejects notions of progress that see the loss of wild things as an acceptable cost for a higher standard of living. He privileges direct experience over technological mediation when

---

68 Theodor Fontane, *Große Brandenburger Ausgabe*, ed. Gotthard Erler, Gabriele Radecke, and Heinrich Detering, 44 vols. in 12 parts (Berlin: Aufbau, 1994–) [*GBA*], Part I, vol. 17, 63; Theodor Fontane, *The Stechlin* (Rochester, NY: Camden House, 1995), 41.

69 Gottfried Keller, *Sämtliche Werke und Ausgewählte Briefe*, edited by Carl Hanser, 3 vols. (Munich: Hanser, 1958), vol. 1, 267–68.

70 Herman Melville, *Moby-Dick* (New York: W. W. Norton & Co., 2002).

71 John Burroughs, "Real and Sham Natural History," *The Atlantic Monthly*, March 1903. For brief accounts of the history of the "Nature Faker" controversy, see S. K. Robisch, "Ecological Narrative and Nature Writing," in *A Companion to American Fiction, 1865–1914*, ed. Robert Paul Lamb and G. R. Thompson (Malden, MA: Blackwell., 2005), 187–89; and David Thomas Sumner, "'That Could Happen': Nature Writing, the Nature Fakers, and a Rhetoric of Assent," *ISLE* 12, no. 2 (2005): 40–46.

26 ♦ INTRODUCTION

he writes, "For us of the minority, the opportunity to see geese is more important than television, and the chance to find a pasque-flower is a right as inalienable as free speech."[72] For Leopold, representation is subject to external reality. "One must make shift with things as they are,"[73] a realist claim the book enacts both through its descriptions of flora and fauna and Charles Schwartz's accompanying illustrations. The problem of the "truth" of nature and its mediation is as fraught in twentieth-century nature writing as it was for nineteenth-century realists. Nearly two decades after Leopold, Edward Abbey addressed the problem in the preface to his 1968 book *Desert Solitaire*, writing: "In recording my impressions of the natural scene I have striven above all for accuracy, since I believe that there is a kind of poetry, even a kind of truth, in simple fact."[74] Because language can never completely capture the reality of a place, in his case what is now Arches National Park in Utah, Abbey states: "Not imitation but evocation has been the goal."[75] "Evocation" for him is an assertion of the claim to artistic representation not against the truth claim but through it, since for Abbey "poetry" and "truth" coexist in "simple fact." In his book's representational practice, "evocation" manifests in memorably vivid accounts of the dawn over the desert or the mouse droppings on the floor of his trailer. Annie Dillard, on the other hand, regards the possibilities of representing nature "realistically" in more paradoxical terms. In a passage in her book *Pilgrim at Tinker Creek* (1974) she reports reading Stewart Edward White, who draws a distinction between the "naturally obvious" and the "artificial obvious," the latter being, counterintuitively, the condition for seeing nature. Dillard illustrates the artificial obvious with an anecdote about being the only person among a dozen campers unable to see a large bullfrog. It was not until they told her to look for the color green that she spotted the frog. "When at last I picked out the frog, I saw what painters are up against: the thing wasn't green at all, but the color of wet hickory bark."[76] In other words, only by constructing in her mind a false image of the frog, the artificial obvious, could she distinguish the frog from its surroundings in the first place. The line about what painters are up against links the paradox to aesthetic realism: art has to be in some degree false in order to be true.

The problem of realism and the representation of nature continues on as a throughline to the emergence of ecocriticism at the end of the

72 Aldo Leopold, *A Sand County Almanac, and Sketches from Here and There* (Oxford: Oxford University Press, 1968), vii.

73 Leopold, *A Sand County Almanac*, vii.

74 Edward Abbey, *Desert Solitaire: A Season in the Wilderness* (New York: Ballantine Books, 1971), x.

75 Abbey, *Desert Solitaire*, x.

76 Annie Dillard, *Pilgrim at Tinker Creek* (New York: HarperCollins, 2007), 20.

twentieth century, much of which emerged out of scholarship on nature writing deemed valuable for its realism. For instance, in the introduction to *The Ecocriticism Reader* (1996), Cheryll Glotfelty defines nature writing in terms of its realist claim as "nature-oriented non-fiction," and argues that such a mode of representation is politically important for the lessons it imparts: "In an increasingly urban society, nature writing plays a vital role in teaching us to value the natural world."[77] For Lawrence Buell, referentiality appears as a question of a text's "orientation," such that one of the criteria for an "environmental text" is that it be an "environmentally-oriented work."[78] Patrick Murphy defines ecocriticism as a project that "reinstates referentiality as a crucial and primary activity of literature."[79] Such a reinstatement for Murphy also has the end of orienting a reader's "thinking not only toward the world in the text but also the world in which the text materially and ideationally exists at the moment of reading."[80] For Murphy, along with Glen Love and some others (but by no means all) of ecocriticism's "first wave,"[81] the insistence on referentiality is a corrective to a constructionist position, or more specifically a cultural constructionist position, that they regarded as insisting on textuality and abstraction to the point of reducing nature to little more than a product of discourse.[82] The ecocritical debate about referentiality, in short, picks up on the longer-running problem of mimetic representation

77 Cheryll Glotfelty, "Introduction: Literary Studies in an Age of Environmental Crisis," in *The Ecocriticism Reader: Landmarks in Literary Ecology* (Athens: University of Georgia Press, 1996), xxiii.

78 Lawrence Buell, *The Environmental Imagination: Thoreau, Nature Writing, and the Formation of American Culture* (Cambridge, MA: Belknap Press of Harvard University Press, 1995), 7.

79 Patrick D. Murphy, *Ecocritical Explorations in Literary and Cultural Studies: Fences, Boundaries, and Fields* (Lanham, MD: Lexington Books, 2009), 1.

80 Murphy, *Ecocritical Explorations in Literary and Cultural Studies*, 4.

81 "For first-wave ecocriticism, 'environment' effectively meant 'natural environment.' In practice if not in principle, the realms of the 'natural' and 'the human' looked more disjunct than they have come to seem for more recent environmental critics .... Ecocriticism was initially understood to be synchronous with the aims of earthcare." Buell, *The Future of Environmental Criticism*, 21.

82 See Soper, *What Is Nature?*, 1–14. On the problem of realism and referentiality in ecocriticism and "theory" in general, see SueEllen Campbell, "The Land and Language of Desire: Where Deep Ecology and Post-Structuralism Meet," in *The Ecocriticism Reader*, ed. Glotfelty and Fromm, 124–36; Dana Phillips, *The Truth of Ecology: Nature, Culture, and Literature in America* (Oxford: Oxford University Press, 2003), 3–41; Love, *Practical Ecocriticism*, 1–36; Buell, *The Future of Environmental Criticism*, 29–61; Kate Rigby and Axel Goodbody, "Introduction," in *Ecocritical Theory: New European Approaches* (Charlottesville: University of Virginia Press, 2011), 1; Louisa Mackenzie and Stephanie

as the proper mode of representing nature on the one hand against the artifice of aestheticization on the other, and translates it into a principle of critical practice.

German realism, both as a literary and a critical movement, is ultimately not an outlier relative to other realist traditions, but instead stands in a history of environmental politics and ecological aesthetics that spans the Atlantic and continues into the twenty-first century. However, while we can read both German realist literature and the critical discourse surrounding it within a larger history of environmentalism, that is not to necessarily recover any of these texts for contemporary green politics, particularly of the leftist variety. Stifter's disenchantment with the 1848 revolution hardened a conservatism that shows up in his fiction and his statements about the function of literature. Storm, Raabe, and Fontane, likewise, did not oppose industrial capitalism as such. They were all bourgeois liberals and would not have gone as far as Ernst Rudorff, who, at the end of his essay against industrial development's effects on nature, wrote: "Wer mag von national-ökonomischen Vortheilen hören, der weiß, daß sie um solchen Preis erkauft sind, daß um ihretwillen die Keime zerstört werden, aus denen frisches geistiges Leben erblühen kann!" (Anyone who might hear about national-economic advantages knows that their price is the destruction of the seeds from which fresh spiritual life can blossom!).[83] But that is not to say that they were uncritical of the effects that industrial capital had on social life or the environment. Indeed, one can find among their contemporaries a more nakedly affirmative stance towards environmental transformation than the authors included in this study might have endorsed. Particularly in the 1850s, the critics of German realism tended to regard the everyday life that realist literature represented as an economically grounded one that found its fullest expression in industrial expansion.[84]

Gustav Freytag's 1853 novel *Soll und Haben* (Debit and Credit) is an emblematic example of a German realist text that takes an unambiguously affirmative view of environmental transformation in the service of economic ends and, not incidentally, ethno-nationalist expansion. Freytag was an editor of *Die Grenzboten*, and his novel is the one where the program of aestheticizing everyday life is put most obviously and intentionally into practice. Freytag approvingly uses a quote from his *Grenzboten* colleague Julian Schmidt as the epigraph to the novel: "Der Roman soll

---

Posthumus, "Reading Latour Outside: A Response to the Estok–Robisch Controversy," *ISLE* 20, no. 4 (2013): 757–77; among many others.

83   Rudorff, "Über das Verhältnis des modernen Lebens zur Natur," 276.

84   Peter Uwe Hohendahl, *Literarische Kultur im Zeitalter des Liberalismus 1830–1870* (Munich: C. H. Beck, 1985), 131.

das deutsche Volk da suchen, wo es in seiner Tüchtigkeit zu finden ist, nämlich bei seiner Arbeit" (The novel should seek the German people where they most excel, namely at work).[85] This particular novel finds them at work on nature specifically in the second volume, busy restoring the ruined castle near the town of Rosmin. Rosmin is one of a number of German settlements in ethnically Polish territory where Polish farmers exchange their goods for the "Erfindungen deutscher Industrie" (inventions of German industry), binding them "mit andern Menschen, mit Bildung, mit Freiheit und einem civilisirten Staat" (to other people, to education, to freedom, and to a civilized state).[86] Along with the renovation of the castle, a project that comes at the expense of the jackdaws and other creatures that have found a home in the ruins, the characters engage in projects of landscape transformation, such as redirecting the stream, with the goal of extracting more value from the land.[87] The novel thus binds environmental transformation, commodity exchange, and German colonial expansion within its larger poetic project. It is not entirely uncritical of modern industry, but that criticism is connected to its antisemitism: "good" German industry is contrasted with "bad" Jewish financial capital when Löbel Pinkus and Veitel Itzig conspire to entrap Baron von Rothsattel in a series of ruinous investments in a beet sugar factory. But to the extent that *Soll und Haben* can be said to find "the poetic" in nature, that nature is one that reflects human economic and political forces, even if it implicitly finds earlier stages of industrial development more conducive to poetic representation.

Soll und Haben refracts industrialization, urban development, and landscape transformation through an ideological prism that figures its Germanic characters as agents of historical progress. The authors included in this study consider the poetics and politics of environmental transformation in more nuanced ways. For Adalbert Stifter, whose works *Brigitta*, *Abdias* (1842, revised 1847), and *Der Nachsommer* (1857) are the subjects of chapter 1, the work done on nature is also figured as fundamentally good because it makes manifest the moral order that governs both human behavior and reality in general. I argue that these works constitute a counterfiction to nineteenth-century European environmental history. Stifter's fiction envisions humans intervening in natural systems in ways that parallel the "conquest of nature" as a historical experience, but imagine the work done on nature not in terms of relations of conflict and domination, but an ethics of regard for the integrity of both other humans and non-human beings. But even as the texts present

---

85 Gustav Freytag, *Soll und Haben*, 37th ed., 2 vols. (Leipzig: S. Hirzel, 1891), title page.

86 Freytag, *Soll und Haben*, 2: 112.

87 Freytag, *Soll und Haben*, 2: 13, 177–79.

30 ♦ Introduction

the production of nature within an ethical framework (one that aligns with Stifter's own conservative, anti-revolutionary politics), indications of a more violent relation between human and non-human nature lurk throughout his texts. Signs of a more coercive relationship both to other humans and the more-than-human world appear both in the speech of the characters and in the landscapes themselves, while the possibility that the forces of non-human nature will violently break in from the margins remains a persistent threat. This tension I read not as revealing the falsity of the politics and poetics Stifter proclaims, either in his own voice or through the mouths of his characters, but rather as romantic irony self-reflexively casting the texts' thinking about environmental transformation in a more critical light.

Chapter 2 looks at the representation of environmental degradation in Wilhelm Raabe's late novels *Pfisters Mühle* and *Die Akten des Vogelsangs* (The Birdsong Papers, 1896). In these novels the persistence of the dirty signs of industrialization catalyze a critical re-evaluation of the possibilities for a realism that represents contemporary reality in a way that also has aesthetic status. Both *Pfisters Mühle* and *Die Akten des Vogelsangs* present us with diegetic narrators who witness industrial development and its environmental impact as generational experiences. In the former, water pollution leads to the bankruptcy of the Pfister family mill, while in the latter urban sprawl transforms the Birdsong neighborhood from the idyllic peripheral settlement of the narrator Karl Krumhardt's childhood into the faceless industrial suburb of his present. Both narrators thus tell stories in which environmental transformation undermines any project to represent the world both realistically and aesthetically by any means save a nostalgic turn to a pre-industrial past. Were that all there was to Raabe's novels, then we would be left with an assessment like that of Georg Lukács, who saw Raabe's heroes as following a path of "renunciation" as a means of maintaining "their human integrity in the face of the impending dangers of modern life."[88] But Raabe's realism is also a highly perspectivized one, a fact that causes tensions and ambiguities that are not resolved through whatever strategies the narrators find to live under the circumstances of their times. The narrators of *Pfisters Mühle* and *Die Akten des Vogelsangs* have their own strategies for accommodating themselves to new socio-ecological realities, but the fact remains that they find themselves as writers in a position where environmental degradation resists any attempt to harmonize the mimetic and artistic imperatives of the realist novel.

The third chapter turns to Theodor Storm's 1888 novella *Der Schimmelreiter*. In this chapter, I argue that the dike at the center of the narrative becomes a site of contest between a mythic nature and human

---

88 Georg Lukács, *German Realists in the Nineteenth Century*, trans. Jeremy Gaines and Paul Keast (Cambridge, MA: The MIT Press, 1993), 258.

domination, prompting in turn a realist negotiation with the fantastic. The protagonist Hauke Haien is an engineering autodidact whose model for the dike breaks with received tradition in order to create more arable land for the community against the threat of the sea. He represents an Enlightenment model not only in terms of his rationalistic planning, but in his contrast to the novella's mythical element. The dike is not only a physical barrier separating the community from the natural force of the tides, but functions as a line between the ghosts and fantastical creatures associated with the sea and the processes of social and political transformation landwards, processes Hauke sets in motion when he rises to the station of dikemaster. But the dike is porous in both a literal and figurative sense: literally in that mouseholes threaten its structural integrity, figuratively in the sense that mythical beings like Haien's spectral white horse seem to be able to cross between the reality of the village and the sea as the realm of ghosts, giants, and mermaids. The novella's framing device functions in the narrative structure much as the dike functions within the world of the story: it establishes distance between the outermost frame set in the late nineteenth century and the ghostly story set in the middle of the eighteenth century, serving to stabilize the realist claim against the mythological elements depicted. But even in relegating the main drama to the pre-industrial era in Germany, the novella depicts the transformations of both nature and village life as fundamentally enmeshed in ways that anticipate the socio-ecological changes of the industrial era. The history it constructs, in short, is an environmental history that accounts for Storm's own 1880s present.

The fourth chapter, on Theodor Fontane's *Der Stechlin*, considers how global socio-ecological relations manifest themselves even in the marginal reaches of the March Brandenburg. Environmental transformation in this novel appears as a phenomenon that transcends the local, with the consequence that the separation between human and natural history collapses. Instead of realism's dual claims being cast in a state of precarity, as was the case in the works of Raabe, Fontane re-casts the problem of environmental transformation as one that can be recovered for realist poetics. Telegraph wires, the glass industry, and the eponymous lake itself all undercut the apparent provincialism of the region in which the novel is primarily set, because they embed it in a matrix of nature and capitalism spanning the globe. The novel in turn imagines this matrix as poetic in and of itself because it is a reality that transcends the narrow thinking of its more reactionary characters. I make the case that the reality that is at the basis of the novel's poetics is that of an emerging Anthropocene *avant la lettre*. The "Anthropocene" as we understand it today is an ambiguous concept, and the novel's depiction of the relation between the human and the non-human reflects these ambiguities, both in its implicit thinking about colonial capitalism as enmeshed in more-than-human ecological realities, as well as the possible futures towards which the socio-ecological processes in the narrative point.

From a contemporary perspective, the question of how to represent industrial capitalism and its environmental realities in a manner that is "poetic" might seem thoroughly dated. Rudorff believed that nobody could write poetry about the world of machines, at least not good poetry, but in the years after Fontane died and Raabe hung up his pen, a new generation of poets was doing just that. Georg Heym's poem "Gott der Stadt" (God of the City, 1910) gives a vision of the sprawling industrial metropolis, Ernst Stadler's "Fahrt über die Kölner Rheinbrücke bei Nacht" (On Crossing the Rhine Bridge at Cologne by Night, 1913) depicts the subjective experience of seeing the world rush by through the window of a steam-powered train, and Jakob van Hoddis's "Weltende" (End of the World, 1911) imagines storms and surging seas destroying infrastructure and disrupting the routines of bourgeois life in a modern industrial society.[89] These are canonical poems in German literary history, whereas Wilhelm Müller, whose verses on the pre-industrial Plauen Valley Rudorff so admired, is an obscure poet today. But the language that early-twentieth-century writers found for depicting modern industrial reality did not emerge fully formed like Athena from the head of Zeus. As much as German modernist authors in the early twentieth century stood at the beginning of a subsequent history of artistic innovation, so too did they stand at the end of a history in which authors like Stifter, Raabe, Storm, and Fontane were working through the challenges of representing both the abstract social and material ecological changes that they witnessed in their lifetimes.

---

89 By the time of the Weimar Republic, as Carl Gelderloos argues, authors such as Alfred Döblin and Ernst Jünger "took seriously the functional and formal similarities between what was being discovered about organic life, on the one hand, and the modern, urban, technological world they saw growing up around them, on the other." Carl Gelderloos, *Biological Modernism: The New Human in Weimar Culture* (Evanston, IL: Northwestern University Press, 2020), 6.

1: Environmental Counterfictions: The Ethical Domination of Nature in Adalbert Stifter

IN 1866, A HIKER looking from the town of Kirchschlag down over Linz and the wider Danube Plain would not have beheld the most sublime of landscapes. At least, not according to Adalbert Stifter in his late essay "Winterbriefe aus Kirchschlag" (Winter Letters from Kirchschlag, 1866): "Wir sehen an den heitersten Tagen von unserem Berge hinab über der Donau-Ebene und namentlich über Linz einen schmutzig blauen Schleier schweben, die Ausdünstung der Niederung und insbesonders die Ausdünstung der Menschen, Tiere, Schornsteine, Unratkanäle und anderer Dinge der Stadt" (Looking down from our mountain on the most cheerful days we see above the Danube plain and especially above Linz a dirty blue veil hovering, the emission of the lowland but especially the vapor of people, animals, chimneys, sewage canals, and other things of the city).[1] Stifter, who had come to Kirchschlag believing that the mountain air would help improve his declining health, strikes an anti-urban note in the passage, as he imagines the man in the "Bergklarheit" (mountain clarity) of the hill town being overcome "mit einer Art unheimlichen Gefühles" (with a sort of uncanny feeling) when he looks down and remembers that people actually live out their lives blighted by such bad air.[2] The city and the smog are viewed here from a distance in a scene reminiscent of Caspar David Friedrich's painting *Wanderer over the Sea of Fog*. But unlike Friedrich's figure beholding a sublime mountain landscape, the distance in the "Winterbriefe" is the condition for a different, but by no means unconnected experience: the uncanny, a term that Stifter does not use in an idle way.[3] The smog produces an uncanny effect because it transgresses assumed boundaries between the natural and unnatural. That transgression is also pivotal for Freud's formulation of the uncanny. For Freud the uncanny is a variety of the frightening that arises when the

---

1   Stifter, *HKG*, 8,2: 320.
2   Stifter, *HKG*, 8,2: 320–21.
3   On Stifter as a point where the sublime tips into the uncanny, see Michael Minden, "Stifter and the Postmodern Sublime," in *History, Value, Text: Essays on Adalbert Stifter; Londoner Symposium 2003* (Linz: Adalbert-Stifter-Institut, 2006), 9–21.

familiar presents itself as the unfamiliar and vice versa, a moment captured in the semantic overlap between "heimlich" (literally "homely," but connoting not only "familiar" but also "hidden," "secretive") and its seeming opposite, "unheimlich" ("uncanny," but literally "unhomely").[4] The word "smog" is a portmanteau of "smoke" and "fog," and so reflects the troubled boundaries between the "natural" and the "artificial." While the term is of twentieth-century coinage, Stifter's description captures the way in which distinctions between "the social" and "the ecological" prove to be untenable because the "dirty blue veil" arises both from the trappings of urban-industrial life (smokestacks, sewers, an agglomeration of human and non-human animals, "other things of the city") and the way in which fog "naturally" accumulates over the Danube plain.

The view from outside the city in the "Winterbriefe" enables a perspective on larger socio-ecological relations that would not be apparent from street level down in Linz. The pastoral settings in Stifter's fiction achieve something similar. *Brigitta* (1843, revised 1847), *Abdias* (1842, revised 1847), and his novel *Der Nachsommer* (Indian Summer, 1857) are all set in places away from centers of capital, which enables a perspective on how political and economic power reshapes nature in ways that would not be possible otherwise. We see the cultivation of fields and forests, the laying of roads, and the walling off of gardens, to name a few. It is therefore Stifter's pastoralism that makes him a useful starting point because of how his works imagine nineteenth-century social and economic realities reconstituting the physical world beyond the space of the city or the factory. What is remarkable about Stifter, though, is that while his stories contain such meticulous descriptions of nature as to arguably place him in the genre of nature writing, his stories do not cast such human interventions in nature as intrinsically bad. In fact, the opposite is the case: *Brigitta, Abdias,* and *Der Nachsommer* present the production of nature in accord with a moral-ethical program in which the cultivation of outer nature is also the cultivation of inner, human nature. Relative both to the environmental history of nineteenth-century Europe as well as to the other authors included in this study, the fact that Stfter's texts present the production of nature as essentially good makes them counterfictions to the conquest of nature as a real historical process. To say they are counterfictions is not to say that they construct a utopian parallel universe from the ground up, where everything is better in its oppositeness. Instead they recast the social production of nature through a prism that imagines it free from relations of domination, making a case for the ethical character of the socio-ecological relations they depict, a case that happens to reflect Stifter's own conservative politics. But Stifter's works

---

4   Sigmund Freud, "Das Unheimliche," in *Gesammelte Werke*, vol. 12, ed. Anna Freud (London: Imago, 1947), esp. 230.

are famously two-sided, and his stories fascinate because the moments of conservative moral didacticism are consistently countered by all that threatens to undermine the moral-aesthetic program. In practice, his realism is ultimately a matter of conflict and tension that resists understanding in terms of some sort of hermeneutic reconstruction of textual details into a sensible unity.[5] Even as Stifter's texts seek to imagine environmental transformation free from the relations of domination, signs of a more antagonistic relation between the human and the non-human persist. That fact does not simply belie Stifter's ethical vision. The conflict between the ethical claim on the one hand and the signs of domination both of other humans and the environment on the other is a structural feature of the texts' reflections on environmental ethics. It casts a critical light on the texts' particular vision of the relation between the human and the non-human, so that, in the final analysis, the moral claims the texts make about the production of nature are left in a state of ironic suspension.[6]

In Stifter's fiction, the work done on nature is one of the primary vehicles through which the narratives seek to make apparent the universal ethical order that, in his view, guarantees reality and thus his notion of realism.[7] The basic concept of a moral structure to the universe appears in various forms in his writing at least as early as *Abdias* in 1842, but its most direct formulation is in the preface to the novella cycle *Bunte Steine* (Motley Stones) from 1853, where he states that the goal of his stories is to make visible "das sanfte Gesez" (the gentle law, Stifter's spelling). Stifter argues in the preface that seemingly large things, like storms and volcanic eruptions, might seem great but are in fact small because they are exceptional events. It is in the seemingly small that we glimpse "das sanfte Gesez" at work, because its regularity and consistency is a manifestation of the law as a universal moral structure, meaning that the small is the truly great.[8] The importance of nature stems from the fact that Stifter's realist agenda turns on a homology between inner and outer nature: "So wie es in der äußeren Natur ist, so ist es auch in der inneren, in der des

---

5   Christian Begemann, *Die Welt der Zeichen: Stifter-Lektüren* (Weimar: Metzler, 1995), 2.

6   Stifter is not an author who has often been noted for his irony, but Jochen Berendes makes a convincing case that, in fact, irony is central to his works. See Jochen Berendes, *Ironie—Komik—Skepsis: Studien zum Werk Adalbert Stifters* (Tübingen: Niemeyer, 2009), esp. 7–8.

7   On the concept of reality as guaranteed reality, see Hans Blumenberg, "Wirklichkeitsbegriff und Möglichkeit des Romans," in *Ästhetische und metaphorologische Schriften*, ed. Anselm Haverkamp (Frankfurt am Main: Suhrkamp, 2001), 50–51.

8   Stifter, *HKG*, 2,2: 9–16; Adalbert Stifter, *Motley Stones*, trans. Isabel Fargo Cole (New York: New York Review of Books, 2021), 3–8.

menschlichen Geschlechtes" (As is outward Nature, so too is inward nature, the nature of the human race).[9] His stories figure *cultura agri* as also *cultura animi*, that is, the cultivation of nature is also cultivation of the soul.[10] It is a variation on what Lawrence Buell calls a "myth of mutual constructionism," a myth of the "physical environment (both natural and human built) shaping in some measure the cultures that in some measure continually refashion it."[11] Much contemporary environmentalism holds that "nature seems safest when shielded from human labor,"[12] but for Stifter straightening waterways, planting gardens, taming animals, etc., can not only be done in an ethical way, but can actually help nature become more natural because it reflects the moral order that structures the realm of the sensible.[13]

The counterweight to the "sanfte Gesez" is the fact that in Stifter's stories the relation between human and non-human nature is also shot through with mutual violence. In *Brigitta* wolves break into the estate and threaten the child Gustav, while on the human side one of the most prominent features of the estate is a gallows. In *Abdias* the titular character cultivates a remote Alpine valley, but he is also scarred by pox and loses his daughter in a lightning strike. In *Der Nachsommer* nature is the garden governed in such a way that flora and fauna perfectly serve Freiherr von Risach's design, but it is also the "dunkle Innere der Schlünde" (the dark abyss [of the gorges]) into which the young Risach contemplated hurtling himself when the parents of Mathilde, his love interest, blocked their union.[14] The result of the sheer presence of dark and violent nature is, as Alfred Doppler argues, that the "sanfte Gesez" breaks

9 Stifter, *HKG*, 2,2: 12; Stifter, *Motley Stones*, 5.

10 Hans Dietrich Irmscher, *Adalbert Stifter: Wirklichkeitserfahrung und gegenständliche Darstellung* (Munich: Fink, 1971), 111.

11 Lawrence Buell, *Writing for an Endangered World: Literature, Culture, and Environment in the U.S. and Beyond* (Cambridge, MA: Belknap Press of Harvard University Press, 2001), 6. See also Irmscher, *Adalbert Stifter*, 111.

12 Richard White, "'Are You an Environmentalist or Do You Work for a Living?': Work and Nature," in *Uncommon Ground: Rethinking the Human Place in Nature*, ed. William Cronon, 2nd ed. (New York: W. W. Norton & Co., 1996), 172.

13 For Stifter, "Die Aufgabe des Menschen besteht also darin, *in die Natur eingreifend ihr zu sich selbst zu verhelfen*" (The task of the human consists of *intervening in nature to help it to be itself*). Irmscher, *Adalbert Stifter*, 122. Emphasis in original. See also Herwig Gottwald, "Natur und Kultur: Wildnis, Wald und Park in Stifters Mappe-Dichtungen," in *Waldbilder: Beiträge zum interdisziplinären Kolloquium "Da ist Wald und Wald und Wald" (Adalbert Stifter)*, ed. Walter Hettche and Hubert Merkel (Munich: Iudicum, 2000), 90–107.

14 Stifter, *HKG*, 4,3: 211; Adalbert Stifter, *Indian Summer*, trans. Wendell W. Frye, 3rd ed (Bern and New York: Lang, 2006), 438.

apart "an der Gewalttätigkeit der Natur als auch an den Forderungen des Sittengesetzes, und diese Gewaltherrschaft ist als dunkle Unterströmung in den Stifterschen Texten anwesend und taucht deren Oberfläche in ein Zwielicht von Menschlichkeit und Unmenschlichkeit" (on the violence of nature as well as on the demands of a moral law, and this reign of violence is present as a dark undercurrent in Stifter's texts, casting them in a half-light of humanity and inhumanity).[15] Stifter's realism is not reducible to either the moral laws nor the naked violence, rather, these are best understood as two opposing vectors. The natural environment, then, as an object of human domination and a set of chaotic non-human forces in its own right, derives its importance in Stifter's realist aesthetics from the fact that it is where these two vectors intersect most clearly and consistently.

Making a Friendly Wilderness: *Brigitta*

A "Nichts" (nothing), an "Öde" (barrenness), a "Wüste" (desert): such is the rhetoric the narrator in Stifter's novella *Brigitta* uses to describe the puszta, the steppe region in eastern Hungary. Turning this barren nothing into productive agricultural land is the central project of a man the narrator at first knows only as "the Major," at the end revealed to be Stephan Murai, and Stephan's estranged wife, Brigitta Marosheli. Stephan and Brigitta's marriage, we learn, fell apart years earlier when Stephan was seduced by Gabriele, a local woman whose superficial beauty contrasts with the apparent physical ugliness of Brigitta. During his sojourn at Uwar, Stephan's estate, the narrator has the opportunity to witness how Stephan has changed from a rootless wanderer in Europe capturing the hearts of both women and men into a man bound to his region through his work on the land.[16] At the climax of the novella, Brigitta and Stephan's son Gustav is threatened when wild wolves breach the estate walls; Stephan rescues him, leading Brigitta to recognize him as her husband, thus precipitating the reconciliation of the couple and the restoration of the family.

The work done to transform the puszta into a cultivated, park-like landscape, free of wild animals, has the effect of also completing Stephan's moral improvement from adulterer and wanderer to settled pastoralist. Brigitta undergoes a similar process. Stifter's notion of *cultura agri* as

---

15 Alfred Doppler, "Schrecklich schöne Welt? Stifters fragwürdige Analogie von Natur- und Sittengesetz," in *Adalbert Stifters schrecklich schöne Welt (Eine Koproduktion von Germanistische Mitteilungen und Jahrbuch des Adalbert-Stifter Instituts)* (Linz: Adalbert-Stifter-Institut, 1994), 11.

16 On the same-sex erotics in *Brigitta* see Erik J. Grell, "Homoerotic Travel, Classical Bildung, and Liberal Allegory in Adalbert Stifter's *Brigitta* (1844–47)," *The German Quarterly* 88, no. 4 (2015): 519–24.

cultura animi is made explicit in the account of Brigitta's childhood in the chapter "Steppenvergangenheit" (Steppes in the Past). Here we learn that Brigitta's mother neglected her because of her apparent ugliness, causing the young child to retreat into herself, playing solitary games with stones, uttering strange sounds, and hitting her sisters. When the mother realizes her error and tries to intervene, it is too late because "die kleinen Würzlein, als sie einst den warmen Boden der Mutterliebe suchten und nicht fanden, in den Fels des eigenen Herzens schlagen mußten, und da trotzten" (the little roots that had once looked for the warm soil of a mother's love and had not found it had no choice but to take root in the rock of the child's own heart and there grow obstinate).[17] Little roots, warm soil, and the rock of the heart are all metaphors drawn from external nature to account for the development of Brigitta's own wild inner nature.

Beauty is the key point of aesthetic reflection in *Brigitta*, and its realization in the landscape as well as in the human individual is the problem that unites the thematization of the social production of nature and the more specifically human drama. Whether Brigitta is, in fact, physically ugly is not as clear as it might at first seem: the text presents claims about her ugliness always second hand, and moreover, as we shall see, a key point of the novella is that anyone who finds her ugly does so because they are taken in by superficial appearances, which, as the narrator argues in the opening, is not where true beauty lies.[18] He notes at the opening that we sometimes sense an inner beauty even in spite of an ugly appearance, whereas the features of an individual whom everyone judges to be

---

17 Stifter, *HKG,* 1,5: 447; Adalbert Stifter, *Brigitta: With Abdias, Limestone, and The Forest Path* (London and Chester Springs, PA: Angel Books; Dufour Editions, 1990), 122–23.

18 See, for instance, Ulrich Dittmann, "Brigitta und kein Ende. Kommentierte Randbemerkungen," *Jahrbuch des Adalbert-Stifter-Instituts* 3 (1996): 28. Benno von Wiese likewise points out that in fact Brigitta is a beauty whom most people wrongly consider to be ugly. See Benno von Wiese, "Adalbert Stifter: Brigitta," in *Die deutsche Novelle von Goethe bis Kafka: Interpretationen,* vol. 2 (Düsseldorf: August Bagel, 1956), 207. Alternatively, Patricia Howe argues that it is not that Brigitta is *not* ugly, but that her ugliness is suppressed in favor of the novella's program. Howe argues that the narrator understands that judging Brigitta to be ugly would make him one who only has a superficial sense of beauty. "These insights diminish his narrative's commitment to Brigitta's ugliness. Hence he retards and suppresses it: by confronting it indirectly as mediated through aesthetic distance; by emphasising the beauty of the people and landscape that surround her; and by beginning to redeem her from it before it has been firmly established." Patricia Howe, "Faces and Fortunes: Ugly Heroines in Stifter's *Brigitta,* Fontane's *Schach von Wuthenow* and Saar's *Sappho,*" *German Life and Letters* 44, no. 5 (1991): 428.

beautiful appear "kalt und leer" (cold and empty) to us.[19] This, the narrator says, is one of life's mysterious "Dinge und Beziehungen" (things and relationships) that escape rational understanding and instead have a mysterious effect on the soul.[20] Beauty in the novella's opening thus raises the larger epistemological question of how we can know the essence of something when that essence is not visible on the surface. The narrator ultimately decides that the ability to sense true beauty defies explanation, concluding "daß es nicht zu viel ist, wenn wir sagen, es sei für uns noch ein heiterer, unermeßlicher Abgrund, in dem Gott und die Geister wandeln" (that it is not too much to say that there exists for us a bright and unfathomable abyss in which God and the spirits move).[21] The narrator's suggestion is that intuition for true, inner beauty is an abyss because it is mysterious, but "we" know that it is connected to the divine. Brigitta and Stephan both situate it at the root of their own moral improvement, enabling in turn their reconciliation. In an apparent anticipation of Stifter's main concept from the 1853 preface to *Bunte Steine*, Brigitta even speaks of "ein sanftes Gesetz der Schönheit, das uns ziehet" (a gentle law of beauty which attracts us), a phrase which also appears in the first version of the story from 1843.[22]

Yet the "bright and unfathomable abyss" metaphor also undercuts beauty and the human sense thereof as stable guarantors of a moral order. Helen Watanabe-O'Kelly renders "heiter" as "bright," but it could also be translated as "cheerful" in the sense of mood. Abysses, however, are not known to be particularly bright or cheerful, leaving the possibility of chaos and meaninglessness. Of course, we could just as easily say that while abysses in general might not be bright or cheerful, this one is. Such assent to this theoretical argument does not remove the negative connotations of emptiness, danger, meaninglessness, and chaos the image of an abyss implies. God and the spirits are supposed to lend the abyss meaning, but the fact that they simply dwell therein suggests that they are subject to the abyss, not the other way around. In revising the story Stifter kept the abyss metaphor but removed the figure of "ein unerforschlicher Engel der Tugend und Schönheit" (an inscrutable angel of virtue and beauty) that allows us to recognize those qualities in others, meaning that the abyss ultimately stands alone as the ultimate instance that structures the reality of the novella's realism. The result is that "bright and unfathomable

---

19 Stifter, *HKG*, 1,5 : 411. Stifter, *Brigitta: With Abdias, Limestone, and The Forest Path*, 97.

20 Stifter, *HKG*, 1,5: 411; Stifter, *Brigitta: With Abdias*, 97. See also Walther Hahn, "Zu Stifters Konzept der Schönheit: 'Brigitta,'" *VASILO* 19, no. 3/4 (1970): 150.

21 Stifter, *HKG*, 1,5: 411; Stifter, *Brigitta: With Abdias*, 97, translation modified.

22 Stifter, *HKG*, 1,5: 473; 1.2: 255; Stifter, *Brigitta: With Abdias*, 141.

40 ♦ Environmental Counterfictions

abyss" is ironic in the romantic sense in that both terms contradict each other and yet are equally true. But in this case, irony does not efface the implications of chaos and danger, which are very much qualities of both inner human nature and outer non-human nature in the novella.

The suggestions of meaninglessness and emptiness is mirrored in the steppe landscape. Upon arriving in the puszta, the narrator encounters nature as an overwhelming void, to which the gardens of the estates will later contrast. He reports:

> Anfangs war meine ganze Seele von der Größe des Bildes gefaßt: wie die endlose Luft um mich schmeichelte, wie die Steppe duftete, und ein Glanz der Einsamkeit überall und allüberall hinaus webte:—aber wie das morgen wieder so wurde, übermorgen wieder—immer gar nichts, als der feine Ring, in dem sich Himmel und Erde küßten, gewöhnte sich der Geist daran, das Auge begann zu erliegen, und von dem Nichts so übersättigt zu werden, als hätte es Massen von Stoff auf sich geladen—es kehrte in sich zurück, und wie die Sonnenstrahlen spielten, die Gräser glänzten, zogen verschiedene einsame Gedanken durch meine Seele, alte Erinnerungen kamen wimmelnd über die Haide, und darunter war auch das Bild des Mannes, zu dem ich eben auf der Wanderung war ....[23]

> [At first my whole soul was filled with the immensity of the scene— the way in which the boundless air caressed me, the fragrance of the [steppes,] and the way the shimmer of solitude spread everywhere and over everything. But when it was the same the next day and again the day after—nothing but the fine round in which heaven and earth met in a kiss—then the spirit became accustomed to it, the eye began to succumb and to become as sated by nothingness as though it had loaded itself with masses of material and to turn inwards and, while the rays of the sun played and the grass shimmered, various stray thoughts moved through my soul, old memories came thronging over the heath and among them was the image of the man I was now walking to meet ....]

The uncultivated puszta has an overwhelming effect owing to its sheer size and monotony. But it becomes apparent in the subsequent account of the journey to the estate that the puszta is hardly the void the narrator implies it is in this passage: there is air, grass, and sky, and his journey will take him across waterways and into communities of unsettled rustics. Be that as it may, the initial encounter with the vastness of the steppe has a powerful effect on the subject, turning the narrator at once back within himself while also confronting him with his own suddenly externalized

---

23 Stifter, *HKG*, 1,5: 413; Stifter, *Brigitta: With Abdias*, 98.

memories. These old memories, which seem to roll towards him from across the landscape, bend the narrative itself backwards as they lead the narrator into an account of when he first met Stephan, "the Major," during his travels in Italy. Given the power of the landscape to thus overwhelm the human subject, cultivation becomes a re-assertion of human will over an objectified autonomous nature, a dualism that, in turn, can be as much the basis for conservation as conquest.

The signs of a more coercive relationship to nature are everywhere in and around the estates of Uwar and Marosheli. As he passes for the first time with Brigitta through the estate at Marosheli, for instance, the narrator marvels at its fields, avenues, and vineyards, all of which he presents as beautiful relative to the field of stones without. Part of the beauty of the estate comes from the implementation of monoculture. When the narrator observes that "nicht ein Gräschen war zwischen [den Stangeln des Maises]" (there was not a blade of grass between [the maize stalks]),[24] he reminds us with his praise that the order he sees comes at the cost of other plant life. The tour of Uwar in the chapter "Steppenhaus" (House on the Steppes) gives the narrator the chance to actually see the work that goes into creating and maintaining the estate landscape: Stephan orders the construction of drainage ditches, they supervise a group of women dusting off the rare and expensive camellias in the estate greenhouses, and they visit spots where soil is imported from other areas on the backs of mules and mixed together for the flowers. The tour of Uwar, in sum, reveals to the narrator the actual work that goes into the cultivated nature he saw in finished form at Marosheli.

The result of this work is a nature that has a very different character than the uncultivated puszta beyond, a difference made vividly present to the narrator when he reports looking out over the vineyards of Marosheli to the landscape beyond the estate, which he characterizes as a stony field bathed in red, a stark contrast to the "kühlen grünen Frische" (cool green freshness) within.[25] The narrator calls the estate a "park," which he describes as "eine freundliche Wildniß, sehr gut gehegt, rein gehalten, und von Wegen durchschnitten" (a [friendly] wilderness, very well tended, [kept clean,] and dissected by paths).[26] The order, cleanliness, and accessibility of the place describe a park well enough, and more to the point, these are the things that make parks very human constructions. The term "friendly wilderness" is an ironic phrase on several levels. At the most obvious level, it anthropomorphizes what is supposed to be decidedly not human. But the characterization reflects a shift in

---

24 Stifter, *HKG*, 1,5: 419; Stifter, *Brigitta: With Abdias*, 103.
25 Stifter, *HKG*, 1,5: 419; Stifter, *Brigitta: With Abdias*, 103.
26 Stifter, *HKG*, 1,5: 428; Stifter, *Brigitta: With Abdias*, 109, translation modified.

European thinking about wilderness as a concept. Prior to the nineteenth century, "wilderness" connoted terror and moral confusion.[27] The entry for "Wildnis" in the Grimms' *Deutsches Wörterbuch* makes it sound quite unfriendly. "Wildnis" is an "unbewohnte, unwegsame Gegend" (uninhabited, impassable area) or more commonly a "dichter Wald" (thick forest). It is a thing that is defined by its wild qualities, that is, "wildheit, etwas wildes" (wildness, something wild) and historically connoted "wirr, seltsam, häszlich, unrein" (tumultuous, strange, ugly, dirty). It is also semantically related to "Wüste" (desert) and "Öde" (barrenness), the terms the narrator applies to the uncultivated puszta.[28] Regarding the English equivalent, Roderick Nash points out at the openings of his classic study *Wilderness and the American Mind* that etymologically "wilderness" combines "wild" with Old English "dēor," meaning "animal" or "beast." "Wilderness" thus connotes the absence of humans, but also suggests that the wilderness is "a region where a person was likely to get into a disordered, confused, or 'wild' condition."[29]

From the perspective of the historic connotations of wilderness/Wildnis, the "friendly wilderness" in *Brigitta* may be an oxymoron (of which there are many in Stifter's oeuvre). But by the turn of the nineteenth century "wilderness" was undergoing a semantic shift both in Europe and North America away from such negative connotations as tumultuous or dirty to being connected instead to beauty, or more than that, the sublime. This shift in meaning, for which the Romantic movement is in no small part responsible, culminates in the term's use in much contemporary environmental parlance, where "wilderness" is a reservoir for renewal and reconnection to the Earth outside of industrial modernity. Edward Abbey says that the very term wilderness "draws all whose nerves and emotions have not yet been irreparably stunned, deadened, numbed by the caterwauling of commerce, the sweating scramble for profit and domination."[30] Not that the term is strictly positive even among environmentalists after the turn of the twentieth century. Even for Abbey, "wilderness" includes such not friendly things as "disease and death and the rotting of the flesh."[31] The wilderness concept in *Brigitta* straddles both the historic negative connotations and its more positive revaluation.

---

27 William Cronon, "The Trouble with Wilderness, or, Getting Back to the Wrong Nature," in *Uncommon Ground*, ed. Cronon, 70–71.

28 See "Wildnis," in *Deutsches Wörterbuch von Jacob Grimm und Wilhelm Grimm*, vol. 30, www.woerterbuchnetz.de/DWB/wildnis. On this topic see also Gottwald, "Natur und Kultur."

29 Roderick Frazier Nash, *Wilderness and the American Mind*, 5th ed. (New Haven, CT: Yale University Press, 2014), 2.

30 Abbey, *Desert Solitaire*, 207. For an account of the semantic shift of "wilderness" see Cronon, "The Trouble with Wilderness," 70–75.

31 Abbey, *Desert Solitaire*, 208.

But what makes the "friendly wilderness" in *Brigitta* representative of a shift in the concept is not only that this wilderness has positive associations, but that it alerts us to the social character of wilderness. It is, in that sense, not unlike the concept of wilderness William Cronon critiques in the North American context: "It is not a pristine sanctuary where the last remnant of an untouched, endangered, but still transcendent nature can for at least a little while longer be encountered without the contaminating taint of civilization. Instead it is a product of that civilization, and could hardly be contaminated by the very stuff of which it is made."[32] Critics of Cronon's argument see in claims like this a "postmodern" "nature-skeptical" position that can be a Trojan horse for environmental politics,[33] although Cronon's essay is less "nature-skeptical" than his critics allege. Cronon sees value in the term "wilderness," and ends the essay with a call to think in terms of the more holistic term "wildness" as a means of seeing the totality of nature as our species' "home."[34] The characters in *Brigitta* imagine their work as achieving such a home in nature, a belief that we can easily see in some of the novella's idiosyncratic compounds. "Steppenhaus" (House on the Steppes), for instance, suggests an embeddedness of the house specifically and the domestic more generally in the ecosystem of the Steppes. "Gartenwald" (garden-forest) similarly underscores the moment of cultivation, and may be read as echoing the phrase "friendly wilderness" inasmuch as there is a possibility that "Wald" and "wild" have a common etymological root.[35] Others, though, point to the persistence of violent tension within the holism of social nature. "Wolfshunde" (wolf-hounds) is an example, while "Galgeneiche" (gallows-oak) suggests that the tree's defining characteristic is its purpose of killing those who transgress the social order.

It is the creation and reinforcement of a social hierarchy with Stephan, Brigitta, and the other estate owners on top that both determines and is determined by the creation of a "friendly wilderness." "Wilderness" in the North American context, as William Cronon points out, is also a product of the expropriation of native peoples.[36] In *Brigitta* the creation of the estates has brought about a displacement of the local people through enclosure, making formerly pastoral nomads into wage

---

32 Cronon, "The Trouble with Wilderness," 69.

33 See, for instance, George Sessions, "Reinventing Nature, ...? A Response to Cronon's *Uncommon Ground*," *The Trumpeter* 13, no. 1 (1996): n.p.; and Love, *Practical Ecocriticism*, 20–21. William Cronon addresses such criticisms in the foreword to the paperback edition of *Uncommon Ground*. See William Cronon, "Foreword to the Paperback Edition," in *Uncommon Ground*, ed. Cronon, 19–22.

34 Cronon, "The Trouble with Wilderness," 87–89.

35 Nash, *Wilderness and the American Mind*, 2.

36 Cronon, "The Trouble with Wilderness," 79–80.

44 ♦ Environmental Counterfictions

laborers. During the tour the narrator and Stephan spot a group of workers busy draining a swamp to lay a road, about whom Stephan says: "dies seien Bettler, Herumstreicher, selbst Gesindel, die er durch pünktliche Bezahlung gewonnen habe, daß sie ihm arbeiten" (these were beggars, tramps, scaff and raff, whom he had got to work for him by giving them prompt payment).[37] The indirect discourse combined with the German subjunctive "dies seien" (more literally, "these be") establishes some rhetorical distance between the narrator and Stephan's condescending assessment, even though the narrator's tone is generally one of awe at the work he sees and at the person directing it. Even the people on the estate who still hold to a nomadic lifestyle, the local "Zigeuner" (gypsies), also find themselves in service to Stephan, supplying musical entertainment for the workers at lunchtime.[38]

What the novella effectively depicts is primitive accumulation in Marxist parlance: the estate stands on land previously held in common by nomadic people, who are then turned into a working class. Of course, from the narrator's perspective, that is not how it looks at all. Enclosure, displacement, and the establishment of a working class actually appear to him as a collective shift to a more ethical pastoralist life based on a better relationship to the land.[39] If it is hierarchical, then from his perspective that is hardly a bad thing, because Stephan's work cultivating both external nature and his own internal nature has elevated him to a position where he can direct the ethical improvement of both other people and the land. When the narrator encountered Stephan for the very first time, it was beside a smoking vent on Mt. Vesuvius, which, given the homology between inner and outer nature in the novella, symbolizes Stephan's own inner tumult. But seeing Murai on the estate wearing local garb the narrator remarks that he appears "so zu der Umgebung stimmend, daß es schien, ich hätte ihn immer so gesehen" (so in keeping with his entire surroundings that it seemed as though I had always seen him like this).[40] Murai, for his part, understands himself to have arrived at a point in his life where he is in a position to implement a paternalistic pedagogical program. He tells the narrator:

Vielerlei Volk ist in dem Lande, manches ist ein Kind, dem man vormachen muß, was es beginnen soll. Seit ich in der Mitte meiner Leute lebe, über die ich eigentlich mehr Rechte habe, als ihr euch

37 Stifter, *HKG*, 1,5: 428. Stifter, *Brigitta: With Abdias, Limestone, and The Forest Path*, 110.

38 Stifter, *HKG*, 1,5: 429; Stifter, *Brigitta: With Abdias*, 110.

39 On the relation between *Brigitta* and the pastoral mode see Walter Haußmann, "Adalbert Stifter, Brigitta," *Der Deutschunterricht: Beiträge zu seiner Praxis und wissenschaftlicher Grundlegung* 3, no. 2 (1951): 38–41.

40 Stifter, *HKG*, 1,5: 427; Stifter, *Brigitta: With Abdias*, 108.

denket, seit ich mit ihnen in ihrer Kleidung gehe, ihre Sitten theile, und mir ihre Achtung erworben habe, ist es mir eigentlich, als hätte ich dieses und jenes Glück errungen, das ich sonst immer in der einen oder der andern Entfernung gesucht habe.

[There are all manner of people in our land, many of them still children who have to be shown what to do. Since I have been living in the midst of my people, over whom I have more rights than you think, since I have been going around with them in their costume, taking part in their way of life, and since I have won their respect, it seems to me as though I have gained many a happiness I had looked for in various distant spots in vain.[41]]

What makes the workers "children" is their closeness to nature to the point where, as Barbara Osterkamp points out, they are effectively cast *as* nature, with Stephan's power resting on a mutual acknowledgment of the legitimacy of his tutelage.[42] By embracing aspects of the local lifestyle, such as the clothing, he gives himself and therefore the changes that he institutes the appearance of being connected to the place in a way that has the effect of naturalizing them. Russell Berman's argument about Freiherr von Risach in *Der Nachsommer* could just as easily apply to Stephan: "Stifter proclaims the desideratum of a natural fraternity in which the artificiality of hierarchical etiquette has disappeared, but his own utopian schemes reproduce the signs of status in terms of the exigencies of the division of labor," leaving Stephan, in this case, in a "privileged position" where the labor process is an "aesthetic spectacle."[43]

The upshot is that Stephan is figured as a pastoral ideal even as both the narrator's characterization and his own claims about himself admit of his will to dominance. That makes him a prime example of one of the contradictions that structures Stifter's fiction, and, more broadly, the pastoral tradition. As a trope that focuses on rural land in opposition to cityscapes, the pastoral has appealed to writers critical of mass urbanization and industrialization from Romanticism down to the contemporary environmental movement.[44] But, as Lawrence Buell observes, "historically, pastoral has sometimes activated green consciousness, sometimes euphemized land appropriation. It may direct us toward the realm of physical nature, or it may abstract us from it."[45] Both tendencies in the

---

41 Stifter, *HKG*, 1,5: 437; Stifter, *Brigitta: With Abdias*, 116.

42 Barbara Osterkamp, *Arbeit und Identität: Studien zur Erzählkunst des bürgerlichen Realismus* (Würzburg: Königshausen & Neumann, 1983), 136.

43 Russell Berman, *The Rise of the Modern German Novel: Crisis and Charisma* (Cambridge, MA: Harvard University Press, 1986), 109.

44 Garrard, *Ecocriticism*, 37–65.

45 Buell, *The Environmental Imagination*, 31.

pastoral that Buell identifies appear when the narrator draws an explicit comparison between Murai and the classical pastoral of antiquity. He says: "Die Einsamkeit und Kraft dieser Beschäftigungen erinnerte mich häufig an die alten starken Römer, die den Landbau auch so sehr geliebt hatten, und die wenigstens in ihrer früheren Zeit auch gerne einsam und kräftig waren" (The solitude and the strength of these occupations reminded me frequently of the strong ancient Romans who had loved agriculture so much and who, at least in the earlier period, had also liked to be solitary and strong).[46] The comparison to the Romans detaches Stephan from his historical context within the Austrian Empire of the nineteenth century and instead depicts him as a timeless figure of virtue. Viewed from the perspective of the novella's didactic-aesthetic program, the pastoral here is environmentally virtuous insofar as it designates the sort of harmonious social and ecological relations that Stephan claims to embody. The specifically masculinist characteristics "solitary and strong" do not appear in the narrator's imagination as connected in any way to the domination of humans or non-human nature. But even here the narrator takes a self-skeptical tone, suggesting that such a condition is not sustainable in the long term when he alludes to the thesis that, unlike the "earlier period" of Roman history, late antiquity was a time of decadence and thus fall.

Stephan's ethical ambivalence is only accentuated as the narrator shifts in the same passage from seeing him as the embodiment of the pastoral to seeing him as an Edenic figure: "In ihrer Einfalt und Mannigfaltigkeit, in dem ersten Zusammenleben mit der Natur, die leidenschaftlos ist, gränzt sie zunächst an die Sage von dem Paradiese" (In its simplicity and variety, in this first coexistence with nature, which is without passion, [the vocation of the farmer] borders above all on the myth of paradise).[47] The credibility of the comparison to both classical bucolic and Biblical Eden depends on the weight we give to the phrase "borders on." In terms of the rhetoric of paradise, Uwar (and Marosheli) do border on paradise to the extent that Murai appears to the narrator as one with the world around him, "beyond the sin of individuation, beyond the tangle of desires that prevents man from being at one with himself," as Martin and Erica Swales put it.[48] But this prelapsarian state is contingent on a postlapsarian reality: Adam and Eve must toil on "cursed" ground after God casts them from Eden (Genesis 3:17–24), and by figuring the puszta as a "desert" "barrenness," *Brigitta* imagines it in just such postlapsarian terms. The invocation of paradise here thus frames the project of environmental transformation in terms of what Carolyn Merchant has called a

---

46 Stifter, *HKG*, 1,5: 437; Stifter, *Brigitta: With Abdias*, 116.
47 Stifter, *HKG*, 1,5: 437; Stifter, *Brigitta: With Abdias*, 116.
48 Martin Swales and Erika Swales, *Adalbert Stifter: A Critical Study* (Cambridge: Cambridge University Press, 1984), 99.

"recovery narrative," a story of returning humans to the garden of Eden by way of science and capitalism.[49] Merchant argues that the recovery narrative legitimates environmental transformation and settlement in the context of American history,[50] and it is deployed to similar effect in *Brigitta*. The invocation of Eden is political insofar as it functions to naturalize, and therefore normalize the labor relations and transformation of the environment on the estate.

The rhetoric of the classical and the Edenic lend Stephan the appearance of being outside of history, but in reality the production of nature at the estates is eminently historical. First, in the sense that the novella encodes Hungarian nationalist politics and the history of land reforms in the kingdom, aspects that Stifter accentuated in the 1847 revision.[51] But more than that, the characters understand themselves to be part of a world-historical process. Stephan tells the narrator, for instance: "Die ganze Welt kömmt in ein Ringen sich nutzbar zu machen, und wir müssen mit. Welcher Blüthe und Schönheit ist vorerst noch der Körper dieses Landes fähig, und beide müssen hervorgezogen werden" (The whole world has entered on a struggle to make itself [useful] and we must go with it. The body of this country is capable of great flowering and beauty, and both must be cultivated).[52] Stephan's use of the reflexive when he says that the country must "make itself useful" ideologically ascribes historical agency to the landscape itself, while the passive "must be cultivated" rhetorically subtracts the humans who actually do the cultivation.

Stephan's claim about the role he and the other local estate owners are playing in world history is still highly abstract, but elsewhere the novella connects cultivation and environmental transformation more explicitly to the historical realities of nineteenth-century political ecology. When looking at the vineyards of Uwar, for instance, the narrator feels moved to compare them to those of the Rhine, suggesting at the very least a fraternal connection between a cultural landscape with a significant place in German nationalist imaginaries and a region subject to a German-speaking aristocracy.[53] The most explicit moment, however, is when Brigitta takes him and Stephan on a tour of her estate. The report of the conversation during the tour raises by virtue of association the homology between the cultivation of outer nature and of inner, human nature that is so central for Stifter. They discuss topics such as

---

49   Carolyn Merchant, "Reinventing Eden: Western Culture as a Recovery Narrative," in *Uncommon Ground*, ed. Cronon, 133.

50   Merchant, "Reinventing Eden," 137.

51   Richard Block, "Stone Deaf: The Gentleness of Law in Stifter's *Brigitta*," *Monatshefte* 90, no. 1 (1998): 17–18, 24–28.

52   Stifter, *HKG*, 1,5: 436; Stifter, *Brigitta: With Abdias*, 115, translation modified.

53   Stifter, *HKG*, 1,5: 419; Stifter, *Brigitta: With Abdias*, 103.

the improvement of the common person, exemplary "Vaterlandsfreunde" (friends of the fatherland), the preparation and use of the soil, and the straightening of the Danube. The mention of the work on the Danube is significant because it takes the conversation to a specific hydrological project of the kind that both enabled and was enabled by political and economic centralization in the German-speaking countries from the eighteenth century onwards.[54] The discussion of the preparation and use of the soil, meanwhile, reflects the development of chemical fertilizers in the 1840s. Justus Liebig's book *Die organische Chemie in ihrer Anwendung auf Agricultur und Physiologie* (Organic Chemistry in its Application to Agriculture and Physiology) appeared in 1842, and the appearance of his "Chemische Briefe" (Chemical Letters) in the *Augsburger Allgemeine Zeitung* between 1842 and 1844 inspired Stifter to write to the newspaper's editor, Aurelius Buddeus, proposing a set of "aesthetic letters," which never got written.[55] The subtle reference to Liebig casts Stephan's remark about the puszta engaged in a global struggle to make itself useful in a different light. As Greta Marchesi argues, Liebig's work on chemical fertilizers "involved a profound reenvisioning of organic development, distilling complex processes to a series of chemical relationships easily recognized in any geographic context," making him an agent in "a broader midcentury reconsideration and reorganization of capitalist agricultural production."[56] "The chemical model of soil fertility," she goes on to argue, "was a key product of this crucible of creative destruction."[57] While the characters see their work as part of a global project, they do not understand it as advancing a capitalist socioeconomic order aimed at the production of surplus value. We might read that as a reflection of a utopian scheme, to borrow Russell Berman's phrase,[58] but the logic behind that scheme is the logic that makes it an environmental counterfiction, as one of the more obvious moments where the novella refracts existing political and ecological circumstances through a moral prism.

Chemical fertilizers and the straightening of the Danube are two concrete historical examples of the production of social nature. The characters do not see them in terms of a "conquest of nature," of course, but instead imagine them as larger-scale corollaries of the production of a "friendly wilderness" at the estate. But the older, negative connotations of wilderness, and specifically the implication of the term Roderick Nash

54 Blackbourn, *The Conquest of Nature*, 6–12

55 Adalbert Stifter, *Sämmtliche Werke*, ed. August Sauer, vol. 17 (Prague: Calve; Reichenberg: Kraus, 1904), 247.

56 Greta Marchesi, "Justus von Liebig Makes the World: Soil Properties and Social Change in the Nineteenth Century," *Environmental Humanities* 12, no. 1 (2020): 206.

57 Marchesi, "Justus von Liebig Makes the World," 206.

58 Berman, *The Rise of the Modern German Novel*, 109.

underscores of wilderness as a place of wild animals and where any human might get into a "wild" condition, returns most forcefully in the scene when Stephan and Brigitta's son Gustav is menaced by wolves. The episode begins as Stephan and the narrator are riding along a newly laid road, itself a sign of work on nature beyond the limits of the estates. When they hear gunshots, Stephan races ahead, and when the narrator catches up he sees that the shots were fired by Gustav in an attempt to defend himself against the wolves. Stephan swoops in, moving against the wolves "mit der Wuth seiner vor Angst und Wildheit leuchtenden Augen" (with the anger in his eyes, blazing with fear and wildness) making him "fast entsetzlich anzuschauen, ohne Rücksicht auf sich, fast selber wie ein Raubthier" (almost terrible to behold: with no thought for himself, almost like a beast of prey).[59] The description is a far cry from the narrator's earlier impression of Stephan as an ideal pastoral type, enjoying a passionless first coexistence with nature, and instead is closer to the wildness implied in their first meeting, when he saw Stephan at the edge of a steaming volcanic vent on Mt. Vesuvius. In the wolf scene, the violence of external nature is matched by the violence of Stephan's internal nature, serving as a violent mirror image to the notion of *cultura agri* as *cultura animi.*

Wilderness as violent, chaotic, and ultimately not so friendly is reflected in the landscape in which the scene takes place, the gallows between the estates of Uwar and Marosheli. The wooden gallows stands near the oak tree it superseded, the so-called "gallows-oak." Far from being a symbolic divide between cultivated and uncultivated landscapes, as Benno von Wiese argues, or an "alien body" in the world of the estates, as Rosemarie Hunter-Lougheed claims,[60] the gallows and the gallows oak together collapse the nature/culture binary in the same way that the scenes of the social production of nature on the estate do, while also symbolizing most obviously the violent undercurrent beneath the characters' utopian thinking. The tree is a living organism, the wooden gallows is made out of dead trees, so that the natural thing and the human construction share an affinity because of their very material and the social function they serve. Their marginal location does not so much suggest that they are aberrations as that they embody realities that the estate owners would rather suppress.

The threat the wolves pose, though, is eliminated and the wildness they bring out in Stephan passes. The wolves that are not shot dead on the spot are hunted down and Gustav is rescued. Brigitta arrives that

---

59   Stifter, *HKG,* 1,5: 470; Stifter, *Brigitta: With Abdias,* 138.

60   von Wiese, "Adalbert Stifter: Brigitta," 199; Rosemarie Hunter-Lougheed, "Adalbert Stifter: Brigitta (1844/47)," in *Romane und Erzählungen zwischen Romantik und Realismus: Neue Interpretationen,* ed. Paul M. Lützeler (Stuttgart: Philipp Reclam jun., 1983), 366.

evening at Gustav's bedside, and the shock of the events prompts Stephan to reveal himself to Brigitta as her estranged husband, leading to their reconciliation and thus the restoration of the family. The apparent restoration in both the family sphere in particular and the estate as a "friendly wilderness" unto itself makes the wolves an example of a pattern in Stifter's works of what Sean Ireton identifies as "disruptive nature," a passing phenomenon involving a tripartite schematic of order—disruption—reinstated order.[61] But, as Ulrich Dittmann argues, the fact that disruptive nature is the condition for reconciliation at the end forbids a reading of the wolves in simple binary terms as an anti-civilizational force.[62] The chaos is structural for the harmonious end. What's more, just as the work done on the estates is supposed to be part of a global project, so too do the wolves indicate the persistence of chaos from non-human forces at the planetary level. Stephan remarks: "Es muß einen harten Winter geben, und er muß in den nördlichen Ländern schon begonnen haben, daß sie sich bereits so weit herab drücken" (It must be a hard winter, and it must have begun already further north, since they are already pressing so far south).[63] If Murai's deduction is, in fact, correct, then the wolf attack stands at the end of a causal chain that begins with distant climate variation. Social nature as part of a world-historical process of political and aesthetic becoming is matched by the unpredictable effects of the atmosphere as a non-localizable planetary system.

The closing scene implies also a restoration of the estate's transregional connections as something fundamentally good. Those connections are instantiated in the narrator's return to his homeland by foot. He describes setting off with an insistence on his ethnic identity, saying: "Im Frühjahre nahm ich wieder mein deutsches Gewand, meinen deutschen Stab und wanderte dem deutschen Vaterlande zu" (In the spring I put on my German costume again, took my German walking-stick and set off on foot towards my German homeland).[64] He marches west and crosses the Leitha, the Danube tributary that had historically marked the eastern border of the Duchy of Austria. The insistence on his Germanness, the journey to Austria by foot, and the crossing of what was in the Austrian Empire a border of more cultural than political significance suggests a harmonious conservation of difference within a fundamental unity of east and west. By contrast, the puszta he leaves behind him lies at the western

61   Sean Ireton, "Between Dirty and Disruptive Nature: Adalbert Stifter in the Context of Nineteenth-Century American Environmental Literature," *Colloquia Germanica* 44, no. 2 (2011): 161–62.

62   Dittmann, "Brigitta und kein Ende," 26. See also Hunter-Lougheed, "Adalbert Stifter: Brigitta (1844/47)," 378.

63   Stifter, *HKG*, 1,5: 470; Stifter, *Brigitta: With Abdias*, 139.

64   Stifter, *HKG*, 1,5: 475; Stifter, *Brigitta: With Abdias*, 143.

ENVIRONMENTAL COUNTERFICTIONS ♦ 51

edge of the Great Eurasian Steppe, an ecoregion extending to the far east of the Eurasian landmass. The directionality of the narrator's walk, in other words, with all of its cultural and political implications, stands in tension with the directionality of the steppe as a more-than-human ecosystem. "Alles war nun gut" (all was now well), the narrator insists before his departure, but the latent violence in Stephan's character, and the threat of intrusion from the larger ecosystem beyond the estate walls, are not removed because a few wolves have been shot.[65] The possibility that a chain reaction in non-human natural systems might still lead to chaos in the world of the estates can only be inferred at the end of *Brigitta*. Cause and effect and the question of whether there is ultimate meaning behind the workings of nature, however, are the central theoretical problem in another story from the *Studien*, the novella *Abdias*.

Alienation and Immanence: *Abdias*

If *Brigitta* idealizes a "first coexistence with nature," that ideal finds a contrasting image in *Abdias*. The story tells the life of Abdias beginning with his childhood in a community of fellow Jews occupying the ruins of a lost Roman city in the Atlas Mountains, which stretch across the Maghreb in northwest Africa. His father sends him out as a young man, and he travels the world learning to become a trader, becoming fabulously wealthy but horribly scarred from a case of pox he contracted during his travels. Back in his community, he manages to make an enemy of the character Melek by refusing him a loan, and Melek ultimately plunders the Roman city. During the attack, Abdias's wife dies in childbirth, and so Abdias takes his daughter Ditha to Europe, where he purchases land in a remote Alpine valley that he then proceeds to cultivate. The second half of the novella concerns his time in the Alps, where he and his daughter live an isolated life. The major plot turn in this part of the novella is the discovery that Ditha is blind, until one evening she is struck by lightning and miraculously gains the power of vision. The story ends, however, when another storm rolls in and a second bolt of lightning strikes Ditha, killing her on the spot, leaving Abdias to live out the rest of his life sitting on a bench in front of his house, staring at the sun in stupor. Like *Brigitta* and *Der Nachsommer*, the cultivation of nature and the cultivation of the self is a core theoretical concern to *Abdias*. But unlike Brigitta, Stephan, and Risach in *Der Nachsommer*, Abdias never realizes the pastoral ideal the other characters embody.

Ditha's recovery of sight and then ultimate death through two freak natural events makes her an example of the philosophical problem raised at the opening of *Abdias*, namely the extent to which humans are

---

65 Stifter, *HKG*, 1,5: 475; Stifter, *Brigitta: With Abdias*, 143.

52 ♦ Environmental Counterfictions

delivered unto the laws of nature, which have something "schauderndes" (terrifying) in their "gelassenen Unschuld" (innocent indifference).[66] The narrator considers the possibility that the inexplicable events that befall us are simply a matter of fate, the dumb workings of the cosmos to which even the gods are subject, or perhaps destiny, that is, the notion that what appears to be the indifferent effects of natural laws are actually ordained by a higher power. But then the narrator raises another possibility, that "eine heitre Blumenkette" (a [cheerful] chain of flowers) is strung through the universe, beginning with human rationality and ending in God's hand.[67] This possibility—and the narrator is clear that it is only a possibility— would mean that the reality we encounter in the novella is another one of Stifter's guaranteed realities, with the divine hand stabilizing the causal chain. That is a contrast with the cause-and-effect relation behind the wolf attack in *Brigitta*, where it is simply climatic forces that drive the wolves south. The wolf episode at least had meaning to the extent that it catalyzed the restoration of the family, but the narrator of *Abdias* says that the main character's life will not so much provide answers as to whether there is something meaningful behind the seeming dumb mechanics of nature, but rather only raises questions of why.

Where in *Brigitta* nature was mostly the object of conquest, in the ruined city where Abdias spends his childhood it is nature that reconquers the human construction. The city, we are told, is not on any maps, architectural features litter the site as rubble, and its water infrastructure is dry and crumbling. Already we see in the Jewish community the opposite of the pastoral ideal from *Brigitta*, insofar as the community has no active relationship with its environment. The fact that an ancient city is allowed to crumble also stands in marked contrast to *Der Nachsommer*, where Risach is extensively engaged with the preservation and restoration of old things, especially the ancient Greek statue. A lack of genuine connection to the local environment is an antisemitic stereotype, a sentiment made most explicit in the narrator's remark that "düstre, schwarze, schmutzige Juden gingen wie Schatten in den Trümmern herum, gingen drinnen aus und ein, und wohnten drinnen mit dem Schakal, den sie manchmal fütterten" (Dark, melancholy, dirty Jews moved around in the rubble like shadows, went in and out among it and lived in it with the jackal, which they sometimes fed).[68] Whether and to what extent the novella is anti-Semitic has been a topic of debate in scholarship on *Abdias*. Ruth Klüger, for one, has argued that *Abdias* is not really antisemitic because Abdias is

---

66 Stifter, *HKG*, 1,5: 237; Stifter, *Brigitta: With Abdias*, 21.
67 Stifter, *HKG*, 1,5: 238; Stifter, *Brigitta: With Abdias*, 22.
68 Stifter, *HKG*, 1,5: 240; Stifter, *Brigitta: With Abdias*, 23.

not a negative figure.[69] Nevertheless, Abdias himself reflects a number of antisemitic stereotypes, such as the Wandering Jew, a fixation on money, and isolationism.[70] These aspects of his character inform his relation to nature, as Martha Helfer shows.[71] Ironically, Jason Groves demonstrates that the text does construct Abdias as having a relation to at least a part of non-human nature through its pattern of comparing him to stone, metal, and the inorganic generally as a way of capturing his obstinacy.[72]

His failure to achieve a "first coexistence with nature," in any event, not only marks him as "other" in comparison to characters like Stephan and Risach who are at least presented as having a relation to place, but marks him out as at best an ambivalent figure from an environmental politics that sees place-connectedness as an ecological virtue. For Lawrence Buell, place connection is not itself an index of any sort of ecological right thinking, but nevertheless "it seems indisputable that the self-conscious commitment to place … would more likely produce or accompany environmental responsiveness than would atopia or diaspora."[73] The diaspora remark aside, "place" in this line of thinking requires a "deep and often contemplative familiarity with local fauna and flora, soil qualities, geologies, and the like, as well as the intricate history of human occupancy, environmental modification and the embedding of human labor in the land, particularly in the built environment," as David Harvey characterizes

69 Ruth Angress [Klüger], "Wunsch- und Angstbilder: Jüdische Gestalten aus der deutschen Literatur des neunzehnten Jahrhunderts," in *Kontroversen, alte und neue: Akten des VII. Internationaler Germanisten-Kongreß* (Tübingen: Niemeyer, 1986), 93.

70 See Joseph Metz, "The Jew as Sign in Stifter's Abdias," *Germanic Review* 77, no. 3 (2002): 220. Metz sees, however, in the novella's deployment of anti-Semitic imagery another example of the double nature of Stifter's realism. On the one hand, Metz argues, the anti-Semitic stereotypes fall short of their function as a reality-stabilizing device, while secondly the text seems "to double back on itself and undermine its tropology of anti-Semitism, including both the expected verification of anti-Semitic knowledge by a future science and the current overwhelming chain of anti-Semitic signifiers strung throughout the narrative" (225).

71 Martha Helfer, "Natural Anti-Semitism: Stifter's Abdias," *Deutsche Vierteljahrsschrift für Literaturwissenschaft und Geistesgeschichte* 78, no. 2 (2004): 261–86.

72 Jason Groves, "Stifter's Stones," in *A Companion to the Works of Adalbert Stifter*, ed. Sean Ireton (Rochester, NY: Camden House, 2025), 238.

73 Buell, *The Environmental Imagination*, 253. This is not to deny the abuses to which an analytic of place can be put, as Buell acknowledges in his chapter on the concept in his 2001 book *Writing for an Endangered World*. "On the contrary, place attachment can itself become pathological: can abet possessiveness, ethnocentrism, xenophobia." Buell, *Writing for an Endangered World*, 76. Its abuse, Buell argues, does not invalidate its usefulness as an environmental ethic and aesthetic (77–78).

54 ◆ ENVIRONMENTAL COUNTERFICTIONS

it in his critique of the concept. Place, Harvey says, thus constitutes an "alternative esthetic to that offered through the restless spatial flows of commodities and money."[74] As one who spent his early adult life as a travelling trader accumulating wealth, Abdias embodies the flow of money and capital that stands in contrast with place connectedness.

Even after Abdias moves to Europe and begins his work cultivating the Alpine valley, the novella casts him as estranged from nature in a way that Brigitta and Murai were not. Abdias chooses to settle in the valley because it has in his eyes an affinity with his desert home on account of its "Oede und Unfruchtbarkeit" ([waste] and barrenness).[75] He then sets about reproducing his desert home in the Alps by equipping his house with security measures more fitting for the dangers he faced from his old enemy Melek. He decorates it in a way that resembles his rooms in the ruined Roman city, and constructs it with thick walls and small windows in order to keep it cool, "lauter Anstalten, die er in Europa nicht nöthig hatte" (all arrangements that were unnecessary in Europe).[76] Unlike Risach, who is careful to design his garden in such a way that it does not conflict with the laws of nature, Abdias's settlement of the valley speaks to an inability or unwillingness to adapt to his new environment. He is likewise slow to appreciate the resources available in the valley. For instance, he is at first careful not to use up too much water from his well, remembering how quickly the water table in the high desert of the Atlas Mountains sank once the rains had stopped. Only after two years does he realize he will not be able to consume all of the water that is at his disposal.

The most dramatic illustration of Abdias's failure to achieve a meaningful, organic connection with non-human nature is in the scene where he shoots his dog Asu. The incident is one of the clearest cases of his inability to properly understand the non-human, even when that "non-human" is a domestic animal with an understanding of human social cues. One day, Abdias is riding his donkey through the valley when Asu begins making strange noises and running wildly back and forth. Rabies has struck other dogs in the region, we learn, and so Abdias is concerned that Asu too may have contracted the disease. Abdias sees that Asu will not cross a stream, that he is foaming at the mouth and behaving in a seemingly erratic fashion, and, concluding that Asu is indeed infected, puts him out of his seeming misery. Shortly thereafter Abdias realizes that he had left a bag of money behind, and returning to the spot finds that

74 David Harvey, *Justice, Nature, and the Geography of Difference* (Cambridge, MA: Blackwell, 1996), 303.

75 Stifter, *HKG*, 1,5: 302; Stifter, *Brigitta: With Abdias*, 66, translation modified.

76 Stifter, *HKG*, 1,5: 304; Stifter, *Brigitta: With Abdias*, 68.

before dying Asu had dragged himself back to the location where Abdias had left it. The dog was not rabid, but instead was trying to alert Abdias to his oversight. The dog, in short, had both the power to communicate and at least the sense that a sack of money was not something one should leave behind. For his part, Stifter believed that animals had an interiority and speculated about the possibilities for animal communication.[77] In an 1845 essay fragment "Zur Psichologie der Tiere" (On the Psychology of Animals), for instance, he states that since his childhood he rejected the notion that animals do not have a capacity for reason, and he speculates about the discoveries that might be made if only we had grammars to understand their languages.[78] In *Abdias*, a novella that thematizes sight versus blindness, and where Asu is specifically referred to as one of the "sehenden Wesen" (sighted beings), the shooting is surely a sign of Abdias's inner blindness.[79] Abdias's inner blindness, though, is ironically countered by his keen observation of the dog's behavior, which could objectively be understood as the symptoms of rabies. The tragedy of the episode is that Abdias was not blind to the signs, which he read at least plausibly, but rather he failed to understand the message Asu was attempting to communicate.

But *Abdias* is more than a story of what a "first coexistence with nature" is not. Stifter imagines a third way in which the human can relate to the non-human through the figure of Abdias's daughter Ditha. Ditha is born blind, a fact that Abdias is alerted to when observing the ways in which his daughter has not achieved the developmental milestones of early childhood. She is like Brigitta in that her development in these years does not make her adequately socialized; but whereas Brigitta was a violent child, by the age of four Ditha barely moves and is not walking or even crawling on her own. Also like Brigitta, Ditha produces strange sounds in place of speech; but whereas Brigitta's sounds are specifically ones she invented on her own, we are told that Ditha "lallte ... seltsame Töne, die keiner der menschlichen Sprachen ähnlich waren" (babbled strange incomprehensible sounds unlike any human language),[80] a phrase that at least signals the possibility that she is speaking a non-human language.

---

77 See Alois Hofman, "Die Tierseele bei Adalbert Stifter," *VASILO* 13, no. 1/2 (1964): 6–15.

78 Stifter, *HKG*, 8,2: 13–14.

79 Stifter, *HKG*, 1,5: 315; Stifter, *Brigitta: With Abdias*, 76. The English translation incorrectly states that Abdias is the "sighted being" in question. See also Johann Lachinger, "Adalbert Stifters 'Abdias': Eine Interpretation," *VASILO* 18, no. 3/4 (1969): 107–8; Gunter Hertling, "Der Mensch und 'seine' Tiere: Versäumte Symbiose, versäumte Bildung. Zu Adalbert Stifters Abdias," *Modern Austrian Literature: Journal of the International Arthur Schnitzler Research Association* 18, no. 1 (1985): 19.

80 Stifter, *HKG*, 1,5: 308. Stifter, *Brigitta: With Abdias*, 71.

As Kelly Middleton Meyer characterizes it, "for Ditha, there is neither a mirror stage nor a resulting division between subject and object, self and other. Instead she experiences life as a continuous interpenetration of self and world precluded by the advent of vision."[81]

Abdias interprets his daughter's lack of movement and lack of language as signs that she does not yet have a "soul" (*Seele*).[82] Viewed from the perspective of the novella's opening, not having a soul entails not having reason, which the narrator says is "das Auge der Seele" (the eye of the soul) and the final link in the chain of flowers that stretches between the human brain and the hand of God.[83] Whether she has a soul or not, Ditha experiences the world in a non-dualistic way. Her father sees that as something that must be corrected, but it also means that she does not see the world in a way that much contemporary environmental thought sees as furnishing a conceptual framework for the domination of nature.[84] As opposed to dualism, "an alienated form of differentiation, in which power construes and constructs difference in terms of an inferior and alien realm," as Val Plumwood defines it,[85] Ditha is one who experiences continuities, making her a figure of environmental immanence. In contemporary environmental thought, "immanence" is a "notion of being different *from* but simultaneously being a part *of* that from which one is different," and thus "is the perhaps most general conceptual basis of ecological thought and an ecological attitude."[86] In the first version of *Abdias* from 1842, the narrator characterizes both Abdias and Ditha as alienated from their surroundings when he says that Abdias "war wie ein fremder Baum in diesem Lande und seine Tochter ein fremder Apfel auf diesem Baume" (was like an alien tree in this country and his daughter an alien apple on this tree).[87] The line does not appear in the 1847 version, however, leaving an even sharper contrast to her father's alienation from the environment. Ditha's relation to nature is so passive that when she goes outside she lies in the grass of the garden so still that dew collects on her body. More tellingly, her body is connected to the atmosphere to such an extent that changes in temperature and humidity cause a shaking

---

81 Kelly Middleton Meyer, "'Sohn, Abdias, gehe nun in die Welt ...': Oedipalization, Gender Construction, and the Desire to Accumulate in Adalbert Stifter's 'Abdias,'" *Modern Austrian Literature: Journal of the Modern Austrian Literature and Culture Association* 35, no. 1/2 (2002): 12.

82 Stifter, *HKG*, 1,5: 309; Stifter, *Brigitta: With Abdias*, 71.

83 Stifter, *HKG*, 1,5: 238; Stifter, *Brigitta: With Abdias*, 22.

84 See Garrard, *Ecocriticism*, 23–36.

85 Val Plumwood, *Feminism and the Mastery of Nature* (London: Routledge, 1993), 42.

86 Hanjo Berressem, "Ecology and Immanence," in *Handbook of Ecocriticism and Cultural Ecology*, ed. Hubert Zapf (Berlin: Walter de Gruyter, 2016), 85.

87 Stifter, *HKG*, 1,2: 150.

in her limbs. The doctor is unable to find a cause, and so explains it away as being about her physical growth, but the fact that his explanation does not account for the correlation between the tremors and atmospheric changes casts doubt on his scientific explanation.

Blindness as a condition enabling a non-dualistic relation to the non-human is only cast in further relief when Ditha is struck by lightning and miraculously gains the power of sight. After the strike, which appears to take place during puberty,[88] she is able to see her surroundings, but without the ability to orient herself in a world where she is a subject among objects: she has trouble walking because the sight of things on the ground overwhelms her, and she becomes confused when looking too closely at a tree or a fold in her father's clothing, thinking that these things suddenly occupy the entire world simply because they occupy her entire field of vision. Abdias's solution to the crisis brought about in Ditha's consciousness is a pedagogical project of reorientation in order to train her in "dem neuen Reich des Sehens" (the new realm of sight).[89] Instead of seeing herself and all the other things around her as part of a whole, she is taught to see her world as a collection of discrete things: sky versus clouds versus ground versus grass, all illuminated by "die Sonne, die Lampe des Tages, die nach dem Schlummer immer komme, den Tag mache und den Augen Kraft gebe, alles sehen zu können" (the sun, the lamp of the day, which always came after sleep, making the day and giving the eyes the power to see everything).[90] The implication here is that the ability to perceive the sun's light even separates out night and day and waking from sleeping as similarly discrete things.

This pedagogical program of getting her to conceive of the world in dualistic terms proceeds slowly and is at best partially successful. She struggles to name trees, flowers, and colors correctly, "insbesondere wenn Farben und Klänge zugleich sich in ihrem Haupte drängten" (especially when colours and sounds crowded together in her head).[91] When she first sees flax blossoms, she sees them as different, but still part of the sky: "Vater, sieh nur, wie der ganze Himmel auf den Spitzen dieser grünen stehenden Fäden klingt!" (Father, just look at how the whole sky is singing on the tips of those green upright threads!).[92] Not incidentally, the flax also invokes the blue flower as a famous symbol for infinity coming out of the Romantic movement. The fact that she looks at blue flowers and hears the sky singing is a symptom of synesthesia, something we

---

88 "Ditha war beinahe völlig herangewachsen" (Ditha was almost fully grown). Stifter, *HKG*, 1,5: 318; Stifter, *Brigitta: With Abdias*, 78.

89 Stifter, *HKG*, 1,5: 326; Stifter, *Brigitta: With Abdias*, 86.

90 Stifter, *HKG*, 1,5: 325; Stifter, *Brigitta: With Abdias*, 83.

91 Stifter, *HKG*, 1,5: 325; Stifter, *Brigitta: With Abdias*, 83.

92 Stifter, *HKG*, 1,5: 330; Stifter, *Brigitta: With Abdias*, 86.

58 ♦ ENVIRONMENTAL COUNTERFICTIONS

see again when the narrator reports her speaking of "violetten Klängen" (violet sounds).[93] Her synesthesia both resists the mode of seeing at the core of her father's pedagogical program and also preserves her previsual way of being in her world. Timothy Morton has argued for the productivity of synesthesia in a broader process of "dissolving the subject-object dualism upon which depend both aestheticization and the domination of nature."[94] Hence the narrator's statement about Ditha's life: "So lebte sie eine Welt aus Sehen und Blindheit, und so war ja auch das Blau ihrer Augen, so wie das unsers Himmels, aus Licht und Nacht gewoben" (So she lived in a world made of sight and blindness, like the blue of her eyes which, like that of our sky, is woven out of light and night).[95] This conclusion about her life announces the persistence of her immanent, non-dualistic way of being in the world. Her eyes are like the sky not only because they happen to be the same color, but the statement that both are woven of light and night contradicts what Abdias teaches her in his attempt to train her in seeing night and day as entirely separate things. The very phrasing in the German "so lebte sie eine Welt," likewise implies a greater immediacy through its use of the accusative.[96] Stifter could have used a prepositional phrase, the way Helen Watanabe-O'Kelly does by translating the phrase as "so she lived in a world." Indeed, his phrasing is an unusual one, then as now. The entry for "leben," "to live," in the Grimms' *Wörterbuch* states that with the accusative plus a time or object marker, "leben" connotes "durchleben," "lebend durchmachen," or "verleben," all of which imply lived experience in English.[97] In spite of the fact that she has gained sight, and her father is busy training her in

---

93 Stifter, *HKG*, 1,5: 330; Stifter, *Brigitta: With Abdias*, 86.

94 Timothy Morton, *Ecology Without Nature: Rethinking Environmental Aesthetics* (Cambridge, MA: Harvard University Press, 2007), 162.

95 Stifter, *HKG*, 1,5: 330; Stifter, *Brigitta: With Abdias*, 87, translation modified.

96 In a previous version of this argument, I stated that the phrase was in the genitive: "so lebte sie einer Welt" (Alexander Robert Phillips, "Adalbert Stifter's Alternative Anthropocene: Reimagining Social Nature in *Brigitta* and *Abdias*," in *German Ecocriticism in the Anthropocene*, ed. Caroline Schaumann and Heather Sullivan [New York: Palgrave Macmillan, 2017], 79–80). While it appears as a genitive phrase in the six-volume Insel edition of 1959, it is an accusative phrase in both the Prague-Reichenberg edition and the *Historisch-Kritische Gesamtausgabe*. Stefl explains his editorial interventions in the afterword, but does not account for this particular discrepancy. See Adalbert Stifter, *Gesammelte Werke*, ed. Max Stefl (Frankfurt am Main: Insel, 1959), vol. 2, 693–708. The reading with the accusative, "so lebte sie eine Welt," is based on the authoritative editions, but the basic point about the language implying a greater immediacy stands either way.

97 "leben," in *Deutsches Wörterbuch von Jacob Grimm und Wilhelm Grimm*, 33 vols. (Leipzig: Hirzel, 1853–1971), vol. 12, www.woerterbuchnetz.de/DWB/leben.

dualistic thinking, the text still describes her mode of being in terms of a passive contiguity between herself and the non-human.

In the end, though, it appears that Ditha's immanence with her environment cannot last, at least not while she remains alive. She is killed when she is struck by lightning a second time, but in the moments preceding her death, she begins excitedly talking about the flax field that her father had planted for her after seeing her enthusiasm for the blossom. But the way she speaks about the field suggests that she has at last come around to seeing nature not as an extension of herself or that which extends through her, but something that can be exploited as a resource. In a meandering speech she tells her father that the flax plant "ist ein Freund des Menschen" (is man's friend) because it provides the raw materials for cloth that serve human needs from birth to the grave.[98] She begins to sound very much like one of Stifter's cultivating types and is promptly struck dead.

Ditha's sudden death is the kind of natural event that defies meaning-making. In dying she achieves a higher level of immanence with nature than she ever did during her lifetime, as her body becomes a source of nutrients for plants, a point the story makes when it mentions that she was buried and "aus Dithas Glieder sproßten Blumen und Gras" (out of Ditha's body grew flowers and grass).[99] The novella assures us at its close that the valley is fruitful and the owners who take ownership of it after Abdias's death have, with their sons, expanded the house and made it more beautiful. One way to make sense of this ending is that the subsequent cultivation of the valley lends sense to Abdias's and Ditha's deaths, which are links in the chain of flowers metaphor from the opening, a meaning signaled by the literal flowers that spring out of Ditha's corpse. But that more harmonious environmental future happens over Abdias's and Ditha's dead bodies and the extermination of their family line, demanding yet again that we be skeptical of the sunny description of the fruitful valley and its beautiful house at the close of the story.

Ethical Prometheanism: *Der Nachsommer*

The connection to the local environment that Stephan and Brigitta achieve but Abdias does not is the ultimate telos of the narrator Heinrich Drendorf's process of *Bildung* in Stifter's 1857 novel *Der Nachsommer*. The story, to the extent that this famously slow and descriptive novel has any story at all, concerns the relationship between Heinrich, child of a merchant family in a thinly veiled Vienna, and the Freiherr von Risach, owner of the Asperhof estate, which Heinrich prefers to call the Rosenhof

98 Stifter, *HKG*, 1,5: 340; Stifter, *Brigitta: With Abdias*, 93.
99 Stifter, *HKG*, 1,5: 341; Stifter, *Brigitta: With Abdias*, 94.

because of Risach's many well-tended rose bushes. Risach mentors Heinrich in science and aesthetics, guiding his upbringing to the point of his marriage to Natalie, daughter of Mathilde of the Sternenhof estate, who, we learn, was Risach's love interest in his youth but whose parents blocked the union. When Heinrich announces in the final sentence of the novel that he has laid the foundations for a family with his marriage, that he will continue to pursue the sciences, and promises "ich werde meine Habe verwalten, werde sonst noch nüzen, und jedes selbst das wissenschaftliche Bestreben hat nun Einfachheit Halt und Bedeutung" (I shall administer my property, shall be useful in other ways, and everything, including my scientific endeavors, has now gained significantly in clarity, solidity, and importance),[100] he makes clear that his full integration into the society in and around Risach's estate, the archetypal end of the Bildungsroman, is predicated on his own relation to nature as scientist and estate manager. In this he follows his mentor Risach, whose cultivation of his estate is based on close observation of nature and an ecological understanding that blends both the findings of science and a more heuristic knowledge of the environment. In the introduction to this book I mentioned the famous "weather conversation" when Heinrich and Risach first meet. Heinrich is seeking shelter because he is convinced a storm is about to break, but Risach argues that it will not. After the storm does not, in fact, take place, Risach reveals to Heinrich that the reason he was able to accurately predict the weather was by observing the local animals, which is to say, he made an accurate prediction heuristically. At the same time, he does keep informed of the natural sciences as a set of methods and disciplines: Alexander von Humboldt's writings feature prominently in his private library, and he has a collection of scientific instruments for predicting weather.[101] However, just as Stephan's connection with nature justified a social hierarchy, so too does it seem that Risach's knowledge leaves him in a privileged position in an order that structures the work humans do on the rest of nature. In one scene, while waiting to see whether the storm will, in fact, arrive, Heinrich observes workers cutting grass, and says to Risach that they, too, seem to think the storm will not come, to which Risach bluntly replies that they know nothing about the weather, and are only cutting the grass because he told them to.[102]

100 Stifter, *HKG*, 4,3: 282; Stifter, *Indian Summer*, 478–79.

101 See also my own reading of the scene in Alexander Robert Phillips, "Cheerful Terror: Stifter and the Aesthetics of Atmosphere," in *A Companion to the Works of Adalbert Stifter*, ed. Sean Ireton (Rochester, NY: Camden House, 2025), 287–89.

102 Stifter, *HKG*, 4,1: 75; Stifter, *Indian Summer*, 47. In his classic study of *Der Nachsommer*, Horst Glaser characterizes Stifter's "restorative utopia" as a caste society, one that wants capitalism without class conflict. See Horst Albert Glaser, *Die Restauration des Schönen: Stifters "Nachsommer"* (Stuttgart: Metzler,

Risach's deep knowledge of local ecosystems adds a dimension to the "first coexistence with nature" that Stephan and Brigitta embodied. He is a Promethean figure, whose knowledge and forethought is put to use in a project of dominating nature at the estate. However, his is a soft Prometheanism, unlike, for instance, the Prometheus of Goethe's poem, who takes unabashed pride in his own creations and general stance of defiance against the gods.[103] Instead, knowledge of nature means that Risach can work not in defiance of, but in accord with, its immutable laws in order to realize his design. Christian Begemann characterizes the relation between the self and nature that Risach embodies as a "narzißtisch[e] Dialektik" (narcissistic dialectic) between a self-centered enclosure in one's own interiority and an imagined expansion into the universe, the traces of which show up especially in Risach's garden.[104]

Risach delivers a lengthy explanation of how he has engineered his garden to be a harmonious ecosystem in the chapter "Der Abschied" (The Departure). A garden is, by definition, as social as nature gets, being the product of human planning and cultivation in the service of very human goals. The way Risach deploys his knowledge of nature to serve his own ends, and the paradoxes that arise therefrom, become especially clear when he describes how he has put the birds to use in maintaining the garden. He ensures that fresh food and water are provided for them, and in return they help keep the vermin under control and provide him with the pleasure of their song. Ostensibly it is a symbiotic relationship, one that Risach sees as ensuring the birds' freedom, but the irony in his insistence is that signs of a more coercive relationship still slip in to this speech meant to prove that he is not like those who would dominate nature in a cruder way. When it comes to the practice of encaging birds and keeping them indoors he says:

> Wenn [der Vogel] jung oder sogar alt gefangen wird, vergißt er sich und sein Leid, wird ein Hin- und Widerhüpfer in kleinem Raume, da er sonst einen großen brauchte, und singt seine Weise; aber dieser Gesang ist ein Gesang der Gewohnheit, nicht der Lust.

1965), 1–3. More recently, by contrast, Robert Leucht has argued against a reading of the estate as being *merely* a conservative utopia, showing instead that a variety of utopian concepts come together in the novel. Risach's attitude towards his workers, though, is a moment of conservative sentiment due to its investment in the maintenance of social hierarchy. See Robert Leucht, "Ordnung, Bildung, Kunsthandwerk. Die Pluralität utopischer Modelle in Adalbert Stifters *Der Nachsommer*," in *Figuren der Übertragung: Adalbert Stifter und das Wissen seiner Zeit*, ed. Michael Gamper and Karl Wagner (Zürich: Chronos, 2009), 291.

103 Johann Wolfgang von Goethe, *Werke*, ed. Erich Trunz, vol. 1 (Hamburg: Christian Wegner, 1964), 44–46.

104 Begemann, *Die Welt der Zeichen*, 343.

62 ♦ Environmental Counterfictions

Wir haben an unserm Garten einen ungeheuren Käfich ohne Draht Stangen und Vogelthürchen, in welchem der Vogel vor außerordentlicher Freude, der er sich so leicht hingibt, singt, in welchem wir das Zusammentönen vieler Stimmen hören können, das in einem Zimmer beisammen nur ein Geschrei wäre, und in welchem wir endlich die häusliche Wirthschaft der Vögel und ihre Geberden sehen können, die so verschieden sind und oft dem tiefsten Ernste ein Lächeln abgewinnen können... . [Die Leute] wollen dieselben genießen, sie wollen sie recht nahe genießen, und da sie keinen Käfich mit unsichtbaren Drähten und Stangen machen können, wie wir, in dem sie das eigentliche Wesen des Vogels wahrnehmen könnten, so machen sie einen mit sichtbaren, in welchem der Vogel eingesperrt ist, und seinem zu frühen Tode entgegen singt. Sie sind auf diese Weise nicht unfühlsam für die Stimme des Vogels, aber sie sind unfühlsam für sein Leiden.

[If [the bird] is caught young or even old, he forgets himself and his misery, becomes a creature that hops back and forth in a small space when he otherwise needed a large one, and sings his song; but this song is one of habit, not of joy. Our grounds are actually a colossal cage without wire, bars or doors where the birds sing from an extraordinary joy that comes to them so readily, where we hear a medley of many voices which would only be a discordant scream in a room together, and where we can observe the birds' housekeeping and behavior which is so different and can often make us smile even when things are gloomiest... . People want to enjoy them; they want to enjoy them from up close, and since, [unlike us], they are incapable of making a cage with invisible wire and bars, where they could observe the true nature of the birds, they make a visible cage in which the bird is locked and sings until his premature death. People are not without feeling for the bird's song, but they are without feeling for his suffering.[105]]

For Risach, people who keep birds in cages err in terms of both ethics and aesthetics. The ethical problem is that the cage does not afford the bird the space it needs, leading to the aesthetic problem that the bird produces not the pleasant song it would under "natural" conditions, but instead a disharmonious screech. In his view, keeping birds in cages means that aesthetics actually trumps ethics, since those who do so have feeling for the bird's beautiful sound but no feeling for its suffering. Risach's garden is therefore more ethical because it is seemingly more "natural" than the birdcage. Its design is rooted in his deep knowledge of the flora and fauna of his region, and more generally the garden is less confining and

105 Stifter, *HKG*, 4,1: 161; Stifter, *Indian Summer*, 95–96.

the bird is in more natural surroundings. Or so the bird thinks. As if it were not clear from the lengthy description of the human planning that went into the garden's creation, Risach all but acknowledges the fact that the garden is no space of freedom for the bird when he calls it a "colossal cage without wire bars or doors." The birds might not be confined in cages, but Risach is still manipulating them because he enjoys their song as much as those who put birds in literal cages, and more than that, the birds are also working for him in the sense that they provide him with no-cost pest control. As Lars Rosenbaum points out, Risach not only is consistent in talking about the birds as workers, but has considered their presence in terms of a cost/benefit analysis, choosing to accept the damage they do to the fruit crop in light of the larger profit he gains from them.[106] The birds sing "naturally" only because they do not recognize their environment as anything but natural, and so they serve their function within the gardener's larger design.

The question that the production of nature in this example raises regards the conditions of freedom for birds and, by extension, other life forms, including human beings. Are the birds unfree because they are unwittingly serving human designs? Risach's answer is no, and he might be right. If we accept Risach's argument, then the garden agrees with Aldo Leopold's famous land ethic, which holds that "a thing is right when it tends to preserve the integrity, stability, and beauty of the biotic community. It is wrong when it tends otherwise."[107] The garden might be designed to subtly manipulate the birds into serving Risach's purpose, but if the bird behaves in the garden as it would in a forest because it does not recognize the difference, then it is no less free and its song is no less "natural" than it would be in the wild. In that respect, the garden reflects the thesis of Stifter's essay "Der Staat" (The State), which appeared in April 1848, just after the outbreak of revolution. Stifter argues that the state, in placing limits on individual freedom, actually guarantees freedom by allowing every person to realize their full essence.[108] And yet none of that does away with the coercion. The invisible birdcage metaphor leaves us with the paradox of avian freedom in unfreedom, but elsewhere the violence is far more naked. The redstarts are a bird species that do not target pesky caterpillars, but instead hunt the honeybees Risach raises, and, in spite of his careful planning, he has no better solution to their predation of his bees than to shoot them dead. "The 'order' of the Rosenhaus

---

106 Lars Rosenbaum, "Absence and Omnipresence: On the Significance of Waste in Stifter's *Der Nachsommer*," trans. Sean Ireton, in *A Companion to the Works of Adalbert Stifter*, ed. Ireton, (Rochester, NY: Camden House, 2025), 215–16.

107 Leopold, *A Sand County Almanac*, 224–25.

108 Stifter, *HKG*, 8,2: 27–39.

64 ♦ Environmental Counterfictions

thus seems to devolve into a kind of military order whereby disruptive elements are summarily eliminated," as Lars Rosenbaum puts it.[109]

All of that assumes, though, that we accept a dichotomy in which non-human life is free in a nature without humans, and unfree once humans start exerting any sort of control. But the notion that nature is a realm of freedom is no more self-explanatory than the concept of nature itself. It is a notion Theodor Adorno critiques, not incidentally by considering birdsong as an instance of natural beauty. In *Aesthetic Theory* (1970) he writes: "The song of birds is found beautiful by everyone; no feeling person in whom something of the European tradition survives fails to be moved by the sound of a robin after a rain shower. Yet something frightening lurks in the song of birds precisely because it is not a song but obeys the spell in which it is enmeshed."[110] Birdsong might be an instance of natural beauty, and natural beauty might be liberatory "because it recollects a world without domination," Adorno says, even if such a realm "probably never existed." But Adorno argues that the experience of natural beauty and its recollection of freedom also depends on a "genius" that has arisen out of the "amorphousness" of primordial nature, which enabled it to have a concept of freedom in the first place: "The anamnesis of freedom in natural beauty deceives because it seeks freedom in the old unfreedom."[111] We might speculate in response to Adorno about what freedom means to a bird, but this is not the space. What matters is that Risach imagines the birds to have a sense of freedom that is expressed in their song. The invisible birdcage, then, would be a tacit acknowledgment that the garden reproduces nature and with it Adorno's "old unfreedom." This tacit acknowledgment is not a slip of the ideological mask, one that might lead us to think that the birds would be even better off somewhere else, say in some primeval forest that by 1857 we would be hard pressed to find in Europe anyway. Rather, it is an irony that the birds are their most natural selves in the artificial, unfree space of the garden.

If there is a single natural thing in the novel, though, in which ecology, politics, and aesthetics intersect, it is the cactus *Cereus peruvianus*. The cactus is an index of the realities of global imperialism insofar as its very presence up in the Alps is made possible because of the political and ecological realities of nineteenth-century colonialism. The *Cereus* and other cacti require the maintenance that they do because they are non-native plants that have travelled along the same routes that enable

109 Rosenbaum, "Absence and Omnipresence," 216. See also Begemann, *Die Welt der Zeichen*, 345–46.

110 Theodor W. Adorno, *Aesthetic Theory*, trans. Robert Hullot-Kentor (Minneapolis: University of Minnesota Press, 1997), 66.

111 Adorno, *Aesthetic Theory*, 66.

European empires. Four decades later, as we will see, the aloe plant in Theodor Fontane's *Der Stechlin* would serve a similar signifying function. The *Cereus* first grows neglected at the Inghof, an aristocratic estate neighboring Risach's, in a greenhouse that is far too small for it. Risach ends up acquiring and transplanting it to his own estate. At the Rosenhof, the cactus is placed in a specially constructed greenhouse with a small tower to accommodate its size. For Heinrich, the *Cereus* in its new home is on the way to both self-realization and aesthetic completion: "Ich hätte nicht gedacht, daß diese Pflanze so groß sei, und daß sie sich so schön darstellen würde" (I wouldn't have imagined that this plant was so big or that it would grow so beautifully).[112] He figures the transplantation as yet another example of cultivation that helps a natural form, in this case the cactus, become more natural. At the Rosenhof, the *Cereus peruvianus* is placed not in a pot, as Risach's smaller cacti are, but in the ground itself, and whereas the cramped greenhouse at Inghof forced the cactus to grow sideways against the roof, the new greenhouse "liberates" the plant with its accommodating tower.

Greenhouses are more obviously human constructs than gardens, and Heinrich takes note of how Risach's is engineered to manage light, temperature, and airflow. Transplanting the *Cereus peruvianus* into a structure that allows it more space to grow makes it another instance where cultivation is supposed to make something more natural. Nevertheless, while Risach's greenhouse might be better designed and more accommodating to the cactus than the one at Inghof, it is no less of a container. The irony of the greenhouse is analogous to the irony of Risach's garden cum invisible birdcage: creating an environment in which the organisms can be their "natural" selves, while still serving human ends. The project of "rescuing" the cactus and letting it develop under better conditions at Risach's estate mirrors the work of restoring the ancient Greek marble statue, one of the most important objects in the novel.[113] Risach purchased the statue in Italy from owners who were looking to be rid of it in order to make way for renovations to the hall in which it stood, and had it transported to his estate. Like the cactus, the marble statue was contained in ways that obscured its true nature: in Italy it was kept partially in protective wooden panelling, but more than that it had a coating of plaster that led the owners and Risach to believe it was made of nothing but plaster.[114] The cactus seems to signal that it has become its more natural self in its new home when it finally blossoms, a blossoming

---

112 Stifter, *HKG*, 4,2: 20; Stifter, *Indian Summer*, 185.

113 Catriona Macleod explores the affinity between the cactus and the statue in *Fugitive Objects: Sculpture and Literature in the German Nineteenth Century* (Evanston, IL: Northwestern University Press, 2014), 123–42.

114 Stifter, *HKG*, 4,2: 76–80.

66 ♦ Environmental Counterfictions

that has symbolic significance, as it coincides with Heinrich and Natalie's marriage.[115] Unlike the statue, however, the fact that the cactus is a living, growing organism means that it is not a mere object for unidirectional human labor, and this plant in particular, being thorny, puts up resistance. The gardener alerts us to this fundamental irony in the cactus's being when he says of the *Cereus peruvianus* and the other cactuses in Risach's collection: "Die Stellung ihrer Bildung ist so mannigfaltig, die Stacheln können zu einer wahren Zierde und zu einer Bewaffnung dienen, und die Blüthen sind verwunderlich wie Märchen" (Their forms are so manifold; the spines can serve as a true adornment but at the same time as a weapon; the blossoms are as wondrous as a fairy tale).[116] The variety of forms the cactus can take resists efforts at aesthetic shaping, and the thorns are outright violent, features that combine with the form and the marvelousness of the flowers, which the gardener talks about as more fantastic than real, to produce an overall experience of aesthetic pleasure.

The fact that all but a few key scenes take place in mountainous countryside does not mean that *Der Nachsommer* does not also give us a glimpse of a dawning industrial economy, with all of its ecological consequences. Indeed, such scenes underscore that while the characters might figure the rural estates as utopian alternatives, they are as structured by the shift to an industrial economy as the city. As a merchant's son, Heinrich is very much a child of capital, and seeing where goods come from is foundational to his process of Bildung. And so, after setting off from his family home into the mountains, but before meeting Risach, Heinrich visits sites of agriculture and industrial manufacture. He visits first vineyards and flax fields, then comes to an industrial valley. This is a place where a number of factories are "zerstreut" (scattered), language that evokes planless sprawl, limited only by the fact that the factories are all clustered around the stream on which they rely for power. The stream, Heinrich says, is particularly favorable to industry because of its regular flow and the fact that it does not freeze over easily. That the shift to a hydrocarbon economy has not yet occurred here is trivial compared to the fact that Heinrich limits his description of the stream to an evaluation of its use value. His education in the mountains will effect a shift in his apprehension of the natural environment. For now, though, Heinrich looks at the valley through the eyes of a member of the urban bourgeoisie at an early stage of industrial capitalist development. The presence of the factories is a reminder of the interpenetration of "the city" and "the country" both because they are places that convert the raw materials of

---

115 Stifter, *HKG*, 4,3: 271; Stifter, *Indian Summer*, 472. See also Macleod, *Fugitive Objects*, 139.

116 Stifter, *HKG*, 4,1: 133; Stifter, *Indian Summer*, 80.

nature into products for the market, but also because their owners all live in the city.

On the other hand, being driven by water power, industrial production in this valley happens under an energy regime that, in the language of contemporary environmentalism, is at least more sustainable. But the factories are still embryonic forms of their environmentally more deleterious coal-burning successors, as Karl Marx notes in his discussion of water-driven mills in his account of machinery and large-scale industry in the first volume of *Capital*.[117] From Heinrich's perspective, though, this valley would be a positive counterexample to another valley he later visits, one badly blighted by charcoal production. The ground is covered in black from the wagons carrying charcoal, kilns are scattered throughout the forest, and the inn Heinrich checks into has walls covered in moss and a garden where nothing but chives will grow. The charcoal produced in the region is ultimately bound for the city, another sign of the way in which urban and industrial realities are inscribed on the landscape of this seemingly remote place.

Standing over this valley like Caspar David Friedrich's iconic wanderer, Heinrich makes a crucial admission that the destruction he sees stems from a human "Trieb, die Natur zu besiegen" ([drive] to conquer nature), one that also motivates the people in mountain regions to "zähmen" (to tame) the mountains they love through climbing.[118] Heinrich is also talking about himself as a human who goes into the mountains and has inner drives, and indeed, as Sean Ireton points out, Heinrich's striving for scientific knowledge is balanced by his love of climbing as a means of physical play.[119] But his expeditions into the mountains also open up his consciousness to the fact that the Earth's history is far vaster than his own human timescales. The sudden awareness of the vastness of the Earth and its history happens in the chapter "Die Erweiterung" (Expanding the Horizons). The scene in question begins when Heinrich is on his way to do a survey of Lauter Lake. He passes a pile of stones (*Geschiebe*) that have been dredged from a riverbed for road construction. The

---

117 Karl Marx and Friedrich Engels, *Capital: A Critique of Political Economy*, vol. 1 (New York: Penguin, 1990), 497–99.

118 Stifter, *HKG*, 4,2: 185; Stifter, *Indian Summer*, 277, translation modified. Heinrich's remarks not only reflect on the environmental ambivalence of his own expeditions, but of mountaineering as an emerging pursuit in the nineteenth century. On the history of mountaineering and its environmental politics see Caroline Schaumann, *Peak Pursuits: The Emergence of Mountaineering in the Nineteenth Century* (New Haven: Yale University Press, 2020).

119 Sean Ireton, "Geology, Mountaineering, and Self-Formation in Adalbert Stifter's *Der Nachsommer*," in *Heights of Reflection: Mountains in the German Imagination from the Middle Ages to the Twenty-First Century* (Rochester, NY: Camden House, 2013), 198–99.

68 ♦ Environmental Counterfictions

construction site affords us another glimpse of the conquest of nature: the construction of the road alters the landscape to make the mountains more accessible. But what Heinrich focuses on is not the physical change to the mountain landscape, but the materials and their geologic history. He regards them with "Ehrfurcht" (a sense of awe) and, as "die Bothen von unserem Gebirge" (harbingers of our mountains), the stones literally stop him in his tracks.[120]

Viewed as a pile of raw material, the stones are shorn of their uniqueness and are reduced to their use value as construction materials, but to a budding geologist like Heinrich, they bring the vastness of geological time powerfully to mind. And yet, as products of geological processes unfolding across timescales that almost escape human comprehension, these stones only remind Heinrich of the limitation of geological knowledge relative to the history of the Earth. The narration switches into a lengthy passage consisting almost exclusively of rhetorical questions:

> Wenn ich die Stücke unbelebter Körper, die ich für meine Schreine sammelte, ansah, so fiel mir auf, daß hier diese Körper liegen, dort andere, daß ungeheure Mengen desselben Stoffes zu großen gebirgen aufgethürmt sind, und daß wieder in kleinen Abständen kleine Lagerungen mit einander wechseln. Woher sind sie gekommen, wie haben sie sich gehäuft? Liegen sie nach einem Geseze, und wie ist dieses geworden? Oft sind Theile eines größern Körpers in Menge oder einzeln an Stellen, wo der Körper selber nicht ist, wo sie nicht sein sollen, wo sie Fremdlinge sind. Wie sind sie an den Plaz gekommen? Wie ist überhaupt an einer Stelle gerade dieser Stoff entstanden und nicht ein anderer? Woher ist die Berggestalt im Großen gekommen? Ist sie noch in ihrer Reinheit da, oder hat sie Veränderungen erlitten, und erleidet sie dieseleben noch immer? Wie ist die Gestalt der Erde selber geworden, wie hat sich ihr Antliz gefurcht, sind die Lücken groß, sind sie klein?

> [When I looked at the inanimate pieces I gathered for my collection, it struck me that here these were lying on the ground; elsewhere colossal amounts of the same material were heaped up to form great mountains; in other places relatively shallow layers alternated in lesser intervals. Where did they come from, how were they formed? Were they formed in accordance with some law or principle—how did this come about? Often there were pieces of a larger body in quantity or individually in places where this larger body itself wasn't found, where they really shouldn't be, where they were quite out of place. How did they come to be there? Why was this particular material found on this spot and not on another? How did the gigantic

120 Stifter, *HKG*, 4,2: 27–28; Stifter, *Indian Summer*, 190.

ENVIRONMENTAL COUNTERFICTIONS ♦ 69

mountain formations come into being? Are they still there in their primeval form or did they undergo changes? Are they still changing? How was the Earth itself formed, how was its countenance furrowed, are the gaps large, are they small?[121]]

Heinrich moves from the small of the stones he is gathering for his personal collection to very large-scale questions about the planet, its processes, and the history of its formation. The long list of rhetorical questions creates a sense of radical openness in the narration, serving to call attention to the limits of geological knowledge. Heinrich's thoughts move from the topography beneath the Lauter Lake, which he has come to survey, to shifts in the landscape over the course of geologic time, to the origins of the region's rock formations, the death of forests, and finally changes to the climate over the course of Earth history and how that changing climate, in turn, has changed the shape of the planet, affected its systems, and even had an impact on its rotation.[122] Many of the questions are concerned with the deep past, but the final paragraph of rhetorical questions turns from Earth history, the only history worth studying, he says, to the distant future:

Die Quellen zu der Geschichte der Erde bewahrt sie selber wie in einem Schriftengewölbe in ihrem Innern auf, Quellen, die vielleicht in Millionen Urkunden niedergelegt sind, und bei denen es nur darauf ankömmt, daß wir sie lesen lernen, und sie duch Eifer und Rechthaberei nicht verfälschen. Wer wird diese Geschichte einmal klar vor Augen haben? Wird eine solche Zeit kommen, oder wird sie nur der immer ganz wissen, der sie von Ewigkeit her gewußt hat?

[The Earth itself preserves the sources of this history in its innermost parts just as in a room for records, sources inscribed in perhaps millions of documents; it is only a matter of our learning to read and not falsify them by eagerness or obstinacy. Who will one day have this history clearly before his eyes? Will ever such a time come, or will only He know it completely Who has known it for all Eternity?[123]]

The question about the Earth as archive feeds back into the novel's realist aesthetics. The hall of records recalls the "book of nature" topos in seeing in the rocks documentation of geological history, and therefore an implicit claim to truthfully tell the "history" or, also, "story" (*Geschichte*)

---

121 Stifter, *HKG*, 4,2: 30; Stifter, *Indian Summer*, 190.
122 Stifter, *HKG*, 4,2: 32; Stifter, *Indian Summer*, 192.
123 Stifter, *HKG*, 4,2: 50; Stifter, *Indian Summer*, 192.

of the planet. And because the Earth preserves the sources of its entire history within itself, it is the most holistic possible text.

Taken at face value, the subordination of human history to the much vaster past and future of the planet assumes a non-anthropocentric worldview, as humans are only a small entry in a vast archive to which they have at most partial access, an "Einschiebsel" (interpolation), a word that, as Jason Groves points out, shares a root with the "Geschiebe," or pile of stones, that sets Heinrich down this line of thought in the first place.[124] That archive is instead most legible to some higher, future reader—one who has the omniscient perspective of God, and whose entry on the scene suggests again that he functions as a guarantor of reality to the extent that the sum of stratigraphically recorded history will present itself to him (although one effect of the rhetorical questions is that it tantalizingly suggests that God is not the only possible future reader). Groves makes the case that the point about humans as an "Einschiebsel" brings us back to Stifter and his views about the events of his own present, because interpolating human history into a stratigraphic record gives it a linearity that smooths out irregularity, inconsistency, and revolution, a linearity that is complicated when the stones are left in a heap.[125]

The image is in line with Stifter's gradualist thinking about both outer nature and inner, human nature. In *Der Nachsommer*, as Sean Ireton points out, the slowness of the narrative and the step-by-step process of Heinrich's *Bildung* are analogous to the novel's Alpine setting, given that mountains also form gradually.[126] Heinrich's own thinking in this passage is gradualist, as he imagines changes to the planet unfolding not in quick events but over timescales far longer than those of a human lifetime. But I find the political implications of the Earth-as-archive metaphor more ambiguous. First, as Timothy Attanucci points out, the hall of records does not have the same consistency as the related metaphor of the book of nature, because books have form and order that halls of records do not.[127] Second, stratigraphy works as a record of geological time because it is visibly layered, a layering that can imply sudden, disruptive changes as much as it implies gradual accumulation over long timespans. In our own time we know how sudden those shifts can be, as with the Cretaceous-Paleogene boundary, the line that marks the asteroid impact scientists now theorize to have caused the extinction event sixty-six

124 Jason Groves, *The Geological Unconscious: German Literature and the Mineral Imaginary* (New York: Fordham University Press, 2020), 76.

125 Groves, *The Geological Unconscious*, 76–77.

126 Ireton, "Geology, Mountaineering, and Self-Formation in Adalbert Stifter's *Der Nachsommer*," 196.

127 Timothy Attanucci, *The Restorative Poetics of a Geological Age: Stifter, Viollet-Le-Duc, and the Aesthetic Practices of Geohistoricism* (Berlin: Walter de Gruyter, 2020), 30.

million years ago that included non-avian dinosaurs. Even without the benefit of contemporary understanding of geological history, reading rocks as documents of Earth's past means taking the lines between the layers as seriously as the layers themselves, and those lines would necessarily suggest some sort of sudden shift to distinguish one from the next. Stifter may dismiss large, catastrophic events as being in truth smaller than gradual processes, but the wolf episode in *Brigitta* and the lightning strikes in *Abdias* are only two examples of singular, catastrophic events from his oeuvre that are more important than he admits in the preface to *Bunte Steine*. Shock and conflict are, ultimately, just as constitutive of both of these catastrophic events as slow changes taking place over long stretches of time are.

Regardless of the interpretive weight that we give either to the layers themselves or the boundaries between them in the rock face, in the end the specific rocks that Heinrich is looking at in this scene have all been quarried to lay down a road, that is, a technology in the conquest of nature. Even as the sight of the stones may prompt Heinrich to think about his surroundings in terms of deep time, they present themselves to him as just such a moment of sudden disruption in longer-term geological processes. Proponents of the Anthropocene thesis today would argue that the road is one instance of global anthropogenic environmental transformations that will themselves eventually constitute a distinct layer of rock, and thus a distinct entry in Heinrich's hall of records. The notion that the human transformation of the natural environment marks a distinct historical turning point will come more sharply into the foreground for the later authors of German realism included in this study. While we might note the differences between Stifter and later realist authors, perhaps attributing them to changes in historical conditions, the environmental imagination in all of their works is animated by the social production of nature in the interests of political and economic power. Wilhelm Raabe depicts the environmental fallout from urban and industrial sprawl more directly than Stifter. But he shares with Stifter a concern regarding a logic of domination of the natural environment, one that constitutes his view of the present more deeply than the mere trappings of industrial modernity.

2: The Styx Flows through Arcadia: Environmental Depredation and Aesthetic Reflection in Wilhelm Raabe's Late Fiction

IN THE WINTER of 1890 to 1891 the city of Braunschweig experienced a precipitous decline in the quality of its drinking water. The cause: beet sugar factories in the surrounding area were releasing such high quantities of hydrogen sulfide—the major byproduct of beet sugar production—into the Oker River watershed that it exceeded the capacity of the leach fields on which the city then relied to purify its water. Wilhelm Raabe described the results in a letter to his daughter Margarethe dated January 17, 1891: "Sei Du froh, daß Du nicht in Braunschweig bist. Der reine Schweinestall! Wir waschen uns nicht mehr, wir putzen uns nicht mehr die Zähne, selbst durch das gekochte Essen schmeckt man das durch zwölf Zuckerfabriken versaute Okerwasser: Pfisters Mühle in fürchterlichster Vollendung!" (Be glad that you are not in Braunschweig. The absolute pigsty! We no longer bathe, we no longer brush our teeth, even in our cooked food one can taste the water from the Oker, spoiled by twelve sugar factories: Pfister's Mill in its most terrible completion!).[1] The letter describes the intrusion of a byproduct of modern industry into a city that in a short essay from 1866 Raabe had praised for embodying the "uralte Pracht und Schönheit der niedersächsischen Bürgerherrlichkeit" (ancient magnificence and beauty of lower Saxon bourgeois splendor).[2] Environmental crisis is here also an aesthetic crisis: quotidian habits of hygiene and consumption are suddenly disrupted as the ugly signs of modern industry move from the duchy's peripheral industrial settlements into the beautiful, pre-industrial urban core. Whether intentionally or not, Raabe's letter contains some

---

1 Wilhelm Raabe, "Letter to Margarethe Raabe," January 17, 1891, Nachlass Wilhelm Raabe, Schriftsteller (1831–1910). H III 10 : 2, Stadtarchiv Braunschweig. The letter is also excerpted in Horst Denkler, "Die Antwort literarischer Phantasie auf eine der 'größeren Fragen der Zeit': Zu Wilhelm Raabes 'Sommerferienheft' Pfisters Mühle," in *Neues über Wilhelm Raabe: Zehn Annährungsversuche an einen verkannten Schriftsteller* (Tübingen: Niemeyer, 1988), 101.

2 Wilhelm Raabe, "Der Altstadtmarkt zu Braunschweig," *Freya: Illustrirte Blätter für die gebildete Welt* 6 (1866): 149.

light irony, as the German "rein" implies purity and cleanliness, so that "der reine Schweinestall" can be translated as "the pure pigsty" as much as "the absolute pigsty." Read in that way, the city is "pure" and "clean" in its dirt and stench. And the stench from the water would have been offensive: hydrogen sulfide happens to be the gas that gives human flatus its characteristic odor. If Raabe's own 1884 novel *Pfisters Mühle* (Pfister's Mill), in which hydrogen sulfide from a beet sugar factory threatens the livelihood of a miller downstream, reaches its "most terrible completion" in the calamity of 1891, then it is because what appeared in the novel as an individual tragedy has since its publication grown into a disaster for an entire city.

It is not because of *Pfisters Mühle* alone that Raabe's fiction has a reputation for being particularly environmental. Industrialization, urbanization, and the impact these processes had on the natural environment appear repeatedly in his works, from his debut novel *Die Chronik der Sperlingsgasse* (The Chronicle of Sparrow Lane, 1856) to his final fragmentary novel *Altershausen* (drafted 1899–1902, posthumously published 1911). Whether such thematic elements make his novels "ecological" was a topic of debate in Raabe scholarship of the 1980s, a debate that took place concurrently with the emergence of ecocriticism as a field. On the one side, Thomas Sporn and Horst Denkler both argued that *Pfisters Mühle* in particular captures a historical environmental reality that lends the novel contemporary relevance.[3] On the other side, Jeffrey Sammons argued against the contemporary relevance thesis on the grounds that it disregarded the texts' historical contexts.[4] Sammons furthermore doubts that Raabe's texts are particularly environmental after all. In the case of *Pfisters Mühle* he writes: "Raabe seems primarily to have viewed the matter of pollution *aesthetically* ... . Strictly speaking, there is no question of ecology, that is, of balance in nature and man's balance with nature. What we have is an offense, but not a threat in the dimensions that enlightened people perceive today."[5] While I agree with Sammons's reservations about the relevance question, and while the narrow definition of ecology he offers is necessary for his argument, subsequent ecocriticism has demonstrated that this definition is not the only way of determining

---

3   Thomas Sporn, "Wilhelm Raabe: Ökologisch?," *Diskussion Deutsch* 12, no. 57 (1981): 56–63; Denkler, "Die Antwort literarischer Phantasie auf eine der 'größeren Fragen der Zeit.'"

4   Jeffrey Sammons, *Wilhelm Raabe: The Fiction of the Alternative Community*, 269–82. For other important entries in the debate from this period, see Hermann Helmers, "Raabe als Kritiker von Umweltzerstörung. Das Gedicht 'Einst kommt die Stunde' in der Novelle 'Pfisters Mühle,'" *Literatur für Leser* 87, no. 3 (1987): 199–211; Heinrich Detering, "Ökologische Krise und ästhetische Innovation im Werk Wilhelm Raabes," *Jahrbuch der Raabe-Gesellschaft* 33 (1992): 1–27.

5   Sammons, *Wilhelm Raabe*, 280–81.

whether a text is "environmental." As Lawrence Buell argues, the label "environmental text" designates more of a spectrum than an absolute category, and Robert Kern points out that texts "are environmental but not necessarily environmental*ist*."[6] But more importantly for my argument, the fact that Raabe's novels understand pollution, and environmental issues more generally, in aesthetic terms is precisely the point. In the letter to his daughter Raabe views the calamity aesthetically in two ways: first as a matter of perception and judgment (bad tasting food, unclean people) and second as a real-world event that completes the meaning of the realist literary text, making a truth claim *post facto*. *Pfisters Mühle* imagined a local ecological problem at what turned out to be a relatively early stage: the annual sugar beet harvest began producing a noticeable decline in the quality of Braunschweig's drinking water in the early 1880s, steadily growing worse each year until the calamity of 1890/91, six years after the novel's publication.[7]

Raabe himself, then, may have regarded his work as "relevant," but its prophetic quality is not the most interesting thing about his realism. Rather, his late fiction especially thinks through the apparent conflict between the mimetic representation of an environmentally degraded world and the aesthetic imperative of literary realism. In *Pfisters Mühle* as well as *Die Akten des Vogelsangs* (The Birdsong Papers, 1896) the dirty signs of industrial modernity function as a generatively destabilizing counterforce to the aestheticization of pre-industrial "green" places. Both stories are told from the perspective of first-person narrators who, while making no secret of their personal commitments as members of the urban bourgeoisie, reflect on their childhoods in idyllic spaces since transformed under the sign of Germany's industrialization. Both texts figure their respective places, the old family mill in the former and the idyllic "old" Vogelsang neighborhood in the latter, as sites of socio-ecological harmony, and situate the realist representation of those places at the core of their poetic projects. The dirty byproducts of industrial capitalism destabilize this project to the extent that they cling to each text's vision of a past ecological holism. But where pollution and sprawl disrupt the vision of a marvelous "Vorwelt" (prior world), as in *Pfisters Mühle*, or the harmonious socio-ecological synthesis of "Nachbarschaft" (neighborhood), as in *Die Akten des Vogelsangs*, it also catalyzes both the texts' reflections

6   Buell, *The Environmental Imagination*, 7–8; Robert Kern, "Ecocriticism: What Is It Good For?," *ISLE* 7, no. 1 (2000): 9–32.

7   Rudolf Blasius and Heinrich Beckurts, "Verunreinigung und Reinigung der Flüsse nach Untersuchungen des Wassers der Oker," *Deutsche Vierteljahrsschrift für öffentliche Gesundheitspflege* 27, no. 2 (1895): 335–36; Christian Behrens, *Die Wassergesetzgebung im Herzogtum Braunschweig nach Bauernbefreiung und industrieller Revolution: Zur Genese des Wasserrechts im bürgerlichen Rechtsstaat* (Hamburg: Verlag Dr. Kovač, 2009), 85–89.

on the conditions of possibility for art and artistic representation in an era of ecological plunder, and from there gives rise to the texts' implicit, self-reflective critique of nineteenth-century industrial modernity.

Where Have All the Pictures Gone?: *Pfister's Mill*

Industrial pollution is central to *Pfisters Mühle*, and its basic plot explains why Raabe would have seen the water calamity of 1890/91 as "its most terrible completion." The central narrative conceit of the novel is that the text we read is identical to the narrator Ebert Pfister's ironically named "Sommerferienheft" (summer vacation notebook), in which he relates the story of how the beet sugar factory Krickerode began releasing hydrogen sulfide into the stream that powered the family mill, causing a foul smell that drove customers away from the beer garden operated there, brought the turbines to a halt, and spurred the growth of microorganisms that suffocated all other life in the stream. The fish, Ebert writes, registered "ihr Mißbehagen an der Veränderung ihrer Lebensbedingungen" (their unhappiness with the change in their living conditions) by floating on their backs downstream.[8] Ebert's father, Bertram Pfister, decides to seek legal restitution for the lost business, first enlisting a family friend with the speaking name Adam Asche (*Asche*, ash) to gather scientific evidence against Krickerode. Asche at this time happens to be engaged in putting his own doctorate in natural sciences to use towards the development of a process for industrial laundry cleaning—a process that ironically produces clean clothes but dirty air and water.[9] With Asche's help Bertram wins his suit against Krickerode, but the court victory does not save the mill from insolvency, and so he shuts it down, after which he falls ill and dies. Ebert sells the mill and invests in the factory to be constructed on the site, but before that happens he and his young bride Emmy are allowed to spend a few weeks at the mill, during which time Ebert begins his summer vacation notebook. As Ebert both writes and orally narrates the history of the mill during his last foray there, the architects and the builders of the new factory become an ever-increasing presence, hastening the mill's end

---

8   Wilhelm Raabe, *Sämtliche Werke: Braunschweiger Ausgabe*, ed. Karl Hoppe, 26 vols. (Göttingen: Vandenhoek und Ruprecht, 1966–94) [=*BA*], vol. 16, 52–53.

9   Asche has affinities to Johan Julius Spindler (1810–73). Like Spindler, Asche also opens an industrial cleaning facility on the banks of the Spree in what is now Berlin-Köpenick. Asche is the voice of science in the novel, one of a number of competing discourses around which the text is structured. Sabine Wilke sketches these discourses out in "Pollution as Poetic Practice: Glimpses of Modernism in Wilhelm Raabe's *Pfisters Mühle*," *Colloquia Germanica* 44, no. 2 (2011): 202–6.

as the vacation comes to a close. They are already chopping down the mill's iconic chestnut trees as Ebert and Emmy take leave of Pfister's mill forever.

The novel was inspired by an actual lawsuit brought by the proprietors of the mills at Bienrode and Wenden against the beet sugar factory at Rautheim, all places that have since been incorporated into the city of Braunschweig, over losses incurred by the release of effluent into the Wabe, an Oker River tributary. The suit against Rautheim was one of a series of so-called "Wasserprozesse," or "water trials," in the nineteenth century that smaller businesses and communities filed against polluting industries seeking compensation for losses incurred from reduced water quality.[10] The Wabe is also the stream that flows near the tavern Zum Grünen Jäger, where the *Kleiderseller*, the *Stammtisch* Raabe participated in until the death of his daughter Getrud in 1892, used to hold its meetings. Along the way the author saw first-hand the impact of hydrogen sulfide on the stream's ecosystem, inspiring some of the descriptions of environmental depredation in *Pfisters Mühle*. The city of Braunschweig had established its first water filtration facilities in 1865, but local water purification systems were unable to keep pace with the amount of effluent coming from the booming beet sugar industry. By the 1880s Rautheim alone, for instance, was producing thirty to forty cubic meters of waste water for every single beet processed for sugar. With twenty-five thousand tons of beets processed in one season, the factory was releasing up to a million cubic meters of waste water. The problem would not be ameliorated until the city opened new water purification facilities in 1895.[11]

Prior to the debate in the 1980s over the question of just how "environmental" Wilhelm Raabe really was, literary scholarship on *Pfisters Mühle* tended to subordinate the depiction of the environment to the novel's social concerns, where industrialization and pollution are devices by which the novel represents the condition of the individual in the wake of rapid social and technological change. In his 1937 biography of Wilhelm Raabe, notorious for framing the author as a protofascist, Wilhelm Fehse casts the environmental concern as being a matter of conservative resistance to a crass modern industrial capital.[12] Hermann

10   For an example of such a trial, see the 1890 ruling of the Royal Provincial Court at Bielefeld in the case of Overbeck and the City of Herford vs. Hoffmann's Starch Factory, published as Bayerl and Troitzsch, "Der 'Wasserprozeß' gegen Hoffmanns Stärkefabriken (1890)."

11   Blasius and Beckurts, "Verunreinigung und Reinigung der Flüsse nach Untersuchungen des Wassers der Oker," 335–36; Behrens, "Die Wassergesetzgebung im Herzogtum Braunschweig," 85–89.

12   Wilhelm Fehse, *Wilhelm Raabe: Sein Leben und seine Werke* (Braunschweig: Vieweg, 1937), 494. On the politics of Fehse's book and its influence on Raabe reception, see Jeffrey Sammons, *The Shifting Fortunes of Wilhelm Raabe: A History*

Pongs likewise sees the novel as striking more of an anti-technological stance, while Barker Fairley argues that the pollution problem is only a part of the larger problem of how one adapts to a changing world.[13] Some of the first, and most important, critics to take the environmental thematic seriously were not literary scholars, but natural scientists. The earliest essays exploring the novel's engagement with science appeared in 1925 in a pair of essays by limnologist August Thienemann, himself a significant figure in the history of German conservationism,[14] followed in 1959 by bacteriologist Ludwig Popp and in 1985 by chemist Elisabeth Vaupel.[15]

The scientific commentaries, perhaps understandably, tend to put greater weight on the scientific and historical dimensions. Ludwig Popp, for one, regards the novel as a factual report.[16] But the narrator Ebert announces the interplay between environmental crisis and aesthetic crisis in the opening section, an intentionally cliché lament on the impossibility of aesthetic representation that he himself calls an "unmotivierte Stilübung" (unmotivated stylistic exercise).[17] Here at the beginning of his notebook Ebert connects his own dilettantism to the socio-ecological conditions of industrial modernity. The ironic opening line of this ironically dubbed summer vacation notedbook reads, "Ach, noch einmal ein frischer Atemzug im letzten Viertel dieses neunzehnten Jahrhunderts!" (Ah, once more a fresh breath of air in the last quarter of the nineteenth

---

of Criticism as a Cautionary Tale (Columbia, SC: Camden House, 1992), 40–43. The Stadtarchiv Braunschweig contains letters from Fehse's fellow POWs in the Soviet camp at Torgau reporting that before his death of flu, Fehse wished to publish a new edition of the book with significant cuts and revisions. See Hippe, "Letter to Käthe Fehse," November 19, 1948, G IX 32 : 36 # 14, Stadtarchiv Braunschweig. It seems likely that his intention was to paint a portrait of the author less obviously in the service of National Socialist cultural politics.

13 Hermann Pongs, *Wilhelm Raabe: Leben und Werk* (Heidelberg: Quelle & Meyer, 1958), 492–93; Barker Fairley, *Wilhelm Raabe: An Introduction to His Novels* (Oxford: Clarendon Press, 1961), 43.

14 See Thomas Kluge and Engelbert Schramm, *Wassernöte: Umwelt- und Sozialgeschichte des Trinkwassers* (Aachen: Alano, 1986), 169–72; Blackbourn, *The Conquest of Nature*, 232.

15 August Thienemann, "Wilhelm Raabe und die Abwasserbiologie," *Mitteilungen für die Gesellschaft der Freunde Wilhelm Raabes* 15 (1925): 124–31; August Thienemann, "'Pfisters Mühle.' Ein Kapitel aus der Geschichte der biologischen Wasseranalyse," *Verhandlungen des Naturhistorischen Vereins der preußischen Rheinlande und Westfalens* 82 (1925): 315–29; Ludwig Popp, "'Pfisters Mühle.' Schlüsselroman zu einem Abwasserprozeß," *Städtehygiene* 2 (1959): 21–25; Elisabeth Vaupel, "Gewässerverschmutzung im Spiegel der schönen Literatur," *Chemie in unserer Zeit* 19 (1985): 77–85.

16 Popp, "'Pfisters Mühle.' Schlüsselroman zu einem Abwasserprozeß," 22.

17 Raabe, *BA*, 16: 9.

century!).[18] Alluding to Christoph Martin Wieland's 1780 epic *Oberon*, he continues: "Noch einmal sattelt mir den Hippogryphen;—ach, wenn sie gewußt hätten, die Leute von damals, wenn sie geahnt hätten, die Leute vor hundert Jahren, wo ihre Nachkommen das 'alte romantische Land' zu suchen haben würden!" (Saddle up my hippogryph once again;—oh, had they known, the people back then, had they had a sense, the people a hundred years ago, where their descendants would have to seek "the old romantic country!").[19] "The old romantic country," he then informs us, has succumbed to the trappings of modernity: the desert over which Wieland's Oberon flew is now crisscrossed by railways and telegraph lines, Kidron's waters power paper mills, and on the banks of the rivers that flow out of Eden one finds "noch nützlichere 'Etablissements'" (more useful "establishments").[20] These real-existing places with mythical associations have undergone a thorough disenchantment as, like Pfister's own mill creek, they have become subject to industrial exploitation. With the imminent demolition of his own family mill, the poetic for Ebert is not spatially removed, as for Wieland, but temporally removed as one of "der Vorwelt Wundern" (the prior world's marvels): "zehn Schritte weit von unserer Tür liegen sie—zehn, zwanzig, dreißig Jahre ab" (They lie ten steps away from our door—ten, twenty, thirty years away) at a time before the redirection of streams, the arrival of the railway, and the implementation of monoculture.[21]

Ebert's poetic project, accordingly, is to capture the memory of the mill as one of the world's prior marvels. He sets up a dichotomy of the past as a period of organic wholeness opposed to a fallen present, a narrative encapsulated in the image of the polluted mill creek: "Erfreulich war's nicht anzusehen. Aus dem lebendigen, klaren Fluß, der wie der Inbegriff alles Frischen und Reinlichen durch meine Kinder- und ersten Jugendjahre rauschte und murmelte, war ein träge schleichendes, schleimiges, weißbläuliches Etwas geworden, das wahrhaftig niemand mehr als Bild des Lebens und des Reinen dienen konnte" (It was not cheerful to behold. The lively, clear river, which had rustled and murmured throughout the years of my childhood and youth had become a sluggishly crawling, slimy, white-blue something, that really could not have served anyone as an image of life and purity).[22] In changing the chemical composition of the creek, Krickerode renders it in Ebert's eyes at once no longer a thing of nature, for one, and more specifically no longer an example of natural beauty. It is not even a natural creek anymore, but an indeterminate

18 Raabe, *BA*, 16: 9.
19 Raabe, *BA*, 16: 7.
20 Raabe, *BA*, 16: 8.
21 Raabe, *BA*, 16: 8.
22 Raabe, *BA*, 16: 53.

"something." At one level, Ebert constructs here a "mythography of betrayed Edens" central to what Lawrence Buell calls "toxic discourse;" indeed the entire plot can be read as "an awakening to the horrified realization that there is no protective environmental blanket, leaving one to feel dreadfully wronged."[23] But the betrayed Eden myth here proceeds from a symbolic overdetermination of a topographical feature whose use-value was not just as a source of power for the mill or pleasure for the day-trippers, but as an image of "life" and "purity." What shines through in the plasticity of his description is that the polluted creek is not entirely unnatural, either. The foul stench and the discoloration are organic, the latter caused by the microorganisms that feed off of the hydrogen sulfide from the beet sugar factory. The microorganisms mean that the problem with the stream is not that it is an image of death as opposed to life, but instead the problem is one of too much life. It is the slimy, ugly nature that disrupts the harmonious functioning of the stream and the socio-ecological sphere around the mill. Adam Asche, who as an industrialist himself is unabashed about his role in destroying the environment in the service of production, puts the problem in Darwinian terms when he reminds Bertram that "Pilze wollen auch leben, und das Lebende hat Recht oder nimmt es sich" (fungi also want to live, and living things have the right to do so, or else they claim it).[24]

What Ebert stylizes as "the old romantic country," it turns out, is riddled with similar contradictions. Like the valley of water-powered factories in *Der Nachsommer*, the mill is but an embryonic form of the factory that will ultimately rob it of the environmental conditions upon which it depends. Raabe makes that relation explicit briefly in his 1867 novel *Abu Telfan*, in which the ruined mill is described as the factory's "Schwesterchen" (little sister).[25] While Krickerode transforms the stream into an open sewer in the service of production, the mill, the water wheel, the weir, and the restaurant benches likewise extend processes of labor and consumption from the structure itself into the surrounding ecosystem. It is not merely that the internal contradictions of the mill are inscribed everywhere on the environment, but that the mimetic imperative Ebert as an author sets himself functions as a backdoor for everything that cuts against the grain of his assumptions about pre-industrial nature.

The perspectivization is by design: in spite of its plot, *Pfisters Mühle* presents us with a cast of characters for whom the integrity of nature is a secondary concern at the most. "Jeder Mensch ist Partei in der Welt"

---

23 Buell, *Writing for an Endangered World*, 30–54, here 36. See also Wilke, "Pollution as Poetic Practice."

24 Raabe, *BA*, 16: 91.

25 Raabe, *BA*, 7: 70–71.

80 ◆ THE STYX FLOWS THROUGH ARCADIA

(Everyone is a partisan in the world), as Bertram sighs at one point.[26] His court fight is, like the historical water trials, a conflict between competing business interests, and as such the trial and the decision in favor of the mill are weak examples of ecojustice at best. His lawyer Riechei, another speaking name (from "riechen," to smell), takes the case in order to garner fame for himself, all the while wondering why the Pfisters did not also invest in Krickerode. Asche speaks the most openly and the most consistently about how his commitments and those of the other characters on the side of the mill render the lawsuit quixotic. He prefaces his oath to gather scientific evidence on Bertram's behalf by characterizing himself as one "der die feste Absicht hat, selber einen sprudelnden Quell, einen Kristallbach, einen majestätischen Fluß, kurz, irgendeinen Wasserlauf im idyllischen grünen Deutschen Reich so bald als möglich und so infam als möglich zu verunreinigen" (who is himself determined to dirty as shamelessly as possible any bubbling spring, crystal brook, or majestic river, in short, any waterway in the idyllic green German Empire).[27] Asche speaks here not only as one who has conflicting commitments, but as the ambivalent voice of science and technology, a person who both scientifically uncovers the reality of environmental depredation while also advancing it.[28] Even the notebook itself is caught up in this network of partisanship: as Gerhard Kaiser points out, Ebert's trip into the past takes place against the rapidly approaching terminus of the mill's existence, so that the farther he goes into the past, the closer the text arrives at the mill's destruction.[29]

But the apparent allegiances of the notebook do not amount to a disregard for nature or an uncritical endorsement of environmental degradation. Instead Ebert's own striving towards mimetic representation allows for moments of dissonance that cast all the characters and their assumptions about nature in a more critical light. Early in the novel, for instance, he recalls standing atop the mill as a child and looking out "in einer hellen, weiten, wenn auch noch grünen, so doch von Wald und Gebüsch schon ziemlich kahl gerupften Ebene" (in a bright, broad plain, still green even if it has been stripped bare of forests and bushes).[30] His description admits of the violence that had already been visited upon nature, and he admits that even in those days the cultural landscape was dotted with

26 Raabe, *BA*, 16: 92.

27 Raabe, *BA*, 16: 67.

28 Sabine Wilke traces out Adam Asche's function as speaking in a specifically scientific register of toxic discourse in "Pollution as Poetic Practice," 202–6.

29 Gerhard Kaiser, "Der Totenfluß als Industriekloake: Über den Zusammenhang von Ökologie, Ökonomie und Phantasie in 'Pfisters Mühle' von Wilhelm Raabe," in *Mutter Natur und die Dampfmaschine: Ein literarischer Mythos im Rückbezug auf Antike und Christentum* (Freiburg im Breisgau: Rombach, 1991), 83.

30 Raabe, *BA*, 16: 11.

factory smokestacks. This prompts him to further note that if he found the view beautiful, it was only because he was unlike the rural youth who stand "auf zu gutem Fuße, um sich viel aus [der Natur] zu machen" (on much too familiar grounds to think much about [nature]).[31] The fact that Ebert distinguishes himself from the rural youth is by itself remarkable, given that he grew up in the mill, a fixature of the rural landscape. He justifies the difference by saying that even in his childhood he was mentally drawn to the city, of which he mostly saw air pollution, saying its presence was manifest in the landscape in the form of the "Dunstwolke und die Türme im Nordosten von unserm Dörfchen" (cloud of haze and the towers to the northeast of our little village).[32]

The real difference, though, is less where Ebert's heart was, then or now, as much as his way of perceiving the landscape. He is able to see the beauty of the landscape, in spite of the smokestacks and in spite of the deforestation, because he views nature from an aestheticized distance. He intuits Theodor Adorno's observation about the historical contingency of the appreciation of natural beauty: "Times in which nature confronts man overpoweringly allow no room for natural beauty; as is well known, agricultural occupations, in which nature as it appears is an immediate object of action, allow little appreciation for landscape. Natural beauty, purportedly ahistorical, is at its core historical; this legitimates at the same time that it relativizes the concept."[33] Adorno regards the cultural landscape as a useful reminder of a world prior to the current state of the domination of nature, what Ebert conceives of as "the old Romantic country" and the "the prior world's marvels" at the opening. For Adorno, such perception of nature may be "poisoned," but it is at least better than "an ahistorical aesthetic consciousness that sweeps aside the dimension of the past as rubbish."[34] Adorno admits that nostalgic perceptions of pre-industrial cultural landscapes as better will persist "so long as progress, deformed by utilitarianism, does violence to the surface of the earth," but there is still value in such an experience of natural beauty: "Rationalization is not yet rational; the universality of mediation has yet to be transformed into living life; and this endows the traces of immediacy, however dubious and antiquated, with an element of corrective justice."[35] Ebert's depiction of nature around the mill, in his childhood as well as in his present, is ideological in that it both admits and sublimates the signs of historical developments that will ultimately spell doom for the mill. But that does not invalidate his memory of the landscapes of his childhood nor the

31 Raabe, *BA*, 16: 11.
32 Raabe, *BA*, 16: 11.
33 Adorno, *Aesthetic Theory*, 65.
34 Adorno, *Aesthetic Theory*, 65.
35 Adorno, *Aesthetic Theory*, 64.

experience he and Emmy have of the rural landscape during their summer vacation as an alternative, however anachronistic, to the environmental realities of their urban industrial present.

Their encounter with nature, then, may have something akin to the corrective justice Adorno sees in the traces of immediacy contained within the experience of natural beauty, but in the novel it is the supposedly immediate view of nature that reveals the characters' own partisan ways of seeing. Ebert's wife Emmy, a Berlin native, has an especially keen awareness of the extent to which her perception of nature is contingent upon her urban bourgeois subjectivity. Early in the novel she finds herself sitting alone and contemplating a stork by the stream, and she tells Ebert how she is struck by the relatively unmediated encounter with a wild animal, imagining the bird saying: "Siehst du, ich stehe nicht bloß im Bilderbuche und sitze im zoologischen Garten gegen eine halbe Mark Eintrittsgeld an Wochentagen, sondern—" (You see, I don't just appear in picture books and sit in the zoo to be viewed on weekdays for half a mark's admission, but—).[36] Here Ebert cuts her off with an affectionate, but no less demeaning taunt that prevents Emmy from developing the insight further. But the point that she is building towards is crucial for the novel's overall aesthetic reflection: as a born urbanite, her view of the non-human environment is more thoroughly conditioned by cultural institutions that mediate the non-human world, in this case zoos and print media. But the difference is only one of degree. The experience of nature in the encounter with the stork only seems unmediated simply because it is less mediated than at home in Berlin.

Scholarship on the novel has long treated Emmy in a reductive way, viewing her as a naïve young urbanite.[37] That is, in fact, the way that

36 Raabe, *BA*, 16: 13.

37 Critics have made this argument with varying degrees of sympathy for Emmy's character. To cite a few examples: Horst Denkler characterizes the contrast that she poses as being a question of the "nüchtern-praktische Vernunft der Großstädterin" (urban woman's sober-practical reason). Denkler, "Die Antwort literarischer Phantasie auf eine der 'größeren Fragen der Zeit,'" 98. Barker Fairley recognizes that Emmy is a more observant character than her age might let on, but discusses her perceptiveness only in terms of Ebert's problematic attraction to such ghostly places as the mill and the cemetery that her father enjoyed visiting. Fairley, *Wilhelm Raabe*, 46. Martin Swales reads Emmy in a more differentiated way. He rightly insists that her intelligence should not be underestimated, and that her "weltliche—ausgesprochen gegenwartsbezogene—Anwandlung ist aber keineswegs eine Verscheuchung der (poetischen, sprich artistischen) Bilder" (worldly—markedly present-oriented—disposition is not at all a shying-away from the [poetic, that is, artistic] images). Martin Swales, *Epochenbuch Realismus: Romane und Erzählungen* (Berlin: Schmidt, 1997), 138. Swales still, however, credits the "wo bleiben alle die Bilder" question to Ebert, and characterizes Emmy as "eine praktische,

Ebert depicts her in his notebook, where, as Sabine Wilke points out, female speech functions like the pollution and other signs of modern industry, so much discarded wreckage that Ebert would like to exclude from the master plot.[38] The text indicates that in spite of their affection, the antagonism in their relationship is mutual. For instance, Emmy's pet name for Ebert is "Mäuschen" (little mouse) and his pet name for her is "Mieze" (kitty). Yet in spite of Ebert's habit of cutting off Emmy's speech, the encounter with the stork is only one of the important insights that inform the novel's theoretical reflections for which Emmy deserves credit. As it happens, it is she who supplies the question that is at the core of the novel's reflections on aesthetics in the era of Krickerode. In a conversation Ebert recalls having with Emmy during their honeymoon, she wonders: "'Wo bleiben alle die Bilder?' das ist eine Frage, die einem auf jeder Kunstausstellung wohl einige Male ans Ohr klingt und auf die man nur deshalb nicht mehr achtet, weil man dieselbe sich selber bereits dann und wann gestellt hat" ("Where do all the pictures go?" That is a question that one picks up now and again at each art exhibition and

---

lebenslustige junge Frau, die ihren Mann aus dem Bann des Vergangenen reißt" (a practical, vibrant young woman who pulls her husband from out of the spell of the past). Swales, *Epochenbuch Realismus*, 137. "We might call her Thoroughly Modern Emmy," Jeffrey Sammons writes, and while he argues against a reading of her as "a complacent representative of the crass modern," his grounds for this is that "Raabe has given her too many attractive and loving features." Sammons, *Wilhelm Raabe*, 276. Markus Winkler is also more sympathetic to Emmy, but still sees her only in terms of her admittedly many naïve moments in the novel, which only serve the novel's aesthetic reflection insofar as they prompt Ebert to reflect on the act of narration. According to Winkler, Emmy "nimmt also selbst Partei für die industriell organisierte Herrschaft des Nutzens; der scharfe, bisweilen komische Kontrast zwischen diesem Pragmatismus und Eberhards Versuch, sich erzählend und schreibend in die schöne Vergangenheit zu versenken, ist demnach die Fortsetzung des kulturellen Konflikts zwischen dem Nützlichen und dem Schönen" (takes up the cause for the industrially organized domination of utility; the sharp, sometimes humorous contrast between this pragmatism and Eberhard's attempt to retreat into the beautiful past by narrating and writing is thus the continuation of a cultural conflict between the useful and the beautiful). Markus Winkler, "Die Ästhetik des Nützlichen in 'Pfisters Mühle': Problemgeschichtliche Überlegungen zu Wilhelm Raabes Erzählung," *Jahrbuch der Raabe-Gesellschaft* 38 (1997): 26. Harald Tausch also emphasizes Emmy's function as breaking melancholic reflections through her various interruptions. Harald Tausch, "Wasser auf Pfisters Mühle. Zu Raabes humoristischem Erinnern der Dinge," in *Die Dinge und die Zeichen: Dimensionen des Realistischen in der Erzählliteratur des 19. Jahrhunderts*, ed. Sabine Schneider and Barbara Hunfeld (Würzburg: Königshausen & Neumann, 2008), 188–89, although the "wo bleiben alle die Bilder" speech is arguably one of the most profoundly melancholic moments in the novel.

38   Wilke, "Pollution as Poetic Practice," 205–6.

that one only considers because one has also asked himself that now and again).[39] The implications go beyond painting to call into question art in the broadest sense as well, including literature and thus the text itself.[40] Emmy expresses a "melancholisches Unbehagen" (melancholic discomfort) when she wonders what becomes of all of the paintings that are never seen outside of the galleries: "Und immer malen die Herren Maler andere, wenn es auch von Jahr zu Jahr so ziemlich die nämlichen bleiben" (And so the painters paint others, even if they remain more or less the same from year to year).[41] Emmy's question, which Ebert appropriates as a recurring motif in his narrative, leads into a rather lengthy essayistic discourse on the ephemerality of art in a time of mass production, embodied in the Krickerode factory.

The response Ebert offers Emmy to the question of "where do all the pictures go" is both highly metaphysical and deeply condescending: "Es sind nur die Umrisse und die Farben, welche wechseln; Rahmen und Leinwand bleiben. Jaja, mein armes Kind, es würde uns, die wir selber vorübergehen, den Raum arg beschränken im Leben, wenn alle die Bilder blieben!" (It is only the outlines and the colors that change; frame and canvas remain. Yes, my poor child, we who are ourselves ephemeral would find our space in life badly cramped if all the pictures remained!).[42] Ebert's argument is one of fundamental continuity in spite of the appearance of historical change, and, in the context of the present in which Ebert writes, there might be hope in his claim: the era of Krickerode will pass, just as the era of the mill is passing, but the essence of the world will go on. But the hope it offers is also flimsy. The experience of the mill stream shows that there is no stable essence, no norm in nature or elsewhere that will stay forever constant. If the essence of art remains, then we can take the long view and see the production and the reception of artworks as rising above immediate historical conditions. At the same time, the immediate context of Ebert's statement makes it difficult to accept as a particularly earnest vision of historical change. First, his answer is as much an attempt to silence Emmy's uncomfortable observations as it is a serious theoretical statement. Second, the hope Ebert's response offers still implies an eternal return, such that the work of art follows the model of mass production that transforms the environment: every year another exhibition, another sugar harvest, another release of hydrogen sulfide disrupting the river ecosystem and fouling the air. The long view dispenses with the immediate reality of what is taking place, and so the notion of continuity seems all the weaker for being made at the moment

39 Raabe, *BA*, 16: 30.
40 Kaiser, "Der Totenfluß als Industriekloake," 86–87.
41 Raabe, *BA*, 16: 31.
42 Raabe, *BA*, 16: 31.

that the mill and its environs are about to be cleared away to make room for yet another factory. Environmental degradation, in short, trumps any hope that might be contained in his response to his wife.

Ebert's response to Emmy's question is, in any event, a preliminary one at best. The closest Ebert comes to a definitive answer is at the moment when the summer vacation ends and the demolition of the mill begins. The first chestnut tree falls as Ebert and Emmy board a coach to the train station, setting in motion an experience of acceleration that only sharpens the problems of perception and ephemerality contained in the "where do all the pictures go?" speech.

> Und dann—war Pfisters Mühle nur noch in dem, was ich mit mir führte auf diesem rasselnden, klirrenden, klappernden Eilzuge, vorbei an dem Raum und an der Zeit.
>
> Da brauchte ich dann wohl nicht mehr zu fragen: Wo bleiben alle die Bilder? ... Die von ihnen, welche bleiben, lassen sich am besten wohl betrachten im Halbtraum vom Fenster eines an der bunten, wechselnden Welt vorüberfliegenden Eisenbahnwagens.—[43]

> [And then—Pfister's mill only existed in what I was carrying with me on the rattling, clanking, clattering express train, away past space and time.
>
> So I no longer needed to ask: Where do all the pictures go? ... Those that stay are probably best regarded while in a waking dream, looking out from the window of a train car as it flies past the colorful, shifting world.—]

With the hyphen following "and then," the train gets underway and, at the same time, another of Ebert's marvels of the prior world is lost to the new forces of production. It is the moment when Ebert parts for good from the past that structures his poetic realist project, and he does so within the space of the train, the ultimate sign of industrial modernity. Albrecht Koschorke has argued that at the moment the train leaves the station, the text of *Pfisters Mühle* becomes a substitute for what it refers to, meaning that poetic realism is now only possible in the disappearance of its reality.[44] Christiane Arndt similarly argues that realist texts of this period bear witness to a process of taking leave of an unproblematic concept of mimetic representation even as the attempt to

43 Raabe, *BA,* 16: 156.

44 Albrecht Koschorke, *Die Geschichte des Horizonts: Grenze und Grenzüberschreitung in literarischen Landschaftsbildern* (Frankfurt am Main: Suhrkamp, 1990), 321.

86 ♦ THE STYX FLOWS THROUGH ARCADIA

maintain a relation to reality remains visible on the surface of the text.[45] And yet, the novel imagines the persistence of a relation to the depicted reality in material terms. Ebert tells us his notebook has water damage from when he was caught in a rainstorm while writing, and there is dirt on one of the pages from when the wind picked the paper up and Ebert had to go chasing around a tree to retrieve it. These material leftovers are more than nothing, but not much more, because they have a tenuous status as carriers of the memory of a place. By themselves such small traces would be meaningless. They are only integrated into the poetic project because the realist narrator dutifully records the events that damaged the paper, thereby making the traces legible as leftovers of the storm or the soil under the tree.

Ebert might be mostly sanguine about the story of loss and environmental destruction he relates, but counter to that tone is an apocalypticism that runs through the entire text. For instance, Ebert likens the mill to the church at Sardis, quoting the angel's message that "thou hast a name that thou livest, and art dead" (Revelation 3:1). The split for Ebert between an uneasy, if somber acceptance on the one hand and apocalypticism on the other, is mirrored in two poems that encapsulate the ways in which nature and environment are imagined in the novel. The first is Ferdinand Alexander Schnezler's poem "Die verlassene Mühle" (The Abandoned Mill, 1833), one of the novel's major intertexts. It is not just in our own time that Schnezler has been forgotten; he was regarded as an obscure poet in the 1880s. The memory of his works was fading when Raabe composed his novel, and Ebert himself refers to Schnezler as the "untergegangen[e] Dichter" (the lost poet).[46] The obvious answer to why this poem is so prominent is its thematic affinity to Ebert's own position. The speaker is wandering through a forest when he arrives at the ruins of a mill, apparently without an understanding of how his course brought him there. The building is collapsing in on itself, while the mill's works are silent and covered in moss.[47] As the sun sets and the moon rises, the speaker suddenly sees dwarves emerge out of the bushes carrying sacks of grain for milling, while the machines come back to life. The air fills with the sound of the commotion, which continues until a window opens and a maiden calls an end to the milling. The morning mist then envelopes the mill, and when the speaker returns the following day,

---

45 Christiane Arndt, *Abschied von der Wirklichkeit: Probleme bei der Darstellung von Realität im deutschsprachigen literarischen Realismus* (Freiburg im Breisgau: Rombach, 2009), 13–14.

46 Raabe, *BA*, 16: 133. See also Franz Brümmer, "Schnezler, August," in *Allgemeine Deutsche Biographie*, vol. 32 (Leipzig: Duncker und Humblot, 1891), 173.

47 The poem is printed in Raabe, *BA*, 16: 536.

it is again a ruin, one which haunts him for the rest of his life. Like Ebert, who while writing experiences the past as if it were the present, the speaker's encounter with the mill sparks an uncanny breakdown of experiential reality. In one scene, for instance, Emmy leans out one of the windows of Pfister's mill and calls to Ebert and the old servant Christine to come out of the rain just as Ebert is thinking about the poem. Ebert's description of the moment evokes the maiden in the poem both in terms of imagery and the language he uses to relate being called out of his reverie.

Ebert interprets the poem in a very willful way that reflects his subjective split between acceptance of historical change and muted apocalypticism. He sees "Die verlassene Mühle" as an allegory in which the woman represents poetry, and the dwarves are speculators, those same agents that in Ebert's lived reality are also bringing about the end. If we assume that Ebert's reading is the interpretation that the novel endorses, then the poem is quoted precisely because of its romanticism and its appeal to nature, represented by the mill and its forest environs, all of which stand in opposition to speculative capital and its catastrophic effects on the environment. Accepting Ebert's interpretation might problematically lead us to the kind of conclusion that Wilhelm Fehse draws about the poem, that it is a piece of authentic lyric poetry that Raabe deploys against a trend in the 1880s of poems and verse epics that idealized the German Middle Ages for nationalist ideological ends.[48] The problem with Fehse's reading is that "Die verlassene Mühle" is not an example of "authentic" lyric poetry, but rather post-Romantic kitsch, highly conventional from its subject matter to its very form. His poem adheres to a uniform repetition across its seven stanzas: each stanza consists of eight lines, with a metrical structure that perfectly mirrors the rhyme scheme throughout, save for the last stanza, which introduces slight variation. Its repetitiveness likewise plays out in the story it tells, as the speaker returns to the site of the ruined mill in the poem's final stanza. Schnezler, in other words, is obscure for a reason. The poem belongs to its own kitschy subgenre of *Mühlenromantik*, or "mill romanticism."[49] Its status as kitsch, though, suggests that its inclusion in the novel is about more than the thematic affinity. As an aesthetic category, kitsch is connected to mass production, and in that sense the poem is connected back to all that Krickerode so crassly embodies. And as an author, Ebert is just as inclined towards the

48   Fehse, *Wilhelm Raabe*, 484.

49   For a history of the cultural associations with mills, including a discussion of *Pfisters Mühle*, see Günter Bayerl, "Herrn Pfisters und anderer Leute Mühlen: Das Verhältnis von Mensch, Technik und Umwelt im Spiegel eines literarischen Topos," in *Technik in der Literatur: Ein Forschungsüberblick in zwölf Aufsätzen*, ed. Harro Segeberg (Frankfurt am Main: Suhrkamp, 1987), 51–101.

cliché as is Schnezler, a fact that he at least admits when he calls the opening of his notebook an "unmotivated style exercise."

Part of the appeal of Schnezler's kitschy poem is not just the affinity, however, but that it offers an escapist fantasy. When Emmy calls Ebert back to the present, he thinks that while it might rain, "die alten Bäume [boten noch] ihren Schutz der Poesie" (the old trees still offered on this evening the protection of poetry).[50] But the trees and the poetic escape Ebert finds under them are doomed, and where Ebert tends to muffle the apocalyptic strain in his own narrative, another character, the poet Lippoldes gives it a full-throated return. As an aged representative of genuine poetic ability, Lippoldes is reduced at the end of the nineteenth century to alcoholism as a means of coping with his own status as a living anachronism. His apocalyptic poem "Einst kommt die Stunde" (Soon the Hour Will Come) is an antipode to the Schnezler poem that Ebert prefers. Lippoldes recites his poem at Bertram Pfister's Christmas party, where the sentimental tradition continues, with the scent of baked goods competing with the stench of hydrogen sulfide:

> Einst kommt die Stunde—denkt nicht, sie sei ferne—,
> Da fallen vom Himmel die goldenen Sterne,
> Da wird gefegt das alte Haus,
> Da wird gekehrt der Plunder aus.
> Der liebe, der alte, vertraute Plunder,
> Viel tausend Geschlechter Zeichen und Wunder:
> Die Mutter, das Kind, die Zeit und der Raum!
> Kein Spinnweb wird im Winkel vergessen,
> Was der Körper hielt, was der Geist besessen,
> Was das Herz gefühlt, was der Magen verdaut;
> Und *Tod* heißt der Bräutigam, *Nichts* heißt die Braut![51]

> [Someday the hour will come—think not, it be far—,
> Then the golden stars will fall from the sky,
> Then the old house will be swept clean,
> Then the junk will be cleared out.
> The dear, the old, well-known junk,
> Signs and wonders of thousands of generations:
> The mother, the child, time and space!
> Not even a cobweb in the corner will be forgotten,
> What the body held, what the soul possessed,
> What the heart felt, what the stomach digested,
> And *Death* is the bridegroom, *Nothing* the bride!]

50   Raabe, *BA*, 16: 134.
51   Raabe, *BA*, 16: 85.

The golden stars of the second line are themselves an image of the cliché, but their fall to earth replaces that cliché appearance with apocalyptic significance, evoking the stars falling to earth in Revelation 6:13. The poem moves from there to the annihilation of the domestic and culminates in a nihilistic wedding. As we will see, the clearing away of all things in the household will also be repeated in the 1896 novel *Die Akten des Vogelsangs*. Lippoldes's poem describes an unexpected, fast-moving, all-consuming end of the world. It blends comedy with pathos, breaking down the sort of rigid conventional form that structures "Die verlassene Mühle." For while the first stanza of "Einst kommt die Stunde" also has a more conventional rhyme and meter structure, by the second stanza both fall away as the disaster continues:

> Wie Schade wird das sein! Dann kehrt man dort
> Den guten Kanzeleirat weg und seinen Stuhl,
> Auf dem er fünfzig Jahr lang kalkulierte.
> Vergeblich wartet mit der Suppe seine Alte,
> Nicht lange doch; denn plötzlich füllt ein mächt'ges
> Gestäub die Gasse, dringt in Tür und Fenster—
> Der Kehrichtsstaub des Weltenuntergangs.[52]

> [It will be too bad! Then one will sweep
> The good councilor away and his chair,
> On which he calculated for fifty years.
> In vain his wife will wait with the soup,
> But not for long, for suddenly a mighty dust
> Fills the lane, pushes in through door and window—
> The broom sweepings of the end of the world.]

Heinrich Detering demonstrates that, as the environmental disaster advances, the form of the poem vanishes before our very eyes, just like the world it depicts.[53] The "mighty dust" is reminiscent both of the foul-smelling air that results from the water pollution, and from the clouds of smog that both Krickerode and Asche's factory pump into the atmosphere. Where pollution in Ebert's lived reality has a defined origin, in the poem it seems to come from nowhere, lending it a phantasmagorical quality. The poem ends with the last person laughing as the world is swept away, until he himself disappears as well. Just as the last human disappears into a cloud of dust, Lippoldes later disappears when, in his drunkenness, he falls and drowns in the "trüben Schlammflut" (dark flow

---

52 Raabe, *BA*, 16: 86.
53 Detering, "Ökologische Krise und ästhetische Innovation im Werk Wilhelm Raabes," 19. See also Helmers, "Raabe als Kritiker von Umweltzerstörung."

of ooze) that is the mill stream.[54] With Lippoldes's death, the novel symbolically drowns poetry in an industrial cesspool.

Ultimately, though, the apocalyptic vision goes unrealized, and the disappearance of poetry into industrial pollution is not the end of the story. Instead the novel closes with an image of apparent reconciliation: Ebert Pfister, Adam Asche, and their spouses take tea in view of Asche's massive laundry cleaning facility nicknamed "Rhakopyrgos," a fanciful Greek term of Raabe's invention meaning "rag mountain,"[55] as it belches smog and pumps effluent into the River Spree by Berlin:

> Wir gehen zum Tee unter der Veranda. Nebenan klappert und lärmt die große Fleckenreinigungsanstalt und bläst ihr Gewölk zum Abendhimmel empor fast so arg wie Krickerode. Der größere, wenn auch nicht große Fluß ist, trotzdem daß wir auch ihn nach Kräften verunreinigen, von allerlei Ruderfahrzeugen und Segeln belebt und scheint Rhakopyrgos als etwas ganz Selbstverständliches und höchst Gleichgültiges zu nehmen.[56]

> [We go to tea on the veranda. Nearby the great stain-cleaning facility clacks and rattles and blows its clouds up into the evening sky almost as badly as Krickerode. The larger, if not particularly large river is alive with rowboats and sails, even though we are dirtying it too with all our might, and they seem to take Rhakopyrgos as something self-explanatory and quite unimportant.]

The final scene is remarkable for its dissonance. The people rowing their boats continue to pursue their recreational experience of nature, while the consumption of food and drink appears to be in no way disrupted as it was at Pfister's mill. It is as if the dirtying of air and water were not happening before their very eyes. But beneath Ebert's tone is his knowledge that he is witnessing a developing ecological catastrophe, especially since he draws an explicit comparison between Rhakopyrgos and Krickerode. The difference is that pollution is now both seen and unseen, an accepted part of the environment that nonetheless makes its way into the narrative. Asche's cleaning facility blends into the landscape, and is taken for granted much as Ebert observed that the country youth take nature for granted because of their familiarity with it.

That Rhakopyrgos appears to blend into nature might seem to naturalize the factory at the end, an environmental example of what Georg Lukács saw as "Raabe's dream of reconciliation."[57] Colin Riordan, for one,

---

54 Raabe, *BA*, 16: 152.
55 Raabe, *BA*, 16: 544.
56 Raabe, *BA*, 16: 177.
57 Lukács, *German Realists in the Nineteenth Century*, 265.

makes an ecocritical version of this argument in his survey of ecology and German literature prior to 1914. His thesis about *Pfisters Mühle* is that the novel stages a harmonization process wherein environmental depredation is reconciled with the demands of an industrial nation-state.[58] This reading of the end captures a significant psychological process of adaptation staged in the novel, but in my view it takes the image of the tea party at the end too much at face value. This is a novel, after all, that explicitly thematizes its characters' various partisan commitments, and the characters in the last scene are all on the side of industrial modernity. Therefore their seeming acceptance cannot be taken as the novel's solution to a high capitalism where all that is solid melts into the foul-smelling air.[59] Ebert understands the pollution and its consequences well enough—at least as well as a person of his historical moment would be able. What is gone is not the trouble of pollution, but the trouble of pollution as an aesthetic offense. As Hans Rindisbacher points out, the characters in the scene "reveal their mechanisms of coping essentially as the ideological invocation of *non olet* in an atmosphere that increasingly stinks."[60] They have accepted the ideological illusion that Rhakopyrgos, its effluent, and its smog are "natural" in the most normative sense. What appears to be reconciliation is an instance of one of Raabe's typical narrative strategies: narrating the new—in this case pollution—through familiar forms that reduce the horror, only to make that horror more intensely apparent.[61] The persistence of pollution troubles Ebert's efforts to poeticize the reality of what he sees from the veranda, and moreover implicitly makes a forceful critique about the human ability to adapt to and accept the ongoing destruction of the natural environment.

From Green Hedges to Brick Walls: *Die Akten des Vogelsangs*

Where images of pollution in *Pfisters Mühle* inform the novel's aesthetic reflections, in *Die Akten des Vogelsangs* of 1896 it is urban and industrial sprawl and the perceived banishment of nature that undergird the

---

58 Colin Riordan, "German Literature, Nature and Modernity before 1914," in *Nature in Literary and Cultural Studies: Transatlantic Conversations on Ecocriticism*, ed. Catrin Gersdorf and Sylvia Mayer (Amsterdam: Rodopi, 2006), 322–23.

59 See also Denkler, "Die Antwort literarischer Phantasie auf eine der 'größeren Fragen der Zeit,'" 100.

60 Hans Rindisbacher, *The Smell of Books: A Cultural-Historical Study of Olfactory Perception in Literature* (Ann Arbor: The University of Michigan Press, 1992), 112.

61 Berbeli Wanning, *Die Fiktionalität der Natur: Studien zum Naturbegriff in Erzähltexten der Romantik und des Realismus* (Berlin: Weidler, 2005), 349.

poetic project. *Die Akten des Vogelsangs* reprises the narrative conceit of *Pfisters Mühle* of a first-person narrator, Karl Krumhardt, whose written account of the story constitutes the very text that we the readers hold in our hands. Karl receives one November evening a letter from Helene Mungo née Trotzendorff informing him that their mutual childhood friend, Velten Andres, has died. The arrival of the letter brings back the memory of their childhood in the Vogelsang, a settlement formerly outside of an expanding city somewhere in Germany that over the course of the narrated timeframe is transformed piecemeal from an idyllic neighborhood into an anonymous industrial district. Transported thus back to his childhood Karl, true to his profession as a jurist and bureaucrat, opens a file and begins writing. We learn that he and Velten were friends in the Vogelsang, where they were joined by Helene Trotzendorff, daughter of a family that emigrated to the United States but who has returned to Germany with her mother after her father lost all of his wealth and narrowly avoided a term in Sing Sing Prison. As the three grow up, their paths diverge: Karl studies law and begins a career, Helene emigrates again when her father makes a new fortune, and Velten studies for a time in Berlin before setting off to the United States in pursuit of Helene. But Helene has already married a Chicago millionaire, and so Velten begins drifting through the world, ultimately rebelling against bourgeois notions of property by burning the contents of his mother's house after her death. As with *Pfisters Mühle*, this text also has a certain formal indeterminacy: the former was a summer vacation notebook, while here we have a protocol summarizing a set of documents. As the narrative of an archive of a place, Karl's protocol is even further removed from its referent than Ebert's notebook, which was composed at least partly on site. Raabe's working title, "Aus dem Vogelsang" (From the Birdsong),[62] still suggests a more direct connection to place, whereas the "Akten" ("papers," "files") of the published title underscores the artifactual status of the text relative to a place that essentially no longer exists.[63]

Karl introduces the old Vogelsang by celebrating it as a site of "Nachbarschaft" (neighborhood). "Neighborhood" is a harmonious way of relating to other humans as a community, but it also designates a condition of socio-ecological harmony that lends the old Vogelsang its poetic character.

---

62 Wilhelm Raabe, "Die Akten des Vogelsangs" (1895 1893), Nachlass Wilhelm Raabe, Schriftsteller (1831–1910), H III 10 : 10, Stadtarchiv Braunschweig.

63 "Place" in *Die Akten des Vogelsangs* is an ambiguous value, as John Lyon argues in his book *Out of Place*. The characters "face a painful choice: either relinquish place and the sense of humanity connected with it or hold on to place and find constraint, confinement and alienation from the modern world." Lyon, *Out of Place*, 108.

Auch Gärten, die aneinandergrenzten und ihre Obstbaumzweige einander zureichten und ihre Zwetschen, Kirschen, Pflaumen, Äpfel und Birnen über lebendige Hecken weg nachbarschaftlich austeilten, gab es da noch zu *unserer Zeit,* als die Stadt noch nicht das "erste Hunderttausend" überschritten hatte und wir, Helene Trotzendorff, Velten Andres und Karl Krumhardt, Nachbarkinder im Vogelsang unter dem Osterberge waren. Bauschutt, Fabrikaschenwege, Kanalisationsarbeiten und dergleichen gab es auch noch nicht zu unserer Zeit in der Vorstadt, genannt "Zum Vogelsang." Die Vögel hatten dort wirklich noch nicht ihr Recht verloren, der Erde Loblied zu singen; sie brauchten noch nicht ihre Baupläne dem Stadtbauamt zur Begutachtung vorzulegen.

[And there were gardens adjoining each other and extending their fruit tree branches toward each other, exchanging their plums, cherries, apples, and pears like good neighbors across the green hedges, *in our time,* when the town had not yet passed the hundred-thousand mark and we—Helene Trotzendorff, Velten Andres, and Karl Krumhardt—were neighbor children in the Birdsong at the foot of Easter Hill. Construction debris, [fly ash pavement], sewer and drainage work, etc. were also not to be seen in the suburb called "On the Birdsong" in our time. The birds there had not yet lost their right to sing their song in praise of the earth. They were not yet required to submit their construction projects to the city planning office for approval.[64]]

The narrative arc Karl sketches in this passage is one of progressive alienation from nature, as factories and apartment blocks drive out all that is "green." The pleasant gardens and fruit trees are contrasted with the inorganic human constructions to which they would later give way, but they also relate in this account in a "neighborly" way in that they extend their branches over the hedges, which Karl presents as an image of intact nature.[65] But what emerges in Karl's account without his explicit acknowl-

---

64 Raabe, *BA,* 19: 219; Wilhelm Raabe, *The Birdsong Papers,* trans. Michael Ritterson (London: Modern Humanities Research Association, 2013), 5, translation modified.

65 Irmgard Roebling writes of the hedges: "Die lebendigen Hecken vor und nach der ersten Nennung [Veltens Namens] erscheinen zunächst jeweils abgesetzt von Bildern, die deren Zerstörung in der modernen Industriegesellschaft vor Augen stellen, um dann, aus dieser negativen Perspektive heraus, den Blick zu öffnen auf eine Zeit und ein Dasein in einem letzlich intakten Naturzusammenhang" (The living hedges before and after the first mention of [Velten's] name initially appear offset from images that show their destruction in modern industrial society, so that then, from this negative perspective, they can open up a view to a time and an existence in one ultimately intact natural

edgment is that the hedges also delineate borders between various pieces of property, and it is the relation to property that determines one's place in what Nancy Kaiser calls the Vogelsang's "unconscious hierarchy of residency," which places ownership through inheritance at the top, followed by ownership through purchase, while renters are at the bottom.[66] The hedges are thus organic phenomena in the service of social functions, natural inasmuch as they are living flora, but social in that they are the products of labor and the physical manifestations of property division. Instead of being an image of intact nature, they are a technology of separation. The image of the hedge as a technology of separation happens to be a recurring one in Raabe's fiction, the most significant example being perhaps from his 1891 novel *Stopfkuchen* (Stuffcake, available in English under the title *Tubby Schaumann*), where the main character Heinrich Schaumann tells of being abandoned by the other children under the hedge, hedges which, in that novel's narrative present, are also rapidly disappearing.[67] The hedges make visible the fundamental contradiction of the value of "neighborhood." Being the most prominent "green" objects in the novel, the hedges implicate nature within the social relations that become more visibly inscribed in the material environment during the Vogelsang's transformation. While Karl may not be willing to admit this explicitly, he does include in his papers a letter from Velten, who speaks openly about how the organization of plant life, the "green," anticipates the structures that will be put up in their places: "aus Büschen werden Bäume, aus Bäumen Hausmauern, aus Grün Grau" (Where there were bushes, trees appear; after the trees come walls, green turns to gray).[68]

The invocation of the color green throughout the narrative resembles its use and abuse in contemporary environmental politics as a metaphor for ecological wholeness. It appears thirty-nine times over the course of the Braunschweig edition's 195 pages. The "Grüne Gasse" (Green Lane) is the name of the street that runs through the neighborhood, for instance, and as the factories start to move in, the green becomes something that the remaining residents struggle to conserve. Hartleben, who is the first to sell some of his property for industrial development, retains a small piece of his garden in an effort to cling to the aesthetic pleasure it affords, claiming that with the patch he will have "doch wenigstens was Grünes vom Fenster aus im Auge zu haben" (at least a bit of greenery left to look at from my

---

context). Irmgard Roebling, *Wilhelm Raabes doppelte Buchführung: Paradigma einer Spaltung* (Tübingen: Niemeyer, 1988), 113.

66 Nancy Kaiser, "Reading Raabe's Realism: *Die Akten des Vogelsangs*," *Germanic Review* 59, no. 1 (1984): 5.

67 Raabe, *BA*, 18: 82–83; Wilhelm Raabe, *Novels*, ed. Volkmar Sander (New York: Continuum, 1983), 215.

68 Raabe, *BA*, 19: 328; Raabe, *The Birdsong Papers*, 74.

window).[69] Such conservation efforts reduce the "green" spaces to the status of artifacts which, rather than being a part of some larger green totality, now instead cite the Vogelsang as it existed—or was thought to exist—in the past while also perpetuating a pattern of compartmentalization of space under bourgeois capital. It produces an implicit concept of nature that holds nature to be something outside and away, a thing found in the cemetery and up on the nearby Osterberg (Easter Hill), while the neighborhood itself is sub-divided into spaces of labor (factories), residence (apartment blocks), and pleasure (dance clubs).

In its disappearing act, the color green is not only an index of the extent to which organic things have given way to human constructions, but it ties the physical condition of the Vogelsang to nineteenth-century discourses on the poetic possibilities of realist literature. As discussed in the introduction to this book, in the German realist context, "green" has a special currency as a metaphor for the conditions of possibility of poetic representation in modernity. In his treatise on aesthetics, the Young Hegelian philosopher and literary theorist Friedrich Theodor Vischer offers the metaphor of "die grünen Stellen" (the green places) as an answer to Hegel's claim that poesy had lost its place in a world of prosaic modern social relations.[70] Vischer programmatically argues that "grüne Stellen" are those places that literature can still represent poetically in a world otherwise determined by mechanization, the division of labor, bureaucratization, and more. Raabe was not only versed in mid-century theoretical discourses on realism, but he personally knew Vischer during his stay in Stuttgart from 1862 to 1870, a relationship that soured because Vischer reportedly made fun of Raabe's wife Bertha's north German accent.[71] In *Die Akten des Vogelsangs*, Raabe literalizes Vischer's metaphor of green places in order to subject it to the same relativizing move to which the novel subjects all of the values associated with the old Vogelsang. As in *Pfisters Mühle*, the poesy that the novel seeks to realize is located only in the past, as a recorded memory of a poetic state that has since reached its historical terminus. In the story itself, "the poetic" is literally figured in museal terms. Velten's landlady, the "Fechtmeisterin" (fencing master) Feucht, maintains a collection of memorabilia from student culture at Jena at the turn of the nineteenth century, preserving the memory of the town as a center of Romanticism and home of Friedrich Schiller. The des Beaux family, descendants of French Huguenots who fled to Berlin after the revocation of the Edict of Nantes in 1685, maintain a collection of artifacts, some from their own past, others more recently acquired from France. It is into this "Phantasiestübchen," this "historisch[es]

---

69 Raabe, *BA*, 19: 314; Raabe, *The Birdsong Papers*, 66.
70 Vischer, *Aesthetik, oder Wissenschaft des Schönen*, 1303–7.
71 Raabe, *BA*, Ergänzungsband 4: 46; Raabe, *BA*, Ergänzungsband 2: 450.

Traumstübchen" (little fantasy room, little historical dream room) that Leon des Beaux, who, according to his sister, is unable to separate dream from life, flees for weeks on end when Berlin overwhelms him.[72] Their status as poetic enclaves not apart from, but relative to, urban modernity makes them products of the same processes that produce nature as a thing one finds in the walled-off "green" places of the "new" Vogelsang.

The Osterberg overlooking the Vogelsang exemplifies the reification of both nature that comes with such partitioning of space, and what such partitioning does for the possibilities of aesthetic experience. As the closest thing to sublime nature left in the area, the hill exists in Karl's imagination as a site of poetic transcendence, a quality reflected in the hill's christological name. He describes the hill early in the novel as the "wirkliche Idealität von Zeit und Raum" (true ideal state of time and place).[73] The description comes at the beginning of a pivotal scene in which Karl, Velten, and Helene are all on the Osterberg during a meteor shower making wishes for their futures. Karl insists that they are "im tiefsten Frieden der Natur" (in [the deepest peace] of nature),[74] but this ideal space is and always was the product of human labor. Karl says: "Der Wald war selbst damals schon dort oben von ziemlich wohlgehaltenen Pfaden durchschnitten, wie man heute in den Bädern als 'Promenadenwege' kennt. Hier und da hatte sogar schon irgendein Naturliebhaber und Wohltäter der Menschheit eine Bank aufgestellt" (The woods up there, even in those days, were crisscrossed by fairly well-maintained paths of the kind known today in resort towns as "promenades." Here and there some philanthropic nature lover had installed benches, most of them set back in the woods and bushes).[75] What Karl takes to be nature is the result of the dissonance between the already social character of the environment and his insistence on a mode of poetic perception that admits only of the green surroundings. This dual perception continues through into his representation of the night sky during the "Tears of St. Lawrence," more commonly known as the Perseid meteor shower, which takes place annually around August 10. The reference to St. Lawrence, who Catholics believe was roasted alive during Roman emperor Valerian's persecution of the Christians, foreshadows Velten's burning of the house at the novel's climax, but he has meaning for Karl as well, being also the patron saint of archivists. As for the actual cosmic event, Karl tells us: "Die vereinzelten Sterne zählten nicht; nur die Lichter der Stadt in der Tiefe und die Gaslaternen ihrer Straßen und Plätze gaben einen bemerkenswerten Schein. Im fürstlichen Schloß schien 'irgendwas los zu sein,' denn das

---

72 Raabe, *BA*, 19: 290, 294; Raabe, *The Birdsong Papers*, 40, 50.
73 Raabe, *BA*, 19: 254; Raabe, *The Birdsong Papers*, 27.
74 Raabe, *BA*, 19: 254; Raabe, *The Birdsong Papers*, 28, translation modified.
75 Raabe, *BA*, 19: 254–55; Raabe, *The Birdsong Papers*, 7.

leuchtete sogar sehr hell in die warme Sommernacht hinein und zu dem Osterberge empor" (The scattering of stars overhead didn't count; only the lights of the town down below and the gas lamps of its streets and squares shed a noticeable glow. In the ducal residence there appeared to be "something going on," for its lights shone quite brightly out into the warm summer night and up toward Easter Hill).[76] Illumination technologies extend urban sprawl beyond the city's physical boundaries into spaces not yet penetrated by new construction, such as the Osterberg and the night sky itself. As an author, Karl wants to convey the sublime experience of watching the meteor shower, but the skyglow also enters into the text's realist representation to ultimately stymie the sublime effect.

At the level of plot, the scene on the Osterberg is significant as the moment when the antagonisms between the trio are made most visible. But the place is significant for Karl because it is supposedly radically different from quotidian bourgeois life. Karl describes his ascent of the hill that evening as an escape from the social sphere of the Vogelsang, "aus dem Alltag in den Sonntag" (out of the everyday into the Sunday),[77] thereby figuring nature as somehow separate from daily life. The visible signs of human presence already undercut this imagined separation, but it is the aural experience that ironizes what Karl imagines to be the "natural." He writes:

> Im Walde war es still; wildes Getier, das nächtlicherweile in ihm aufgewacht wäre und sich bemerkbar gemacht hätte, gab's nicht drin; die Fledermäuse, die ihre Kreise um uns zogen, zählten nicht; ihre weichen Fittiche störten den Frieden der Natur nicht. Nur vom Bahnhof her dann und wann das Pfeifen und Zischen einer Lokomotive, und aus den Bier- und Konzertgärten der letzte Wiener Walzer, der Einzugsmarsch aus dem Tannhäuser und der Hohenfriedberger harmonisch ineinaderdudelnd und den Abendfrieden hier oben wenig störend.

> [In the woods all was quiet. Wild animals that would have awakened to go audibly about their nocturnal business no longer lived there. The bats tracing circles around us were almost noiseless; their soft wings did not disturb nature's peace. Only now and then from the railroad station came the whistle and hissing of a locomotive, and from our three beer gardens the final Viennese waltz, the entrance march from *Tannhäuser*, and the "Hohenfriedberger"—all interwoven in a harmonious tootling and causing little disturbance to the evening's peace up here.[78]]

76 Raabe, *BA*, 19: 255; Raabe, *The Birdsong Papers*, 29.
77 Raabe, *BA*, 19: 234; Raabe, *The Birdsong Papers*, 27.
78 Raabe, *BA*, 19: 255; Raabe, *The Birdsong Papers*, 28.

98 ♦ THE STYX FLOWS THROUGH ARCADIA

What undermines the "peace of nature" is not primarily the presence of Helene and Velten, even though Karl calls them "Störenfriede," literally "peace disruptors."[79] Instead the reason is that there is neither "peace" nor "nature" to the "peace of nature" when the woods are full of a tootling, regardless of how harmonious that tootling may be. Second, stillness itself is yet another sign of human intervention misrecognized as nature. Were it not for human intervention, the wild animals would presumably have remained to cause a great deal of noise. The "peace of nature" thus denotes an absence that Karl as a realist narrator cannot fail to draw our attention to, and is no more natural than the industrial sounds or party music emanating from the city. The last we learn of the Osterberg is that by Krumhardt's present its trails have been made more level in the interest of safety, and it is mostly a place where residents of the new Vogelsang parade their fashion. A mass-produced, zinc copy of Canova's sculpture *Hebe* implicitly links this thoroughly socialized natural space to the diminished status of art. The presence of an asylum for the mentally ill only concentrates the Osterberg's function as a place outside of contemporary bourgeois society, being a place officially designated for those who cannot or will not accommodate themselves to it.[80] In sum, the Osterberg has taken on a more pronounced social character as part of the Vogelsang's transformation, but the difference is more of extent rather than kind.

Die Akten des Vogelsangs is a two-layered poetic project: there is Karl's aestheticization of the old Vogelsang, and then there is his subject Velten's attempt to realize a more poetic state of being through the negation of material property. Velten's project culminates in the burning of his family things—his mother's "Herzensmuseum" (museum of the heart)— and the opening of his house to plundering as part of what he calls an "äußerliches Aufräumen zu dem innerlichen" (outward housecleaning to go along with the inner one).[81] This act destroys the last house of the old Vogelsang, completing the colonization of the neighborhood by capitalist relations and raising the question of whether enclaves of poesy are still possible anywhere anymore.[82] The plundering of the house brings Velten to an encounter at the edge of the human when he is approached by the ape man German Fell. "The missing link" who performs in the local freak show, what makes the character puzzling is that he resists

79 Raabe, *BA*, 19: 255; Raabe, *The Birdsong Papers*, 28.

80 See also Eberhard Geisler, "Abschied vom Herzensmuseum: Die Auflösung des poetischen Realismus in Wilhelm Raabes 'Die Akten des Vogelsangs,'" in *Wilhelm Raabe: Studien zu seinem Leben und Werk; Aus Anlaß des 150. Geburtstages (1831–1981)*, ed. Leo A. Lensing and Hans-Werner Peter (Braunschweig: pp-Verlag, 1981), 376.

81 Raabe, *BA*, 19: 370; Raabe, *The Birdsong Papers*, 100.

82 Geisler, "Abschied vom Herzensmuseum," 376–78.

categorization within a Linnaean taxonomic system. Fell is the "von der Wissenschaft so lange und schmerzlich vermißten und endlich gefundenen Anthropomor[ph]" (anthropomorph so long and sorely missed and now at last discovered by science).[83] He is called in the German an "Affenmensch," or "ape-man," but also an "Affendarsteller," which we might legitimately interpret as an actor who is an ape, but also as an actor who portrays an ape. He traverses the line between human subject and animal object: as the missing link he is a matter of scientific study, and as a freak show performer he is there to satisfy his audience's appetite for the bizarre. But this ambiguous ape-man is also a user of language who studied at Hamlet's *alma mater*, the University of Wittenberg. German Fell and his fellow freak show performers clearly represent something other than the bourgeois human, but whereas the others may disrupt normative conceptions of the "natural" through exceptional strength, fire-breathing, or this or that idiosyncratic ability, they only push the boundary of the human. To speak with Darwin they possess "a considerable deviation of structure in one part," "what are called monstrosities."[84] These deviations do not undo their categorization as *Homo sapiens*. German Fell, on the other hand, explodes species categories entirely.[85]

German Fell's entrance is a moment when the verisimilitude of the realist text most obviously breaks down: he is a fantastical incarnation of nineteenth-century debates over Darwinism, and his crossover into the realm of the human happens when he "schien mit einem Male auf allen ihm von der Wissenschaft und den Herren Darwin, Häckel, Virchow, Waldeyer und so weiter auferlegten Wert verzichten zu wollen" (seemed suddenly unwilling to acknowledge the great significance imposed on him by Messrs. Darwin, Haeckel, Virchow, Waldeyer, and the general scientific community).[86] What Karl is referring to here is the historical debate over the "missing link" that Fell embodies, which was an issue because intermediate species are largely to be found only in the fossil record.[87] Rudolf Virchow, one of the more prominent nineteenth-century German skeptics of the theory of evolution, argued that the absence of fossil evidence for what Ernst Haeckel called an ape-man meant that Darwinian theory could not be sustained.[88] Being a living fossil, Fell brings the moment of

83   Raabe, *BA*, 19: 377; Raabe, *The Birdsong Papers*, 104.

84   Charles Darwin, *On the Origin of Species by Means of Natural Selection, or, The Preservation of Favoured Races in the Struggle for Life* (London: Penguin Books, 2009), 49.

85   Darwin acknowledges the contingency of such distinctions in spite of general consensus in *The Origin of Species*. Darwin, *On the Origin of Species*, 54.

86   Raabe, *BA*, 19: 380; Raabe, *The Birdsong Papers*, 107.

87   Darwin, *On the Origin of Species*, 159–65.

88   See Eberhard Rohse's account of the Haeckel-Virchow controversy in "'Transzendentale Menschenkunde' im Zeichen des Affen: Raabes literarische

biological kinship with the non-human out of the distant past and into the immediate present. His appearance as a living being collapses the diachronic into the synchronic and reverses evolutionary time at the moment when the Vogelsang's own not-so-natural evolution from an idyllic settlement outside of the city to an anonymous industrial district completes itself. In doing so he also disrupts an evolutionary telos: not only does he mark the intrusion of the deep past into the present moment, but as a living intermediate species he contradicts any belief in the European human as the pinnacle of biological evolution.[89]

Fell's affinity with Velten is signaled by the shared morpheme in the name (*Fell* and *Vel*ten), and he introduces himself as occupying the next branch over in Yggdrasil, the tree at the center of creation in Norse mythology. "Man kann sich auf mehr als eine Art dran und drin verklettern" (There is more than one way to misclimb up and into it, sir), Fell says.[90] Fell betrays an ironic self-awareness here with the subtle pun on the German word "Art," which means both a way of doing something as well as being a word for species. Yggdrasil has several meanings in this scene. First, as a symbol of a universal totality, it suggests a unity of being that stands in stark contrast to the "green" that is paved over or divided up, as the case may be. Second, Yggdrasil is associated with the tree on which Odin hanged himself, an act of self-sacrifice through which he obtained wisdom.[91] German Fell sees a similar transcendental promise in Velten, telling him that whenever he saw him he would say to himself "auch einmal wieder einer, der aus seiner Haut steigt, während die übrigen nur daraus fahren möchten!" (here's another one who [rises] out of his skin, while most people [simply fly out]).[92] At the same time, Yggdrasil is also a tree, one of the natural things that have disappeared as the Vogelsang has been overtaken by urban sprawl.

But what is significant in Fell's observation is the many ways one can "misclimb" (sich verklettern) in Yggdrasil. While "sich verklettern" can reasonably be translated as "to misclimb," the Grimms' *Wörterbuch* defines it as climbing so high that one cannot get back.[93] To misclimb

---

Antwort auf die Darwinismusdebatte des 19. Jahrhunderts," *Jahrbuch der Raabe-Gesellschaft* 29 (1988): 208–9. For a discourse analysis of the scene, see Florian Krobb, *Erkundungen im Überseeischen: Wilhelm Raabe und die Füllung der Welt* (Würzburg: Königshausen & Neumann, 2009), 202–21.

89   See also Krobb, *Erkundungen im Überseeischen*, 203–4.

90   Raabe, *BA*, 19: 381; Raabe, *The Birdsong Papers*, 107.

91   For an overview of the myths surrounding Yggdrasil, see John Lindow, *Norse Mythology: A Guide to the Gods, Heroes, Rituals, and Beliefs* (Oxford: Oxford University Press, 2002), 319–22.

92   Raabe, *BA*, 19: 381; Raabe, *The Birdsong Papers*, 107, translation modified.

93   "verklettern," in *Deutsches Wörterbuch von Jacob Grimm und Wilhelm Grimm*, vol. 25, www.woerterbuchnetz.de/DWB/verklettern.

here underscores the condition of being stuck on the way to some sort of zenith, placing the subject in an ambiguous position with no way up and no way back. "Sich verklettern" as a condition of life for both Velten and Helene is prefigured in an episode from their childhood when Helene "misclimbs" in Hartleben's tree. Velten is unable to rescue her, and must get help from Hartleben, a failure Velten remembers for the rest of his life. In all cases, misclimbing in the tree has poetological stakes because Velten and, by extension, the novel that is largely about him are not entirely able to access any more holistic alternative condition transcending the everyday. But crucially it does not fall back to earth either, that is, into a sort of empty mimesis of the existing material world. Instead Velten and the novel generally are placed in a precarious state of suspension between the brute material and poetic transcendence.

This state of suspension hangs over the rest of the novel. Velten's death at the end is the fulfillment of his desire to escape all property relations, but in contrast to Odin's arrival at wisdom, Velten's final days are marked by a regression, spent in the room he occupied as a student reading greasy copies of books he enjoyed as a child. Fell, too, whose pursuit of "transzendentale Menschenkunde" (transcendental study of humanity)[94] reverses his position from object of scientific study to subject in pursuit of knowledge, resumes his animal gait after taking leave of Velten. The poetic synthesis of the ideal and the material is not fully realized, and actually appears to collapse back into the material. As Karl remarks upon visiting Velten's empty death chamber, "ich empfand … den Druck der Materie schwerer denn je auf der Seele" (I felt more than ever the weight of material things on my spirit).[95] Karl's feeling of the heaviness of the material, then, is a sense of Velten's inability to achieve a poetic state beyond his class limitations, beyond his body, and beyond the species boundary. Instead Karl's status is closer to that of German Fell, an uncategorizable "leftover" between animal and human.[96] The stakes of this failed transcendence feed back into the text's realism. There is no poetic escape from the material, instead what remains is the persistence of realism's material realia.

Conclusion

When Raabe told his daughter that the Braunschweig water calamity of 1890/91 was a completion of what he had depicted in *Pfisters Mühle*, he implied that the novel and the material conditions in and around

---

94 Raabe, *BA*, 19: 381; Raabe, *The Birdsong Papers*, 107.

95 Raabe, *BA*, 19: 400; Raabe, *The Birdsong Papers*, 119.

96 Barbara Thums, "Vom Umgang mit Abfällen, Resten, und lebendingen Dingen in Erzählungen Wilhelm Raabes," *Jahrbuch der Raabe-Gesellschaft* 48 (2007): 69.

Braunschweig were relatively straightforward complements. While the remark was made off the cuff, it nevertheless touches on core aspects of realist aesthetics. In presenting us with narrators who set themselves the task of writing realistic narratives, be it as a notebook or a protocol based on "files," both *Pfisters Mühle* and *Die Akten des Vogelsangs* foreground and enact their own assumptions about the reproduction of reality through the medium of literature. The texts' insights into realism and ecoaesthetics arise not out of any sort of accordance between text and world, but rather from the friction between environmental depredation and the novels' own implicit and explicit poetics. That the environmental thematic is, in fact, core to Raabe's realism allows us to raise again the question of the extent to which his are "environmental texts." His fiction frequently draws heavily (and often humorously) on his own observations of environmental problems as well as the scientific debates of the day, and the works Raabe produced in his later years especially think critically about historical processes that are not unfamiliar to a contemporary readership.

Raabe's environmental thematic, then, is not some epiphenomenon that happens to stand out to a contemporary readership with a more advanced understanding of the effects of industrial emissions or land use on the quality of life on Earth. Beyond that, how one evaluates the environmental dimension of Raabe's novels relative to contemporary problems depends on one's own set of environmental politics. Thus, how we answer the question of whether Raabe is "environmental" and whether that makes him "relevant" might say more about the readers than it does about the texts. But the fact that those questions can be and have been the subject of debate points to a fundamental ambivalence in Raabe's fiction. The "dream of reconciliation" Lukács saw at work in Raabe's fiction is, in fact, a dream dreamed by characters with a strong stake in the urban, industrial bourgeois cultures that cause the environmental transformations they portray. But the image of Rhakopyrgos, both seen and unseen as it actively dirties the air and water at the end of *Pfisters Mühle*, or the invocation of children in the final pages of *Die Akten des Vogelsangs* both point towards a future the uncertainty of which looms over the endings of both novels, even if the narrators refuse to explicitly contemplate it.

3: Hydrologic Engineering, Social Change, and the Persistence of the Fantastic in Theodor Storm's *Der Schimmelreiter*

ON MAY 1, 1653, an unusual hailstorm struck North Frisia. In his *Nordfresische Chronik* (North Frisian Chronicle, 1666), M. Antoni Heimrich reports that, along with the usual ice clumps, there fell on that day "ein groß geschmeiß einer sonderlichen art von fliegen fast wie ein schnee herunter gefallen, daß man nerlich die augen dafür hat können auffthun" (a large shower of a strange sort, one made up of flies fell like snow, such that it was nearly impossible to open one's eyes).[1] His report of a shower of insects falling from the skies seems fantastic, but is by no means impossible: so-called "rains of animals," while rare, do take place and can be explained scientifically. Other events Heimrich records, however, defy rational explanation. In 1636, on the Feast of the Chair of St. Peter, for instance, he says that a local administrator in the town of Lunden found a *signum sanguinis* around his house, and when he went to wash himself, he discovered five death's heads in his washbasin.[2] Two centuries later, Theodor Storm lifted these events directly out of Heimrich's chronicle for his 1888 novella *Der Schimmelreiter* (The Rider on the White Horse). But whereas Heimrich depicts these incidents straightforwardly as "real" enough that they do not trouble the chronicle's claim to historical truth, in Storm's novella these and similarly fantastic elements can only appear at odds with *Der Schimmelreiter*'s realist claims.

The status of ghosts, mermaids, and the possibly revenant titular horse is determined by the conflict over the construction of a new dike that lies at the heart of the story. *Der Schimmelreiter* places that story within a complex double framing device. The first narrator, an alter ego for the author himself, speaks in Storm's present and recalls encountering the story of the novella in a magazine article from the 1830s that he is

---

1 M. Anton Heimreich, *Nordfresische Chronik: Zum dritten Male mit den Zugaben des Verfassers und der Fortsetzung seines Sohnes, Heinrich Heimreich, auch einigen andern zur nordfresischen Geschichte gehörigen Nachrichten vermehrt*, ed. Niels Falck, 2 vols. (Tondern: Forchhammer, 1819), vol. 1, 90.

2 Heimreich, *Nordfresische Chronik*, vol. 1, 85.

no longer able to find. The second narrator, the journalist who authored the article the first narrator recalls reading, relates the story of Hauke Haien as related to him by a third narrator, the schoolmaster he encountered on the Frisian coast. The schoolmaster, then, takes us to the early to middle decades of the eighteenth century, narrating the life of Hauke, a math autodidact who invents an improved dike model to protect the local community and its *Kooge*, or polders, that is, the arable land gained from the sea. Hauke's innovation is a dike with a gently sloping profile on the seaward side, as opposed to the traditional model of a straight vertical wall. Dikes built according to the old model tended to only last for decades, but, as Hauke explains when he presents his new design to the community, this new model will stand for centuries because it gives the waves no "Angriffspunk" (point of attack).[3] The rhetoric of violent attack here tellingly frames the relation to nature in terms of aggression and conquest. But Hauke will only be in a position to implement his new design once he has obtained the office of *Deichgraf*, dikemaster, and his struggle to obtain that office is what drives the plot in the first half of the story. With help from his father and an advantageous marriage to Elke Volkerts, daughter of the previous dikemaster, Hauke succeeds to the post. He supervises the construction of his new dike mounted on a white horse, which the superstitious characters of the story believe is the same animal whose bones once lay strewn on one of the marshy islands beyond the dikes, but is now risen from the dead. Hauke's life ends during a storm, when rising waters breach the old dike and inundate the polder. Out on the dike attempting to control the situation, Hauke sees his wife and daughter coming for him, but the old dike crumbles beneath them. He follows, they die, and while the land is flooded, his new dike survives and is still protecting the community nearly a century later.

The dike's survival marks the triumph of Hauke's engineering genius, but the rationalism that it embodies is countered by the fact that his ghost haunts it. When we first meet the journalist in the 1830s, he is riding along the dike in a storm when he encounters the spectral horse and rider who pass him twice before vanishing. Taking shelter at an inn, where he meets the schoolmaster who will take over the narrative, he is told that Hauke's ghost continually reenacts the plunge into the breach whenever a storm threatens the community. The very presence of the ghost raises the question of how fantastic and mythical elements can square with the story's own realist claims. One of the effects of the framing device is to separate the realist claim from the fantastic by burying it under layers

---

3   Theodor Storm, *Sämtliche Werke in vier Bänden*, ed. Karl E. Laage (Frankfurt am Main: Deutscher Klassiker Verlag, 1988), vol. 4, 707; Theodor Storm, *The Rider on the White Horse and Selected Stories*, trans. James Wright (New York: New York Review of Books, 2009), 244.

of mediation and uncertainty (the first narrator, after all, is unable to produce his source). Paradoxically, the place to which the fantastic and mythic are banished is the very heart of the novella. It is here that the material reality of the dikes becomes important. Heather Sullivan sees in the sheer materiality of the earthen dikes a means of grounding, in a very literal sense, the novella's realism against its ghostly subject matter.[4] But beyond their sheer materiality as enormous piles of dirt is their function in the landscape as another technology of separation dividing the newly won arable land from the ocean beyond, thus serving the same function as the novella's framing device. The wild ocean is associated for the superstitious characters as well as for a young Hauke with ghosts, mermaids, and fantastic events, things that the dike excludes by virtue of separating land from sea. But, as Anette Schwarz notes, the dike turns out to be "that line of division that enables Hauke to neatly separate spheres and assign beings their proper place, [and] is also the structure that, by its power of delineation, provokes the possibility of transgression and invites questions of belonging."[5] The Hauke Haien Dike is a haunted place in and of itself, but the dikes in general turn out to be eminently permeable, with the revenant horse being the most notable example of a fantastic being that crosses the barrier. Thus, just as the dike turns out to be vulnerable to the forces of nature it is designed to resist, so too does the novella's attempt to distinguish its realism from the fantastic allow for the fantastic to persist, thereby forcing the theoretical negotiation through which the text reflects on its own realist claims.

That the construction of the physical dike effects in turn a defining distinction of realism, namely, its disavowal of the fantastic, is only one half of the argument. The other half is that *Der Schimmelreiter* connects this aesthetic reflection to a social and environmental history of Germany's industrialization. Even as the framing device separates, it implicitly bridges the 1880s with the early- to mid-eighteenth century, thereby connecting the story of Hauke's conquest of nature with the environmental realities of Storm's own industrial age. Jost Hermand has argued that Hauke represents a *Gründerzeit* bourgeois ideal of one who fashions himself as an individual through the pursuit of property and power. In Hermand's view, he is an archetype that feeds, in turn, into a Nietzschean myth of the *Übermensch*.[6] The fact that the main story takes place at the

---

4   Heather Sullivan, "Dirt Theory and Material Ecocriticism," *ISLE* 19, no. 3 (2012): 526.

5   Anette Schwarz, "Social Subjects and Tragic Legacies: The Uncanny in Theodor Storm's *Der Schimmelreiter*," *The Germanic Review* 73, no. 3 (1998): 258.

6   For Hermand, the novella does not uncritically valorize Hauke as a hero, but places him instead in a double light. See Jost Hermand, "Hauke Haien: Kritik

106 ♦ Hydrologic Engineering, Social Change, and the Fantastic

time of the European Enlightenment is crucial to the history the novella constructs, and Hauke's rationalism and resistance to superstition bolster the image of him as an Enlightenment type. But Hauke has another antecedent beyond the myth of the Nietzschean *Übermensch* or that of Prometheus, namely, Goethe's Faust. In the second part of *Faust* (1832), Faust delivers his final monologue looking down on his own dike project, and sees in the conflict with nature the conditions for human freedom. As Kate Rigby argues, however, what Faust and Hauke have in common is less their Prometheanism than the fact that, like Faust, Hauke "falls prey, not so much to the violence of the elements or the backwardness of his compatriots, but to the characteristically modern anthroparchal illusion of unidirectional self-determined human agency."[7] Rigby is certainly correct to argue that the relation between the human and the non-human is not so much one of human reason pitted against the destructive forces of nature, but rather one of "entanglement."[8] But Hauke's illusion of unidirectional human agency nevertheless has consequences beyond being a false way of apprehending the world. As an ideology, it manifests itself in the dike project. As part of the material environment, the dike project, in turn, is as crucial for the text's reflections on environmental aesthetics as it is for the constitution of landscape as such. And for a novella concerned with drawing boundaries, whether in its material universe or at the level of narrative form, the realism of the novella is as entangled in the material ecosystem the dike creates as the land, the water, or the living organisms that populate the story. Hauke's story ends with tragedy, of course, but the fact that his dike stands means that *Der Schimmelreiter* is not a simple cautionary tale about human hubris in the face of natural forces. Beyond Hauke as an individual, the text figures his life as a turning point in how the politics and economy of the community operate, marking the beginning of a period of bourgeois ascendency. The position of dikemaster had been a de facto hereditary post before Hauke, and his project of environmental transformation is animated by a desire to extract more surplus value out of nature.

The tidal variation is the natural force that makes the Frisian setting of *Der Schimmelreiter* so important. The story takes place on the Wattenmeer (Wadden Sea), a stretch of coast running from North Holland up to Denmark. Here the sea flows so far out that the intertidal

---

oder Ideal des gründerzeitlichen Übermenschen," *Wirkendes Wort* 15 (1965): 46–47.

7 Kate Rigby, *Dancing with Disaster: Environmental Histories, Narratives, and Ethics for Perilous Times* (Charlottesville: University of Virginia Press, 2015), 96. On the comparison between Faust and Hauke, see also Sullivan, "Dirt Theory and Material Ecocriticism," 522–26.

8 Rigby, *Dancing with Disaster*, 96.

zone can be measured in kilometers, and at low tide one can hike from the mainland to the nearby islands. The wet, sandy flats exposed when the tide is out are called the *Watt* in Low German, from which the Wattenmeer gets its name. Because of the persistent threat of flooding, dikes, canals, and other hydrological interventions are a major part of the Frisian landscape. In particular, Storm's writing career roughly coincided with the construction of the town and harbor of Wilhelmshaven, a major environmental intervention on the Jade Bay meant to advance the military power of the German state. The Jade Bay, in turn, was created through a series of flooding events in 1164, 1334, 1362, and 1511, all of which eventually destroyed the farms and settlements that had once occupied the area.[9] One of Storm's sources for inspiration was the flood that struck Frisia on October 7, 1756, and indeed, the novella has Hauke and his family die on All Saint's Day of that year.[10] The few weeks' difference, though, points to another catastrophic natural event, namely, the earthquake and tsunami that destroyed Lisbon a year to the day prior to the flood at the story's climax, an event that famously reverberated in European Enlightenment thinking.

The natural qualities of the Frisian coast thus make it a fertile place for the novella's aesthetic reflections as much as for the history it constructs. The Wattenmeer, after all, is an ambiguous zone, not quite dry land but also not quite sea. That ambiguity is bound with the supernatural in the novella's imagination of the uncanny. Along with what Anette Schwarz identifies as the social character of the uncanny in the novella, which she shows is connected to elements of classical tragedy and the struggle of individuals and communities against the inheritance of the past,[11] the uncanny is also the result of the dike as a very material project in the conquest of nature. The parallel repression of the forces of physical nature and the supernatural, only for both to reassert their presence, produces a specifically environmental uncanny. In the case of the environmental uncanny, the uncanny object has a more active, agential status than the mere thing that produces an aesthetic effect. Amitav Ghosh writes: "For what [the environmental uncanny] suggests—indeed proves—is that nonhuman forces have the ability to intervene directly in human thought."[12] In the novella, the appearance of animals that are often at most only semi-tame, atmospheric phenomena like fog, and dead bodies distorted by their time in the sea are all moments when natural forces intervene in the

---

9   Blackbourn, *The Conquest of Nature*, 124–28.

10   Christian Demandt and Philipp Theisohn, eds., *Storm-Handbuch: Leben— Werk—Wirkung* (Stuttgart: Metzler, 2017), 251.

11   Schwarz, "Social Subjects and Tragic Legacies," 253.

12   Amitav Ghosh, *The Great Derangement: Climate Change and the Unthinkable* (Gurgaon: Penguin Books, 2016), 41–42.

108 ♦ Hydrologic Engineering, Social Change, and the Fantastic

social drama, and indicate that nature is not a thing that better technology can more effectively conquer. It is then significant that ghosts, mermaids, and the revenant horse all appear in and around the dike. From that perspective, whether they are experientially "real" or simply optical illusions is beside the point. Storm himself suggested as much in his letter to Gottfried Keller from August 4, 1882, in which he wrote: "nicht daß ich Un- oder Übernatürliches glaubte, wohl aber, daß das Natürliche, was nicht unter die alltäglichen Wahrnehmungen fällt, bei Weitem nicht erkannt ist" (not that I believe in the un- or supernatural, but rather that the natural, what does not fall under everyday perception, is largely unrecognized).[13] Storm's own ambiguous belief in ghosts aside,[14] he places the spectral not in the realm of the supernatural, but rather sees it as belonging to a nature that vastly exceeds human perception and knowledge, a position that allows for the possibility of folding the fantastic into an expanded notion of nature.

Enlightenment, Superstition, and the Realist Claim

The ambiguity around what the novella figures as an Enlightenment ethos arises not just out of the mere fact that the realist novella contains elements of the fantastic, but the fact that those characters who are supposed to be the most representative of rationality are more inclined to the superstitious than the superstitious characters are inclined towards rationality. Hauke, who is at odds with others in his community precisely because of his rejection of superstition, believes in fantastic beings enough that, in one scene early on, he shouts at what appear to be apparitions while standing on the dike. As an adult he utters a blasphemous prayer when his wife seems on the brink of death after a difficult childbirth, and, of course, he sacrifices himself and becomes the ghost that haunts the dike, plot points I will return to. The schoolmaster, who, in the words of the 1830s dikemaster, "gehört zu den Aufklärern" (is a disciple of the Enlightenment), likewise acknowledges his own his inability to break from superstition.[15] His very job is to spread knowledge within his community, buttressing the implicit claim to realism, and yet precisely because of his position he has to preface his account with the caveat: "es ist viel Aberglaube dazwischen, und eine Kunst, ohne diesen zu erzählen" (there's a great deal of superstition mixed up in the story, and it takes

13 Karl E. Laage, ed., *Theodor Storm—Gottfried Keller: Briefwechsel* (Berlin: Schmidt, 1992), 92.

14 For a summary of Storm's views on ghosts and their presence in his oeuvre, see among many others Demandt and Theisohn, *Storm-Handbuch*, 112–17.

15 Storm, *Sämtliche Werke*, 3: 755; Storm, *The Rider on the White Horse*, 283.

some art to tell it truly).[16] It is also telling that in a story where the existence of fantastic beings is something the characters frequently argue about, neither the narrator nor the other characters contest the reality of Hauke's ghost.[17] Counterintuitive though ghosts may be in a "realist" novella, as Christian Begemann argues, they are figures of history's return *par excellence* because they demarcate the position of realism *ex negativo.*[18]

That history is a specifically environmental history. The appearance of the ghost to the magazine journalist establishes the pattern, because the history the ghost continuously reenacts is the disaster of the storm and the flood at the novella's climax. The spectral element, though, also recalls the fantastic quality of wild nature itself, an association that is only thinkable because of the separation the dike establishes between the social nature of the polder on one side and the ocean on the other. That association, and the fact that the barriers between the two are hardly absolute, is established in a scene early in the story. One February the young Hauke hears reports about dead bodies washing up on the beach, having been locked under sea ice since November. The local woman who saw them regarded them as sea devils, with large heads and shiny black bodies, partly decomposed and partly devoured by crabs, much to the horror of the local children. They are not just uncanny objects in general, but specifically things of abjection, which, as Julia Kristeva poetically defines it, is "a massive and sudden emergence of uncanniness, which, familiar as it might have been in an opaque and forgotten life, now harries me as radically separate, loathsome. Not me. Not that. But not nothing, either. A 'something' that I do not recognize as a thing."[19] Ultimately for Kristeva, things derive their abject qualities precisely from their particular forms of transgressiveness: "It is thus not lack of cleanliness or health that causes abjection but what disturbs the identity, system, order. What does not respect borders, positions, rules. The in-between, the ambiguous,

---

16 Storm, *Sämtliche Werke*, 3: 639; Storm, *The Rider on the White Horse*, 188.

17 David Jackson, "'Sie können Ihren eigenen Augen doch nicht mißtrauen': Noch einmal zum zweiten Rahmenerzähler in Theodor Storms *Der Schimmelreiter*," *Schriften der Theodor-Storm-Gesellschaft* 64 (2015): 53–54.

18 Christian Begemann, "Figuren der Wiederkehr: Erinnerung, Tradition, Vererbung und andere Gespenster der Vergangenheit bei Theodor Storm," in *Wirklichkeit und Wahrnehmung: Neue Perspektiven auf Theodor Storm*, ed. Elisabeth Strowick and Ulrike Vedder (Bern: Peter Lang, 2013), 13–14. See also Andreas Blödorn, "Doppelgänger, Geisterseher: Figuren der Spiegelung und der Wiederkehr bei Theodor Storm," *Schriften der Theodor-Storm-Gesellschaft* 66 (2017): 9–27.

19 Julia Kristeva, *Powers of Horror: An Essay on Abjection*, trans. Leon S. Roudiez (New York: Columbia University Press, 1982), 2.

110 ♦ Hydrologic Engineering, Social Change, and the Fantastic

the composite."[20] The corpse, for Kristeva, is "the utmost of abjection" because it is "death infecting life," where "it is no longer I who expel, 'I' is expelled."[21] What had once been beings in the social world, these drowned people have travelled back and forth across the border between the natural and the social that Hauke is so determined to reinforce. They vanished for a period into the open ocean, and have now been ejected back, horrifically altered and changed by the forces of the sea and the wild animals that live there.

Hauke goes to the dike in the hopes of seeing some of these bodies for himself, to no avail. Instead, peering into the steam that rises out of the fissures in the thawing ice sheet, he sees:

> in dem Nebel schritten dunkle Gestalten auf und ab, ... Würdevoll, aber mit seltsamen, erschreckenden Gebärden; mit langen Nasen und Hälsen sah er sie fern an den rauchenden Spalten auf und ab spazieren; plötzlich begannen sie wie Narren unheimlich auf und ab zu springen, die großen über die kleinen gegen die großen; dann breiteten sie sich aus und verloren alle Form.

> [dark shapes were creeping back and forth in the fog ... the dark ones moved with dignity, but they made strange disturbing gestures; they had long noses and necks, and he could see them in the distance, walking up and down beside the steaming cracks in the ice; suddenly, mysteriously, they began to leap up and down like demons, the large ones jumping over the small ones, and the small leaping toward the large; then they thinned out and disappeared.[22]]

It is not clear whether we are to accept these beings as real apparitions or some sort of trick of the light. The schoolmaster, for his part, jumps ahead in the narration and mentions a later scene, when Hauke was with his daughter Wienke seeing the same apparitions. There Hauke assures Wienke that there is nothing to be afraid of, that it is the fishing boats and the crows that only appear monstrous because of the distorting effects of the fog. This explanation, of course, is perfectly plausible and in keeping with the workings of nature. A fata morgana, for instance, also looks like a seemingly fantastic occurrence, but is really no more than an optical effect that comes about as light passes through layers of air differing in temperature. And yet, in that first scene on the dike, the young Hauke responds to the forms as if they were "real" supernatural beings, regardless of what he will tell his daughter many years later. He thinks they might be the

20 Kristeva, *Powers of Horror*, 4.
21 Kristeva, *Powers of Horror*, 3–4.
22 Storm, *Sämtliche Werke*, 3: 644–45; Storm, *The Rider on the White Horse*, 192–93.

spirits of the drowned, or perhaps sea ghosts of Norwegian legend, with a patch of seaweed in place of a face. His call to them, "ihr sollt mich nicht vertreiben!" (I'm going to stand my ground!), is a cry of defiance in the same spirit as the one that animates his project of creating new land from the sea.[23] That suggests that Hauke's skepticism of the supernatural does not come simply from an insistence on empirical truth, but rather an understanding that asserting his will against the forces of nature is also an assertion against the fantastic apparitions that appear there.

From an aesthetic standpoint, the reality or unreality of such apparitions is beside the point, because it is the effect that matters. Indeed, if we accept Hauke's explanation to Wienke that what we see are the images of birds distorted by fog, then the environmental substrate of the novella's uncanny aesthetic is all the more important, resulting as it does from the presence of animals and atmospheric conditions. The birds appear monstrous and distorted no matter what. And if the forms are, in fact, ghosts and devils, then their relegation to the sea beyond the dike and their indifference to human presence only illustrates the vastness and inscrutability of non-human nature, a nature that is irreducible to the aesthetic effects concentrated in one individual of one species. Either way, the specifically environmental nature of the uncanny effect in *Der Schimmelreiter* reflects what is beyond human understanding, whether we accept the fantastic explanation that the shapes are ghosts and monsters or whether we accept the empirical explanation that they are the result of light refracted through steam.

Hauke's excursion to the dike as a child makes clear that the dikes had always served as a barrier between the community of the polder and the fantastic beings of the sea. What is new about the dike design Hauke introduces as an adult, then, is not the spatial division but the break in a cyclical temporality that defines both non-human nature but also has mythic qualities. Hauke's argument for a new dike with a new slope profile rests on the fact that the old dikes had failed roughly at regular intervals: the last collapse took place thirty years before Hauke's present, another thirty-five years before that, another forty-five years previously. And the region is due for another catastrophe. On the one hand, Hauke's insight about the cyclicity of flooding is perfectly scientific. Contemporary hydrology speaks about flooding in precisely Hauke's terms: a decade flood is a flood of such severity that it is statistically likely to occur once every ten years, an even more severe century flood occurring only once every one hundred years, etc. The superstition-averse Hauke, of course, sees the cyclical regularity of the flooding events in terms of the mechanical workings of an otherwise soulless nature, but the novella also suggests that such regularity is not simply a matter of statistics and empirical

23 Storm, *Sämtliche Werke*, 3: 645; Storm, *The Rider on the White Horse*, 193.

observation. Local legend has it, for instance, that a living being must be buried in the dike in order to ensure its integrity. A gypsy child is said to have been buried in the old one, a sacrifice the dike workers would have repeated by burying a dog in the new one had Hauke not intervened and adopted the dog, whom the Haiens name Perle (Pearl). Hauke appears to endorse superstition at last at the climax when he plunges after his family into the breach in the dike, shouting "Herr Gott, nimm mich; verschon die Andern!" (Here, God, take me; but let the others alone!).[24] In sacrificing himself, Hauke repeats the act of sacrifice that legend held had always ensured that the dikes would hold against floods.

The novella's association of the domination of nature, mythic cyclicity, and a logic of sacrifice is comparable to the account Max Horkheimer and Theodor Adorno give of the enlightenment domination of nature in *Dialectic of Enlightenment*. They observe in their reading of the Sirens episode in *The Odyssey* that "every mythical figure is compelled to do the same thing over and over again. Each of them is constituted by repetition: its failure would mean their end."[25] In their account, Odysseus manages to break the cyclical logic animating the mythic characters he encounters by virtue of his own cunning (*List*). Odysseus has his crew plug their ears with wax and orders them to tie him to the mast so that he can both hear the Siren song and still sail past unscathed. For Horkheimer and Adorno, "the detached, instrumental mind, by submissively embracing nature, renders to nature what is hers and thereby cheats her."[26] Hauke's innovative dike design achieves something similar. It promises to break the cyclicity of destructive flooding events not by standing in blunt opposition to the waves, as the traditional vertical dike model did, but instead by accommodating the tidal forces through its gentler slope. Like the Freiherr von Risach in Adalbert Stifter's *Der Nachsommer*, Hauke is able to exert control over the forces of nature by working with and through them, rather than simply against them, thereby more effectively neutralizing the threat the sea poses to the community. The difference between Hauke and Risach is that Hauke does not feel the need to dress up his opposition to nature as an environmental ethic in its own right. For Horkheimer and Adorno, Odysseus's encounter with the Sirens marks the emergence of bourgeois subjectivity in the simultaneous embrace and cheating of nature, setting in motion a dialectic that will collapse in the mythic terror of fascism and the logic of eternal return in mass culture at a moment when the domination of nature has reached an advanced stage where "the

---

24 Storm, *Sämtliche Werke*, 3: 753; Storm, *The Rider on the White Horse*, 282.

25 Max Horkheimer and Theodor W. Adorno, *Dialectic of Enlightenment: Philosophical Fragments*, trans. Edmund Jephcott (Stanford, CA: Stanford University Press, 2002), 45.

26 Horkheimer and Adorno, *Dialectic of Enlightenment*, 45.

HYDROLOGIC ENGINEERING, SOCIAL CHANGE, AND THE FANTASTIC ◆ 113

wholly enlightened earth is radiant with triumphant calamity."[27] As for Hauke, while his new dike holds, he repeats the moment of sacrifice in his spectral existence, perpetuating as a ghost his own mythic cyclicity, appearing at moments when the forces of nature most clearly resist the technology that dominates it.

Yet even as it defies the forces of nature and, with Hauke's design, breaks the cycle of flooding, the dike is as much a locus of the fantastic as it is a barrier. In addition to the legend of the child sacrifice and the later specter of Hauke haunting the structure, the character of Trien' Jans, the witch-like woman who resides in a house out on the old dike, further concretizes the dike's uneasy relation to a realism that defines itself in opposition to the mythic and the fantastic. She is the chief mouthpiece of the superstitious worldview in *Der Schimmelreiter*, and insofar as Trien' Jans falls on the superstitious side of this divide, she becomes a means by which the novella codes a mythic worldview and, by extension, fantastic nature more broadly, as feminine.[28] A key moment when she functions as a means through which the novella works through its truth claims vis-à-vis the fantastic occurs in the scene when she tells Wienke the story about a mermaid trapped in the polder after the closing of the sluices. Trien', who by this point in the story is living at Elke's invitation in the Haien household, claims to have seen the water woman with fish hands swimming through the network of ditches back in the days when she worked as a servant for Elke's grandfather. In Trien's telling, the mermaid not only contrasts with the novella's thematization of Enlightenment notions of rationality, but also with Christian theology. Trien' specifically tells Wienke that while the mermaid appeared to be trying to pray, she could not, because such beings lack a soul. The mermaid alludes to the myth of Undine, the water nymph who can only gain a soul through union with a human, a story that served as the basis for Friedrich de la Motte Fouqué's *Undine* and Hans Christian Andersen's fairy tale "The Little Mermaid," and later, as we shall see, the character Melusine in Theodor Fontane's *Der Stechlin*.

The mermaid's presence within the polder would be a moment of transgression, if it indeed took place. But Trien' Jans's story functions as a moment when the reality of the fantastic is put up for debate. Her truth claim rests on her claim to have been an eyewitness. She says that she saw the mermaid herself, and that the incident took place at a specific moment

---

27 Horkheimer and Adorno, *Dialectic of Enlightenment*, 1.

28 Irmgard Roebling, "'Von Menschentragik und wildem Naturgeheimnis': Die Thematisierung von Natur und Weiblichkeit in 'Der Schimmelreiter,'" in *Stormlektüren: Festschrift für Karl Ernst Laage zum 80. Geburtstag*, ed. Gerd Eversberg, David Jackson, and Eckart Pastor (Würzburg: Königshausen & Neumann, 2000), 183–214.

in the past, meaning that, if we take her at her word, the event is histori-cal and roughly datable, not some fairy-tale "once upon a time." Upon hearing it Hauke admonishes Trien' Jans to keep her stories (*Mären*, from which the diminutive *Märchen*, "fairy tale," derives) to herself, or tell it to the geese and chickens. But when Trien' retorts that the story is no fairy tale, but rather a real event, she suddenly says that her great-uncle was the eyewitness, meaning the basis for the truth claim lies elsewhere. When Hauke seizes on the contradiction, Trien' moves the goalpost by denying that the source matters and taking umbrage at the implication that her relative was a liar. In moving the story to an earlier moment in time and ascribing it to her great-uncle she does exactly what the novella does with its framing device around Hauke's story, that is, establish mediating dis-tance between the reality of the present and the fantastical elements of her anecdote. Her loss of a claim to truth is Hauke's and the schoolmaster's gain, inasmuch as this mythic event loses credibility under basic empiri-cal scrutiny, bolstering in turn the position of both the schoolmaster and Hauke as representatives of enlightenment thinking and, from there, the novella's distinction of its own realism against the fantastic.

The dikes' function as both a barrier, however permeable, and also a locus for the mythic and the fantastic means that they literalize the theo-retical problem at the core of the novella's realism. But they are also real pieces of environmental infrastructure, and the polders that they produce are clear examples of social nature. The status of the fantastic as a problem for realist aesthetics thus collides with the shifting political relations they embody, relations I turn to in more detail.

The Dikes: Poetics and Politics of Separation

As early as the 1840s, Storm saw political symbolism in the dikes so char-acteristic of the Frisian coast. His poem "Ostern" (Easter, 1846/48) stages a scene familiar from *Der Schimmelreiter* as the speaker stands on a local dike looking out at the ocean. The first version of 1846 reads mostly like a conventional nature poem, and indeed, Storm reported being inspired by a walk in his garden.[29] The speaker celebrates the awakening of spring in terms one might compare to Friedrich Gottlieb Klopstock's "Frühlingsfeier" (Spring Celebration, 1759) as he stands atop the dike with the polder on one side, the ocean on the other, hears the sound of church bells, breathes the spring air, and regards the flower buds on the dry side of the dike. He reflects on the spirit of rejuvenation hang-ing in the atmosphere, a spirit connected both to the season and the fact that the day is a celebration of Christ's resurrection. This version is at its most overtly political in its opening line, "Es war daheim auf unserm

29 Demandt and Theisohn, *Storm-Handbuch*, 81.

Meeresdeich" (It was at home on our ocean dike), a line that posits ownership and community, implicitly excluding others.

Who those "others" might be is made more specific in the revised version of the poem from 1848, which contains three new stanzas. On April 23, 1848, after years of increasing calls within Schleswig and Holstein, as well as among German nationalists more broadly, for the two duchies to loosen their ties to Denmark, German forces defeated the Danish at the Battle of Schleswig.[30] In addition to a sharpening of the rhetoric of *Heimat*, or "homeland" with the line, "Und wanke nicht, du feste Heimaterde!" (And falter not, solid homeland ground!), at the end of the first of the new stanzas, the revised version makes the ocean and the dike into symbols for Schleswig's conflict with Denmark. In the second and third of the added stanzas, the speaker is transported back to the previous November, when a storm churned up the ocean, threatening the very dike on which he stands. The thought of how the dike held back the sea prompts for the speaker a moment of jubilation, and he proclaims in the final lines, "Denn machtlos, zischend schoß zurück das Meer— / Das Land ist unser, unser soll es bleiben!" (For the sea retreated with a powerless hiss— / The land is ours, ours it shall remain!).[31] If we read the sea as representing Denmark, then the dike obviously becomes a political symbol because it withstands the onslaught, but more significantly, because it separates the sea from the Heimat soil. That raises the larger question of environmental politics: who has what claims to what nature? "The land is ours," after all, implies the question to which it supplies an answer. The dike in this poem, then, is political both in a symbolic and a material sense. While the storm surge is made to represent a political conflict, the Heimat soil that the dike creates and protects is not simply a symbol for something else. The ground has a literal existence in the poem, on top of which "Heimat" is an extra layer of signification.

In *Der Schimmelreiter* forty years later, the political dimensions of the dike are not limited to what it signifies in the Schleswegian patriotic imagination, but instead both manifests and effects political change in the community. The most significant change Hauke's rise effects is in the position of dikemaster. Before Hauke, the office had aspects of aristocratic culture. The German word for "dikemaster," "Deichgraf" literally translates as "dike count," even though it was not an aristocratic title per se. In Frisia, the position was established at the beginning of the seventeenth century, and the dikemaster was elected by organizations of

---

30 See Thomas Nipperdey, *Deutsche Geschichte, 1800–1866: Bürgerwelt und starker Staat* (Munich: Beck, 2013), 311–12; Demandt and Theisohn, *Storm-Handbuch*, 81.

31 Storm, *Sämtliche Werke*, 1: 56–57.

landowners responsible for the maintenance of the dikes in their region.[32] The requirement that one own land is the key obstacle for Hauke, since the Haiens, in Ole Peters's dismissive words, have "Land, ... das man auf dreizehn Karren wegfahren kann" (property that you could cart away in thirteen wheelbarrows!).[33] Furthermore, by Hauke's time the dikemaster position has become a de facto inherited position, rather than one given on the basis of engineering skill or administrative competence. Hauke's father, Tede Haien, expresses characteristic bourgeois disdain for the aristocratic nature of the office, telling the young Hauke that the current dikemaster is a fool who only has the position because his father and grandfather had it before him, and because he happens to possess twenty-nine fens. The current dikemaster, Tede complains, does not do the actual work of managing the dike, but relies instead on a system of patronage, giving luxurious food to the then-schoolmaster as reward for doing the calculations necessary for planning and maintaining the dikes, and thereby protecting the dikemaster's claim to legitimacy. Another indication that Hauke's rise upsets a specifically aristocratic order lies in the name the new polder is given. It was originally to be named "Carolinenkoog," after some princess, but ultimately bears the name of Hauke Haien himself.

The political conflict, then, is that of Hauke as a self-made bourgeois archetype against an entrenched and, in the eyes of the bourgeoisie, at least, parasitic aristocratic order. By the same token, Hauke's rise to the post is not a triumph for meritocracy. It is facilitated by two turns that are also more aristocratic than bourgeois in nature, or rather, what the bourgeoisie imagine bourgeois nature to be. The first turn that helps his rise is the fen he inherits from his father. On his deathbed, Tede Haien reveals that in spite of his initial skepticism, he felt that Hauke did deserve to be dikemaster, and began working to acquire more property for Hauke to inherit. Part of that inheritance, it turns out, is a fen that formerly belonged to Antje Wohlers. Tede says that the fen was a gift, bequeathed to him because he used to give Antje Wohlers money after she had become old and infirm. The transactional character of this acquisition makes it look less like a thank-you gift and more like Tede was collecting on a debt. The historical reality of life on the Frisian fens bolsters the suspicion that the fens were not given out of mere gratitude. Since at least the seventeenth century, the fens of East Frisia and Oldenburg had been exploited and colonized through the construction of canals and the extraction of peat for fuel, a process that accelerated in the nineteenth century. In the eighteenth century, peat was an important energy source, one that persisted even under the dominance of coal in Storm's own time.[34]

32 Storm, *Sämtliche Werke*, 1: 1092–93.
33 Storm, *Sämtliche Werke*, 3: 665; Storm, *The Rider on the White Horse*, 210.
34 Blackbourn, *The Conquest of Nature*, 144–61.

But fen colonists also found themselves in a condition of precarity to the forces of financial capital. "Failure meant that colonists incurred debts to merchants or peat-shippers, becoming in effect peat-diggers for the profit of others. Or they turned into day laborers on the peat-fired iron works established in some colonies, processing bog iron ore, or limonite."[35] Even if what Tede says about the acquisition can be taken at face value, Antje's physical decline had put her in a position of economic precarity, otherwise she would not have needed financial assistance. Whatever the circumstances, it is the fact of inheritance that matters, because it contradicts the image of Hauke as an archetype of bourgeois self-fashioning.

The second turn that aids his rise to the position of dikemaster is his marriage to Elke Volkerts, daughter of the previous dikemaster Tede Volkerts. While Elke claims that the engagement had taken place long before the dikemaster position had become vacant with the death of her father Tede, she announces it at the moment that Hauke's candidacy for the post is up for discussion. The announcement is a strategic move that shows her also to be a party in actively creating the conditions for Hauke's ascension and, moreover, underscoring that their marriage is at least in part a political union. The political side of the union works because it is also an economic one: the property she brings to the marriage, together with Hauke's inheritance, is sufficient to make Hauke appear as a legitimate candidate for dikemaster, and by marrying into his predecessor's family, the post still follows a line of familial descent.

These facts do not entirely negate the historical shift Hauke inaugurates. Rather, he relates to the aristocratic political status quo as the dike relates to the sea: it works not through stubborn opposition, but an accommodation that beats that which it opposes at its own game. Given the contest surrounding it and the existential stakes of the dike for the community, it is obvious that the office is more than just another bureaucratic position with a narrow mandate. And so once made dikemaster, Hauke wields considerable power both over the community and the environment. His understanding of local hydrology means that, in addition to his main dike project, he is busy constructing numerous new drains and sluices, leaving locals disgruntled over the increased tax burden. The "Vorland" (outland), the tidal flats beyond the dike, is communal property in the sense that all members of the community have a claim to it proportional to their properties behind the dikes. Since Hauke has been expanding his own land holdings, he has also expanded his claim to the ambiguous intertidal zone of the flats. He will thus have that much larger a stake in the arable land of the new polder, meaning he is poised to gain the most value from the project's completion. He stands to be the biggest winner from his own dike project in part also because he now

35 Blackbourn, *The Conquest of Nature*, 155.

possesses the entirety of his former nemesis Ole Peters's property, which he was able to acquire after Ole Peters's best ram drowned in a flood. Ole Peters's loss to the vicissitudes of the Frisian environment is Hauke's gain, such that in this instance he capitalizes far more unambiguously on another's precarity than was the case when his father acquired Antje Wohlers's property. In sum, he is able to wield his political power in service of an infrastructure project that will also happen to enable him to extract more value from the land.

Becoming dikemaster means for Hauke coming into his own as a Promethean type whose forethought is the basis on which he makes the world. That is especially visible when we see him now as dikemaster back on one of the dikes looking out to where his new dike will run, drawing a line and imagining its profile, "welches bis jetzt nur in seinem Kopf vorhanden war" (which so far had existed in his mind alone).[36] Actually realizing the dike means first gaining systematic knowledge of the streams and currents that constitute the complex hydrology of the intertidal zone, and so, resolved to construct his dike, he takes his servant out on a boat and begins mapping and measuring. Such mapping and measuring is an instance of the production of abstract social nature that is the necessary precursor for the polder as an instance of social nature in a historical material sense, one that also demystifies the *Watt* by making it knowable through empirical science.[37] In that sense Hauke's surveying and mapping also serve the novella's realist reflection, insofar as it depicts the landscape "as it really is." That such realist representation serves ends instrumental in the conquest of nature seems less self-explanatory when compared to the moments of surveying in Adalbert Stifter's works. In *Der Nachsommer*, surveying and sketching were likewise ways in which Heinrich Drendorf came to know the landscape. But *Der Nachsommer* figures the act of surveying as an end unto itself, a non-instrumentalized way of knowing nature, and its value lies in an aesthetics of verisimilitude to the forms of the external environment. Hauke's survey drawings, by contrast, are valuable not on aesthetic grounds, but because their verisimilitude is key to dominating nature.

Ambiguous Affinities: Animal Characters in *Der Schimmelreiter*

Hauke may understand himself to be projecting his will onto the forces of nature and subverting them through his own ingenuity, but the novella presents this Prometheanism as illusory. Perhaps the most

---

36 Storm, *Sämtliche Werke*, 3: 690–91; Storm, *The Rider on the White Horse*, 231.

37 Moore, *Capitalism in the Web of Life*, 194–202.

powerful reminder of this fact is the tragic ending, when Hauke and his family are swept out to the ocean where their bodies "allmählich in ihre Urbestandteile aufgelöst sein" (gradually dissolved into their original components), as the schoolmaster puts it, thus becoming part of inorganic nature.[38] But the animal characters in the novella are at least as important as the ocean, the soil, or forces like the weather and the tides. The white horse in the title announces the importance of animals in the story, and the fact that the dike is built to protect livestock as much as the fields themselves indicates the extent to which animals drive the central conflict. In addition to the horse, Trien' Jans's angora cat, the dog Perle (Pearl), and the seagull Klaus turn out also to be important supporting characters in the novella's cast. They also contribute to the environmental uncanny, having one degree or another of familiarity, especially in the cases of those animals with names, but also inscrutability, even in the case of the dog, the tamest and most domesticated of the animal characters. What contributes to the environmental uncanny, as Ghosh formulates it, is becoming aware of how the non-human intervenes in human thoughts, an awareness "that conversations among ourselves have always had other participants: it is like finding out that one's telephone has been tapped for years, or that the neighbours have long been eavesdropping on family discussions."[39] The animals in *Der Schimmelreiter* function in a similar way, their familiarity and also strange otherness makes them "strange strangers," to borrow Timothy Morton's phrasing.[40]

An early and important instance of the ethical status of non-human animals is in the story of Trien' Jans's angora tomcat, whom Hauke, in one of the clearest examples of his aggressive stance towards the non-human, strangles to death. As a youth, Hauke used to go to the beach killing sandpipers, and on his way he would pass Trien' Jans's house on the dike. There he would regularly see her angora cat, and between the two a certain understanding and affinity developed. Both were hunters, and Hauke would share part of his bounty with the cat after a day's killing. One day, instead of his usual gray sandpipers, Hauke had an especially colorful bird—the schoolmaster supposes it was a kingfisher—that he was unwilling to share with the feline. The cat nevertheless made a grab for Hauke's catch, at which Hauke seized the cat by the neck, throttling him in an apparent demonstration of strength. Pointing to the schoolmaster's description of the cat as "diese Unform von einem Kater" (this grotesque specter in the shape of a cat), Elisabeth Strowick sees the cat as an amorphous-spectral figure, and the murder of the cat less

---

38 Storm, *Sämtliche Werke*, 3: 754; Storm, *The Rider on the White Horse*, 283.
39 Ghosh, *The Great Derangement*, 41–42.
40 Timothy Morton, *The Ecological Thought* (Cambridge, MA: Harvard University Press, 2010), 41–44.

the murder of a creature than the violent reinforcement of form against *Unform*.[41] Strowick's argument about *Der Schimmelreiter* is that reality in the novella is always perceived reality.[42] But in spite of the text's strategies of mediation and perspectivization, and also in spite of the moments where it instantiates human perception as a psychic process, the fact is that the scene is very much about the murder of a cat. The scene contains what may be one of the most vivid descriptions of animal suffering in the history of German realism, as the narrator describes in graphic detail the dying cat's panicked kicking and bulging eyes as Hauke squeezes his neck, while Hauke walks away with a badly lacerated arm.

The cat's murder and its aftermath bring into focus the ambiguous ethical status animals have in the novella. Neither companion nor servant capture the reality of the cat because the cat exists enmeshed in the ecosystem of the dike. First the murder of the cat effects a disruption in the workings of that ecosystem. His death means that the rats have no predators, allowing them to destroy Trien' Jans's ducks. Rodents, likewise, are a threat to the stability of the dike construction. We know from elsewhere in the story that mice tend to burrow in the dikes, building holes and tunnels that threaten their overall structural integrity. That fact, in turn, raises the question of how the human characters value the cat, and, by extension, animals more generally. Protecting ducks and the dikes make the cat a useful creature, but Trien' Jans's wail of grief seems to be an obvious sign that she views the cat in more than utilitarian terms. The schoolmaster describes Trien' prostrating herself beside the corpse, cursing Hauke for taking her cat from her, and tenderly gathering up and caring for the body, to which Hauke can only respond with uncomprehending impatience. Her unmitigated grief, then, stands in stark contrast to Hauke's cold sense of victory over a non-human being.

The fact that Trien' mourns the cat the way she does indicates that she respects the animal's life *as* a life in a way that Hauke does not. And yet, from the details in the story, one might wonder to what extent Trien' Jans's grief was connected to the loss of the cat as a lifeform with intrinsic value. The schoolmaster also says that the cat was her "Kleinod" (precious jewel), a status not unconnected with the fact that Trien' Jans's son had given her the cat as a gift before he himself was lost at sea, raising the possibility that her grief is to some degree about the loss of the cat as a kind of souvenir as much as it is for the cat in and of himself.[43] Indeed, when Trien' Jans confronts Hauke's father Tede over Hauke's killing of the cat, she mourns both the loss of a companion as well as the physical

---

41 Elisabeth Strowick, *Gespenster des Realismus: Zur literarischen Wahrnehmung von Wirklichkeit* (Paderborn: Wilhelm Fink, 2019), 200–201.

42 Strowick, *Gespenster des Realismus*, 159–226, here 164–65.

43 Storm, *Sämtliche Werke*, 3: 648; Storm, *The Rider on the White Horse*, 195.

HYDROLOGIC ENGINEERING, SOCIAL CHANGE, AND THE FANTASTIC ♦ 121

comfort he provided: the cat would sit with her while she did her spinning and then lie on her legs, keeping her warm. For his part, Tede Haien only sees the material dimension of the cat's death, and so he offers Trien' money to buy a lamb's pelt for warmth and an opportunity to have the first pick of his own next litter of kittens. He hears Trien' Jans's grief and responds with a logic of equivalence and exchange. The notion that the cat's value was not intrinsic to the animal itself, resting instead in its function as signifier for a deceased human, a kind of souvenir, is one that we can infer more from the schoolmaster's account than from Trien' Jans's actual reaction.

In the end, these facts are not mutually exclusive: another being, human or non-human, is no less a genuine companion with intrinsic value as a lifeform because they also meet basic material needs or remind one of someone or something else. Kate Rigby characterizes the cat as one of Trien' Jans's "familiars" because he retains some agency even as he renders specific useful services. For Rigby, being a "familiar" distinguishes the cat from pet ownership, an institution Hauke inaugurates that relegates animals to a servile status.[44] The dog Perle and the tame seagull Klaus occupy this servile role, in Rigby's view. I would argue, though, that even these have a more ambiguous role than is allowed by the argument that the pet relation is a slave relation. Klaus, for instance, might be tame, but he is not a member of a domesticated species, and he comes and goes as he pleases. The dog Perle is arguably the tamest and most domesticated of the non-human beings (leaving aside the cattle, about which we learn little beyond their mere existence), and yet his closest relation is not to the patriarch Hauke, but to his daughter Wienke. Perle and Klaus might both be Wienke's pets, but her relationship to them is not one of master to slave, but one of affinity, part of an affinity she has with non-human nature generally that stands in sharp contrast to her father's will to dominate.

It should be stated at the outset that the affinity the text draws between Wienke and non-human nature is a problem because it is connected with an apparent mental handicap. Her relationship to language is stunted, and so in the eyes of the community she is simply "schwachsinnig" (feebleminded), as Wienke's mother Elke puts it.[45] To be clear, to say that she has a strong sense of affinity for the non-human is not to say that she is any less of a human being. Instead, we might compare her to Ditha in Adalbert Stifter's *Abdias*, whose blindness was also understood to be a handicap, but which turned out to be the condition for her to experience herself and her natural environment as a continuum in which she was a part, not as a relation of objects relative to herself as

---

44 Rigby, *Dancing with Disaster*, 105.
45 Storm, *Sämtliche Werke*, 3: 731; Storm, *The Rider on the White Horse*, 264.

a supposedly independent subject. Wienke, for instance, tends to speak of herself in the third person, linguistically positioning herself together with everything around her. Given that that is the sum of the evidence of her "feeblemindedness," the text raises the possibility that the judgment is not an objective description of her mental acuity, but a subjective way in which the others make sense of her character and how she relates to the world. The schoolmaster who narrates the story seems to take it at face value, while most of the characters in his narrative are inclined to deem her mentally deficient because doing so fits into their assumptions about the cosmos and divine retribution. For the characters of the Christian reformist community, specifically, Wienke's apparent handicap is God's punishment for a prayer Hauke uttered when Elke was gravely ill from Wienke's birth. In his prayer Hauke stated that God's power was limited by his own wisdom, a statement that he sees as theodiciean but which Ann Grethe, the member of the Christian reformist group who overhears him, interprets as blasphemous because it suggests God is not all-powerful.

Ann Grethe and the Christian reformists concentrate in a singular God a mythical worldview where humans are subject to cosmic punishment for transgression. If we subtract the Christian theological dimension, we are left with a fatalism that sees the relation between humans and non-human nature as a source of mythic terror. In Wienke's case, she seems to become most like the others in the community when she expresses this mythic terror, a moment in which she drops the sign of her supposed "feeblemindedness," the referral to herself in the third person, and adopts the first person. Out on the dike with Hauke she is gripped by fear of the water, but her father assures her: "du bist bei deinem Vater; das Wasser tut dir nichts!" (Your father's here. He won't let the water hurt you). Wienke responds to the second person address in the first person: "es tut mir nichts .... Nein, sag, daß es uns nichts tun soll; du kannst das, und dann tut es uns auch nichts!" (It won't hurt me .... No, tell it not to hurt us. If you tell it that, it won't hurt us).[46] The second person form of address interpellates Wienke as a subject, which, together with the perceived threat of the ocean, prompts her to speak in the first person, as something separate from, in this case, the water: "it won't hurt *me*." When she goes on to use the first-person plural, likewise, she signals more of an affinity to the other human in the scene, her father, than anything else. The moment does not last, though, and when she speaks again, the mythic fear persists, but she refers to herself once more in the third person. The water, by contrast, she perceives as speaking: "Es spricht .... Wienke ist bange!" (It talks .... Wienke is frightened).[47] For Wienke in

46 Storm, *Sämtliche Werke*, 3: 730; Storm, *The Rider on the White Horse*, 263.
47 Storm, *Sämtliche Werke*, 3: 731; Storm, *The Rider on the White Horse*, 263.

this moment nature is animate, possessing a language of its own. That Wienke only has a sense of "me" and "us" as distinct from the ocean when she is with her father on the dike only casts her non-Cartesian relation to the non-human in starker contrast because the pattern is momentarily broken, only to be then restored.

Such a non-Cartesian relation to the non-human also manifests itself in Wienke's relation to non-human animals, specifically the dog Perle and the tame seagull Klaus, her two playmates. There are signs that she recognizes that the animals experience some sort inner life. Trien' Jans tamed Klaus through feeding, but he sits on Wienke's shoulder of his own accord, willingly allowing Wienke to carry him in her apron, which makes the dog Perle jealous. And for all the grief Trien' Jans expressed at the cat's death, it is only Wienke who expresses sorrow over the animal's fate, even years after the fact. We learn that Trien' Jans used the cat's pelt to upholster a footstool, meaning that even in death he still, at least, provides physical comfort, as he did in life. By that point, Trien' Jans has come to regard the cat as always having had a servile function; she tells Wienke that if the cat were still alive, Wienke could ride on his back, a suggestion that evokes a diminutive image of her father riding on his white horse. Instead of taking the suggestion, Wienke begins petting the cat's remains, murmuring "armer Kater" (poor old tomcat).[48] Trien' Jans takes this as evidence of Wienke's handicap, and also as God's punishment of Hauke (whether for the prayer, the killing of the cat, or his general hubris, though, is unclear), and she responds by forcibly placing Wienke on the cat pelt footstool. But what she takes as a sign of Wienke's mental incapacity is an expression of empathy for a being that had been violently killed, a sorrow unconnected to the cat's usefulness as a hunter or any other function he may have had.

Wienke may be exceptional in how she relates to non-human animals, and non-human nature more broadly. But in the final analysis she is not exceptional in the fact of her affinity with non-human animals, a fact perhaps most visible in the relation between her domineering father and the titular white horse. In the minds of the superstitious characters, at least, the animal Hauke rides had been the skeletal remains of a horse that had lain out on Jevershallig, one of the marshy islands, or *Hallige*, that dot the so-called outland beyond the dike. One evening Iven Johns, a local laborer, believes he sees a living horse on Jevershallig in place of the skeleton, but when his companion Carsten takes a boat out to investigate, he reports finding the bones, but no living horse. Iven believes he sees Carsten walk right up to the living horse, but Carsten reports finding only an empty skull, the light of the moon shining into the eye sockets, animated only by a lapwing that happened to

---

48 Storm, *Sämtliche Werke*, 3: 727–28; Storm, *The Rider on the White Horse*, 261.

be amongst the bones. Iven concludes the matter is one of perspective: "von hier aus geht's wie lebig, und drüben liegen nur die Knochen—das ist mehr, als du und ich begreifen können" (If you see it from over here, it's alive. From over there, it's just bones. That's too much for the likes of you and me).[49] If Iven Johns is, in fact, seeing a revenant horse, then this scene would suggest that the fantastic is a reality that not only exceeds human recognition, as Storm claims in his letter to Keller, but always retreats from closer scrutiny. If, by contrast, we assume an empirical perspective, then we have yet another atmospheric distortion, again involving a bird that, in this case, gives the skeleton the appearance of life. If it is the lapwing distorted by the atmosphere, then this is another instance where material reality becomes the basis for the uncanny effect of the revenant horse. But beyond the reality or unreality of the revenant horse, the scene fits into a pattern in the novella where the dike itself is the site from which the fantastic becomes visible, in spite of, or perhaps because of, its separating function.

The possibility that the horse is a supernatural creature matters because it makes the animal a key figure of transgression across the dike. Hauke's acquisition of the horse coincides with the disappearance of the skeleton from Jevershallig. The horse is emaciated when Hauke purchases it, its skeletal appearance suggesting a connection to the vanished bones. The Slovak horse-seller from whom Hauke purchased the animal is also supernaturally coded, having a "braune Hand, die fast wie eine Klaue aussah" (brown hand, that almost looked like a claw) and "lachte wie ein Teufel" (laughing like the devil himself) after the purchase, demonic qualities implicitly associated with his foreignness.[50] If we accept that there is a connection between the appearance of the horse and the disappearance of the skeleton, then the horse transgresses the boundary between two natures of differing social character (the "outland" of the intertidal zone and the polder within) as well as the boundary between the fantastic and the social reality of the community. The horse, however, is not simply significant as another example of the instability of these distinctions. Rather we can trace through the horse a key shift in Hauke's relationship to the non-human. In contrast to the interpretation of the horse as a manifestation of the demonic, both Hauke and Elke understand the animal at first in economic terms, specifically as a non-human thing on which they will have to expend labor and resources, just as labor and resources are expended modifying the landscape. When Hauke first brings the horse home, he and Elke have an argument that revolves around a cost-benefit analysis of returning the animal to health. While he justifies the purchase

---

49   Storm, *Sämtliche Werke*, 3: 700; Storm, *The Rider on the White Horse*, 238.

50   Storm, *Sämtliche Werke*, 3: 703; Storm, *The Rider on the White Horse*, 241, translation modified. James Wright's translation removes the ethnic marker and uses the word "vagabond" instead.

by saying that he will direct his workers to restore the horse to health, in the end Hauke cares for the animal personally, feeding it and helping it recover from the neglect it had previously suffered. The work of restoring the horse unifies him with the animal, as the schoolmaster remarks: "das Pferd schien völlig eins mit seinem Reiter" (horse and rider seemed one creature now).[51] If this is a process of domestication, then it raises the question of who is domesticating whom. "Domesticates," as James Scott observes, do, in fact, have their own active agency, while historically managing crops and tending to livestock also meant that *Homo sapiens,* supposedly the "domesticators in chief," underwent a process of domestication themselves.[52] As always, the statement that horse and rider were one is the narrator's perspective, and he says it only "seemed" so. But the horse will carry Hauke off to the afterlife, which they will spend haunting the dike together forever, fulfilling the unity they had in life.

Needless to say, that unity does not negate Hauke's antagonistic relationship to the non-human. But as we have seen, nature and the non-human are not simply passive objects of human action in *Der Schimmelreiter,* and indications abound in the novella that the horse has agency. For instance, when one of the servants attempts to ride him, the horse leaps away and stands immobile. If we assume the perspective that animals, like non-human nature more generally, are just the objects of conquest, then they become simply victims. Kate Rigby, for instance, regards the relation between Hauke and the horse in these terms in her reading of the description of Hauke's death. Rigby points out that when Hauke sacrifices himself, crying out to God to take him instead of the others, he spurs the horse with him into the breach and thus into doom, making the horse another victim of the human domination of nature.[53] There is, however, enough ambiguity in the schoolmaster's description to call into question the claim that Hauke forced the horse into death with him. Hauke did call upon God to take him instead of the others, and he did spur the horse, but the schoolmaster does not say that he drove the horse into the breach. Rigby reads the "brief struggle" after they fall as evidence of the horse's resistance,[54] but is the horse struggling against Hauke or Hauke against the horse? Or is one or both struggling to stay alive against the force of the water? The schoolmaster does not say. If we factor in the horse's supernatural character, then this scene can just as easily be read as the horse carrying Hauke off to the afterlife as Hauke spurring the horse to its death.

51   Storm, *Sämtliche Werke,* 3: 704; Storm, *The Rider on the White Horse,* 241.
52   James Scott, *Against the Grain: A Deep History of the Earliest States* (New Haven, CT: Yale University Press, 2017), 18–19.
53   Rigby, *Dancing with Disaster,* 105.
54   Rigby, *Dancing with Disaster,* 105.

Two further pieces of evidence ask us to understand the scene from a mythic perspective. First, as Johannes Harnischfeger points out, there were no surviving witnesses to the scene, meaning that there is no basis for the narrator to make an empirical truth claim. Instead, as Harnischfeger notes, the schoolmaster can only pass on a version of events that has come down through collective memory, one that supports the superstitious perspective to the extent that Hauke, the figure of modernity, ultimately commits an act of mythic self-sacrifice.[55] There is no voice of rationality here to negate the mythological account. Second, the schoolmaster reports that after the event the horse bones were seen again on Jevershallig. Regarded from a mythic perspective, then, the reality of human enmeshment with non-human animals becomes a vehicle through which a mythic cycle of violence is reinstated, because the horse takes Hauke back with him to the supernatural realm, willingly or unwillingly. That, in turn, lends credence to the superstitious notion that the stability of the dike was not a matter of engineering genius, but mythic nature having received its sacrifice.

Conclusion

The ending of the novella returns us to the magazine journalist in the 1830s, who describes himself riding along the Hauke Haien Dike "beim goldensten Sonnenlichte, das über einer weiten Verwüstung aufgegangen war" (in the golden sunlight that was shining over a landscape of widespread devastation).[56] The scene is an eerie one. The contrast between the golden sunlight and the devastation from the storm reflects the structural antagonism between human coercion and the forces of nature, Enlightenment and myth, thus signaling an ongoing tension even when Haien's dike design has proved itself. *Der Schimmelreiter* thus imagines a continuing history of antagonism and coercion from the Enlightenment to the 1830s, and by extension down to the *Gründerzeit*. Its claim to realism falls on one side of this relation of mutual antagonism. Trying to separate the "wheat" of empirical reality from the "chaff" of superstition, as the magazine writer would have it, is in this sense not only a hopeless task, it is the wrong question to ask. If, in the collective memory of the people, the dike holds because Hauke, his family, and his animals become the necessary sacrifice, that is a history that has its own reality. If nothing else, the persistence of the fantastic suggests a framework for thinking about those dimensions of socio-ecological relations that for Storm

---

55 Johannes Harnischfeger, "Modernisierung und Teufelspakt: Die Funktion des Dämonischen in Theodor Storms 'Schimmelreiter,'" *Schriften der Theodor-Storm-Gesellschaft* 49 (2000): 34.

56 Storm, *Sämtliche Werke*, 3: 754; Storm, *The Rider on the White Horse*, 284.

exceed human understanding. A key part of the persistence of myth, after all, is the reassertion of mythic cyclicity, something that the dike disrupts but does not break. Hauke's new dike may last for centuries rather than decades, but in geological time the difference between decades and centuries is so marginal as to be insignificant.

4: The Poetics of an Emerging Anthropocene: Theodor Fontane's *Der Stechlin*

B Y THE MIDDLE of the eighteenth century, the Menzer Forest was in the red. As Theodor Fontane tells it in *Wanderungen durch die Mark Brandenburg* (Wanderings through the March Brandenburg, 1862–89), the forest, located around Lake Stechlin in the County of Ruppin north of Berlin, had become a problem for the Prussian government because the cost of managing it was greater than the value it produced in the form of timber and game. One solution was to make the forest a site of glass production, and Fontane writes that at one point curls of smoke were to be seen above the trees by day and the glow of fires by night. Finally, though, the government mulled the idea of using the trees as wood to heat the buildings in Berlin. Tasked with determining how long the forest would last if it were to be cut for firewood, the forestry office confidently asserted, "die Menzer Forst hält alles aus" (the Menzer Forest can withstand anything).[1] What happened next was painfully predictable.

> Die betreffende Forstinspektion wurde beim Wort genommen und siehe da, ehe dreißig Jahre um waren, war die ganze Forst durch die Berliner Schornsteine geflogen. Was Teeröfen und Glashütten in alle Ewigkeit hinein nicht vermocht hätten, das hatte die Konsumkraft einer großen Stadt in weniger als einem Menschenalter geleistet.[2]

> [The respective authority was taken at its word, and lo and behold! Before thirty years had passed the entire forest had flown through Berlin's chimneys. One big city's power of consumption had accomplished in a human lifetime what tar ovens and glassworks had been unable to do in all of eternity.]

The story Fontane tells is one of socio-ecological realities shifting faster than human assumptions about nature. From the perspective of both the state and industry, the Menzer Forest was always little more than a source of value. But while the forest had a long history of exploitation, the extent

---

1 Fontane, *GBA-WMB*, V/1: 346–47.
2 Fontane, *GBA-WMB*, V/1: 347.

of urban development in Berlin and its concomitant "power of consumption" brought the shocking realization that human activity could destroy an entire forest in the span of a few decades.

Fontane's account of the history of the Menzer Forest reflects the emergence of an Anthropocene reality. There is, first, not just the scale of human intervention, but the shock at the scale. Second, when the forest "flew" through Berlin's chimneys, it released what we know now to be a number of greenhouse gases, meaning that its cutting and burning had planetary stakes, however small those stakes may have been in the grander scheme of things. Fontane might not have known how the burning of the Menzer Forest would affect the climate, although Svante Arrhenius first described the greenhouse effect in 1896, two years before the publication of *Der Stechlin*. As Evi Zamenek has pointed out, air quality is a recurring concern for Fontane, in the literal sense that smog and airborne diseases are a topic, in the figurative sense where atmosphere reveals and conceals a social ethos, and finally because Fontane believed his ability to write well depended on breathing good air.[3] Furthermore, Fontane has a sense in the essay that history can be periodized by energy regimes, just as Paul Crutzen and Eugene Stoermer did when they proposed dating the start of the Anthropocene to James Watt's invention of the steam engine in 1784.[4] Berlin switches to burning peat from Linum, a village elsewhere in Brandenburg near Fehrbellin, marking the start of what Fontane calls, albeit humorously, the "Linumer Torfperiode" (Linum peat period) in Berlin's history, which also gestures implicitly to the period that would come after, that is, the coal period.[5] Fontane also characterizes the history of the forest in the rhetoric of conquest, framing its recent environmental history not as one of unsustainable consumption, but as the violent subjugation of the forest to human material demands. He characterizes the felling of the forest as a "guerre à outrance," meaning total war, and while Friedrich II's order to stop the cutting allowed the forest to regenerate, Fontane points out that the Menzer Forest "stieg auf der tabula rasa ihres alten Grund und Bodens *neu* empor" (arose *anew* on the tabula rasa of its old ground), such that the forest as it existed for Fontane was a product of human history, specifically the king's intervention and the fact that energy extraction moved elsewhere, which together inaugurated

---

3   Evi Zemanek, "(Bad) Air and (Faulty) Inspiration: Elemental and Environmental Influences on Fontane," in *German Ecocriticism in the Anthropocene*, ed. Caroline Schaumann and Heather Sullivan (New York: Palgrave Macmillan, 2017), 130–31.

4   Paul J. Crutzen and Eugene F. Stoermer, "The 'Anthropocene,'" *IGBP Newsletter* 41 (2000): 17–18.

5   Fontane, *GBA-WMB*, V/1: 347.

a "Schonzeit und Stillstandsepoche" (time of preservation and epoch of standstill) for the forest.[6]

The essay in which Fontane tells the story, "Die Menzer Forst und der grosse Stechlin" (The Menzer Forest and the Great Stechlin), first appeared in print in 1874, and was included in book form in the *Wanderungen durch die Mark Brandenburg* in 1875. Twenty-three years later, the area would feature in Fontane's final completed novel *Der Stechlin* (The Stechlin, 1898), and here, as in the earlier essay, the enmeshment of the local within global socio-ecological realities is an animating theoretical problem. Smog, urban sprawl, and physical interventions in the landscape appear here as they do in Wilhelm Raabe's fiction, but the ecoaesthetic problem at the heart of *Der Stechlin* does not arise out of the circumstance that industrial capital has buried some "old romantic country," to borrow Ebert's phrase from the opening of *Pfisters Mühle*. Instead, the problem is that the March Brandenburg may have never had much of a poetic character to begin with. The region is famously flat, sandy, and dotted with swamps and marshes. In addition to thematizing the seemingly low aesthetic status of the area, *Der Stechlin* confronts its putative provincialism. The area around the lake is removed from the concentration of capital and political power in nearby Berlin, and the cast of characters can be divided between those who are of a more liberal and "worldly" disposition and those who are more narrow-minded. But what emerges in the depiction of the place is precisely that Lake Stechlin and its environs, far from being a "provincial" place, is a node in global networks of political and economic power, as well as in planetary systems. Telegraph wires, smog, non-native plant species, and the eponymous lake are all signs of how such planetary socio-ecological relations converge in this otherwise out of the way place. The sum of those relations are what constitutes, *avant la lettre*, an emerging Anthropocene reality. The argument I will make in this chapter, then, is that that emergent reality is the basis of the realism of *Der Stechlin*, constituting the text's poetic project. Whereas mid-nineteenth-century theories of realism in Germany tended to regard the relations of industrial modernity as undermining the conditions of possibility for "poesy," *Der Stechlin* sees those signs of industrial modernity inscribed on the Brandenburg landscape as aesthetic precisely because they are manifestations of the area's global connections. As we shall see, though, it does not valorize the production of nature in Brandenburg uncritically or unambiguously, for it also recognizes the environmental destruction industrialization causes and the ways in which the social production of nature can create the conditions for upheaval.

Der Stechlin is primarily a portrait of the German nobility at the end of the nineteenth century centered around a Junker family in the northern

---

6   Fontane, *GBA-WMB*, V/1: 347, emphasis in original.

reaches of the March Brandenburg. Stechlin is the name of the family, the estate, the village, and the lake that is the central topographical feature. The novel is famously plotless. Fontane's own oft-cited summary of the novel from a draft letter to Adolf Hoffmann written in May or June of 1897 reads: "Zum Schluß stirbt ein Alter und zwei Junge heiraten sich;—das ist so ziemlich alles, was auf 500 Seiten geschieht" (At the end an old man dies and two young people get married;—that is pretty much everything that happens in five hundred pages).[7] Fontane is referring to the generational transition that takes place when the old Dubslav von Stechlin dies at the end, and his son Woldemar and bride Armgard assume residence in the manor. Woldemar and Armgard's courtship and ultimate marriage is one of the few lines of plot. However, what becomes clear in the lengthy conversations and the few events that do take place is that this is a world in the throes of a political-economic realignment, even if that reality seems to register only obliquely. The lake is a major symbol for historical change. According to local myth, this lake has the curious property that whenever there is a major seismic event anywhere on the planet, then its waters ripple, and if the event is particularly powerful, such as the earthquake that struck Lisbon in 1755, then a red rooster rises out of the lake and crows into the countryside. The red rooster has a revolutionary significance, but the possibility of revolution remains latent throughout the novel. Nevertheless, the future of the Junker class is increasingly uncertain in the wake of shifting class dynamics under German industrialization. At the opening we learn that the Reichstag representative from the Rheinsberg-Wutz district has died, and in one of the few significant events in the story, Dubslav runs a half-hearted campaign for the seat as a conservative candidate and, in spite of the region's history of voting conservative, loses to the Social Democrat Torgelow. The novel's imagination of historical change runs along a tension between the large and the small. In the lived realities of the characters, epochal change registers mostly at the level of the humorous and trivial, as when the reactionary art professor and Giottonian epigone Cujacius equates the fact that paint now comes in tubes instead of bags as a sign of decadence and the apocalypse.

It might be surprising to some of Fontane's readers that *Der Stechlin* could be subject to ecocritical analysis. In spite of the presence of the lake, the novel has long been regarded as one concerned more with the social and political milieu than with the natural environment. Fontane himself described it as a political novel around the time he was drafting it.[8] The social milieu as subject manifests itself in the conversational form that dominates the novel. Since its publication *Der Stechlin* has been read as

---

7   Theodor Fontane, *Werke, Schriften und Briefe*, ed. Walter Keitel and Helmuth Nürnberger, 22 vols. (Munich: Hanser, 1975) (=*HFA*), IV/4: 650.

8   Fontane, *HFA*, IV/4: 512.

132 ♦ THE POETICS OF AN EMERGING ANTHROPOCENE

a "Plauderroman" or "chit-chat-novel," which for the reviewer who first dubbed it in those terms was something distinct from a novelistic work of art.[9] The fact that conversation drives Fontane's last finished novel would seem to cement his reputation as an author of the Prussian social milieu and make *Der Stechlin* a thoroughly anthropocentric text. "Also wer am meisten red't, ist der reinste Mensch" (And so whoever talks the most is the purest human being), as Dubslav himself tells Woldemar,[10] and so there is a history of reading the novel as one that is really about the social world over the natural, the presence of the lake notwithstanding. Richard Brinkmann's argument is representative of this view: pointing to the fact that Fontane is critical of landscape description, that there is no *Urlandschaft* (primordial landscape) in his novels, and that nature enters into language always bearing the stamp of history, Brinkmann concludes that "alle Beziehungen zwischen Menschen, alle Bezüge, von denen die Rede war, realisieren sich nur im Medium der Gesellschaft" (all relations between humans, all connections discussed, are realized only in the medium of society).[11] Fritz Martini likewise sees in Fontane's work an anthropocentric view that reduces nature to a thing only meaningful relative to human events.[12] Versions of this argument are as old as Fontane scholarship itself, appearing in one of the earliest works of Fontane criticism, Max Tau's study of Fontane's landscapes from 1928, in which Tau argues that Fontane can only be regarded as a depicter of landscapes insofar as these constitute a setting for the human characters in which Fontane is actually interested.[13]

To see *Der Stechlin* as exclusively a social portrait, however, is to see "the social" and "the ecological" as strictly separated domains, a

---

9 A. B., "Review of *Der Stechlin* and *Zwischen zwanzig und dreißig*," *Literarisches Centralblatt für Deutschland*, December 12, 1898.

10 Fontane, *GBA-EW*, I/17: 24; Fontane, *The Stechlin*, 9.

11 Richard Brinkmann, *Theodor Fontane: Über die Verbindlichkeit des Unverbindlichen* (Munich: R. Piper & Co., 1967), 20–25, here 20, 24.

12 Fritz Martini, *Deutsche Literatur im bürgerlichen Realismus, 1848–1898*, 4th ed. (Stuttgart: Metzler, 1981), 742.

13 Max Tau, *Landschafts- und Ortsdarstellung Theodor Fontanes* (Oldenburg: Schulzesche Hofbuchdruckerei, 1928), 8. Similar arguments appear in Peter Demetz, *Formen des Realismus: Theodor Fontane* (Munich: Hanser, 1964), 119; Klaus Scherpe, "Rettung der Kunst im Widerspruch von bürgerlicher Humanität und bourgeoiser Wirklichkeit: Theodor Fontanes vierfacher Roman 'Der Stechlin,'" in *Poesie der Demokratie: Literarische Widersprüche zur deutschen Wirklichkeit vom 18. zum 20. Jahrhundert* (Cologne: Pahl-Rugenstein, 1980), 231; Charlotte Jolles, "Weltstadt—Verlorene Nachbarschaft: Berlin-Bilder Raabes und Fontanes," *Jahrbuch der Raabe-Gesellschaft* 29 (1988): 69; Kurt Weber, "'Au fond sind Bäume besser als Häuser.' Über Theodor Fontanes Naturdarstellung," *Fontane-Blätter* 64 (1997): 141.

distinction that the social character of nature—here and throughout the literature of German realism—renders untenable. Far from diminishing the status of non-human nature in favor of the social, chit-chat is precisely where we can see an environmental unconscious at work. To think about the chit-chat also means thinking about the antithesis of the chit-chat, that is, the moments of silence and suggestion, which constitute a code of their own.[14] Hubert Ohl makes the case that the dialogue reflects a small facet of the larger world surrounding the characters, allowing what lies beyond conversation to appear as living reality.[15] The condition of the natural environment works in similar fashion, not as one topic among many, but as the antithesis to social chit-chat, a fact that the narrator alerts us to when he says at the opening: "Alles still hier" (Everything is silence here).[16] But that does not mean that the reality of the novel's realism lies somewhere beyond conversation in the way that, say, Stifter conceived of "das sanfte Gesez," a greater reality that manifests itself in and through the small. Instead, as Richard Brinkmann argues, conversation is a vehicle suited to Fontane's concept of reality because it allows for the relativity of concepts of reality to emerge and be subject to interpretation and exploration, as opposed to positing a single, objective reality as *the* reality.[17]

Today the label Anthropocene does not describe a single objective reality, save at the most basic level where it reflects the extent of anthropogenic changes to earth systems. Instead it is an umbrella label for a variety of sometimes competing narratives about history and also the future of the planet and the lives lived on it. The fact that "human effects on global systems are time-transgressive and are also spatially and temporally variable" was one of the concerns that the International Union of Geological Sciences cited in 2024 when it announced that its members

---

14 Hans Dieter Zimmermann, "Was der Erzähler verschweigt: Zur politischen Konzeption von Der Stechlin," in *Theodor Fontane, am Ende des Jahrhunderts: Internationales Symposium des Theodor-Fontane-Archivs zum 100. Todestag Theodor Fontanes, 13.-17. September 1998 in Potsdam*, ed. Hanna D. von Wolzogen (Würzburg: Königshausen & Neumann, 2000), 132; Gisela Brude-Firnau, "Beredtes Schweigen: Nichtverbalisierte Obrigkeitskritik in Theodor Fontanes *Stechlin*," *Monatshefte* 77, no. 4 (1985): 460.

15 Hubert Ohl, *Bild und Wirklichkeit: Studien zur Romankunst Raabes und Fontanes* (Heidelberg: Lothar Stiehm, 1968), 187.

16 Fontane, *GBA-EW*, I/17: 5; Fontane, *The Stechlin*, 1.

17 Brinkmann, *Theodor Fontane: Über die Verbindlichkeit des Unverbindlichen*, 150. See also Martini, *Deutsche Literatur im bürgerlichen Realismus, 1848–1898*, 749, 767–70; and Christine Renz, *Geglückte Rede: Zu Erzählstrukturen in Theodor Fontanes "Effi Briest," "Frau Jenny Treibel" und "Der Stechlin"* (Munich: Fink, 1999), 130–33.

had voted against formally adopting the term.[18] The problem of variability, which makes it impossible to reduce the Anthropocene to a single narrative, has been one of the key points of contention for the term's critics, who see a corollary to the problem of spatial variability in the fact that not all humans have contributed equally to current environmental crises, and indeed the Anthropocene entails the suffering of many members of the so-called *Anthropos* at the hands of others.[19] But the Anthropocene can just as easily be said to posit a brighter historical narrative, the "good" Anthropocene of ecomodernists and geoengineers, for whom the negative effects of modernization as a process will be treated by further progress. Clive Hamilton sees in this narrative a form of theodicy that substitutes humans for God, with their creativity and will towards improvement, as the guarantor that good will triumph in the end, such that the Anthropocene posits an "anthropodicy," as Hamilton calls it.[20] The Anthropocene is a useful analytic for my purposes because of its contradictions and paradoxes, the problem of whom it includes and whom it excludes, and the often different narratives of both the past and possible futures that it implies.

Der Stechlin announces repeatedly that its primary concern is with these very tensions and contradictions. One of the first things the narrator tells us about Dubslav von Stechlin is that "Paradoxen waren seine Passion" (Paradoxes were his passion), a statement that could just as easily apply to the novel as a whole.[21] Such paradoxes structure its environmental imagination. The region around the lake is both removed from political and economic power, but bound to the rest of the world through both natural and technological systems. The fact that "Stechlin" is the name of the family, village, and lake suggests an intimate connection between the human and non-human features of the place, and yet the Stechlin family is a living anachronism, even in their own natural habitat, so to speak. Perhaps the biggest paradox is the one already identified: that in spite of the amount of human talk in the novel and the text's focus on the politics, the lake and its mythical associations loom over the human events that drive what little plot there is.

---

18 "The Anthropocene," International Union of Geological Sciences, March 20, 2024, https://www.iugs.org/_files/ugd/f1fc07_40d1a7ed58de458c9f8f24 de5e739663.pdf?index=true.

19 See Eileen Crist, "On the Poverty of Our Nomenclature," in *Anthropocene or Capitalocene?: Nature, History, and the Crisis of Capitalism*, ed. Jason Moore (Oakland, CA: PM Press, 2016), 14–33; and Kathryn Yusoff, *A Billion Black Anthropocenes or None* (Minneapolis: University of Minnesota Press, 2018), among many others.

20 Clive Hamilton, "The Theodicy of the 'Good Anthropocene,'" *Environmental Humanities* 7 (2015): 234–35.

21 Fontane, *GBA-EW*, I/17: 8; Fontane, *The Stechlin*, 3.

"Unpoetic Barrenness" and Anthropocene Poesy

The fact that this area of the North German Plain is stereotyped as somehow aesthetically lesser because it is flat, sandy, and swampy comes up explicitly in a scene towards the end. Dubslav von Stechlin has died and his funeral has just come to its conclusion. The Berchtesgadens and the Barbys set off in one of the coaches, passing down a road lined with willow trees, which are symbolically significant given the occasion. The weather, we are told, is beautiful, mostly overcast but still warmer than in the morning. A column of smoke is visible, larks rise from the fields, and a sparrow sings on a telegraph wire. Surveying the scene, Baron Berchtesgaden announces with astonishment: "Wie schön ... und dabei spricht man immer von der Dürftigkeit und Prosa dieser Gegenden" (How beautiful ... and yet you always hear talk of the unpoetic barrenness of these regions).[22] The statement is significant coming from the mouth of a Bavarian, not only because his positive pronouncement about the Prussian countryside comes in spite of the historical political and cultural divides between north and south Germany, but also because with the Alps to the south, the Danube as a major river, and historically more important cities, Bavaria would seem to be a region of higher aesthetic status than the March Brandenburg.

Brandenburg's "unpoetic barrenness" relative to other regions of Germany and Europe is, of course, a stereotype based on prejudices about the aesthetic value of certain topographical features and urban spaces, but also the supposed nature of the respective regions' inhabitants. What makes the Brandenburg landscape seemingly unpoetic, its relative flatness and sandiness, for which it was known as the "Streusandbüchse des Heiligen Römischen Reiches" (sandbox of the Holy Roman Empire), is the product of alternating periods of glacial advance and retreat during the Pleistocene, from the Elster Glaciation beginning 500,000 years ago to the melting of the region's dead-ice between 29,000 and 22,000 years before the present.[23] Unpoetic barrenness, then, is to a large part the aesthetic result of processes occurring at geological time scales. *Wanderungen durch die Mark Brandenburg,* itself another of Fontane's projects to recover the aesthetic value of the region, addresses the unpoetic barrenness stereotype directly in an essay about the site of the Battle of Fehrbellin, where in 1675 Prussian-Brandenburg troops defeated an occupying Swedish army. Fehrbellin looms large in Prussian historical memory, but when Fontane visits the battlefield he finds a mere potato field, a fact he reads as symptomatic of a northern German culture that

---

22   Fontane, *GBA-EW,* I/17: 454; Fontane, *The Stechlin,* 323.

23   Margot Böse, Jürgen Ehlers, and Frank Lehmkuhl, *Deutschlands Norden: Vom Erdaltertum zur Gegenwart* (Berlin: Springer, 2018), 71–110, here 99.

136 ♦ THE POETICS OF AN EMERGING ANTHROPOCENE

"des poetischen Schwunges entbehre" (does without poetic drive).[24] Fontane's essay posits a certain environmental determinism in suggesting that an unpoetic landscape produces unpoetic people. Unlike the Bavarians, he writes, "es fehlt uns das Bunte der Kostüme und das Kulissenwerk einer Wald- und Bergnatur, und weil wir dieser Requisiten entbehren, mag bis zu einem gewissen Grade die Lust und die Fähigkeit in uns verkümmert sein, ein Schauspiel im großen Stile aufzuführen" (We lack the color of the costumes and the backdrop of a forest and mountain nature, and because we do without these stage props, the desire and ability to put on a show in high style may be withered in us to a certain extent).[25]

The landscape that leads Baron Berchtesgaden to the realization that Brandenburg is a "poetic" place after all is no less socially produced than the potato field near Fehrbellin. The road, the line of willows, and the cultivated field with the larks are all products of human labor. But perhaps the most salient image for what makes Brandenburg poetic after all is the image of sparrows perching on the telegraph wires. In this case, the sparrows, a non-domesticated "commensal" species that co-evolved with humans after the latter's turn to sedentism in the Holocene,[26] sit atop a piece of telecommunications technology, making it hard to draw a clear conceptual distinction between human technology and non-human nature. This image in particular is emblematic not just of social nature in general, but nature as technologically reproducible.[27] The telegraph wire and the plume of smoke are a synecdoche for the Anthropocene: the smog goes into the atmosphere, the glass enters global trade, and the telegraph allows for instant communication between distant places, collapsing a notion of nature built on a simple contrast of nature versus culture. Berchtesgaden, then, is speaking for the novel's project of recovering aesthetic value in the Brandenburg countryside when he finds it anything other than unpoetically barren.

Glass manufacture, telecommunications technologies, and the global connections they forge may mark the technological reproducibility of nature in general, but within the context of the novel they reproduce a specific natural form, that is, the eponymous Lake Stechlin. It might seem to be another of *Der Stechlin*'s many paradoxes that this chit-chat novel opens with a description of the Stechlin landscape, one absent of humans and that hinges on silence. The description of the area with which the

24 Fontane, *GBA-WMB*, V/6: 41.
25 Fontane, *GBA-WMB*, V/6: 41.
26 Scott, *Against the Grain*, 76–83.
27 Gernot Böhme, "Die Natur im Zeitalter ihrer technischen Reproduzierbarkeit," in *Natürlich Natur: Über Natur im Zeitalter ihrer technischen Reproduzierbarkeit* (Frankfurt am Main: Suhrkamp, 1992), 107–24.

novel opens depicts a landscape marked by human history and economy. The area may be sparsely populated, but the chain of lakes to which Lake Stechlin belongs contains plenty of towns and villages, while the forest is dotted with glassworks, tar kilns, and forester's lodges. The lake, part of a chain of lakes, reflects the global connections in human economies. And these lakes are tied to the rest of the planet through Lake Stechlin's telluric connections. As Dubslav puts it, the lake has "Weltbeziehungen, vornehme, geheimnisvolle Beziehungen" (connections with the world ... high-placed, mysterious connections).[28] When Dubslav says that the lake is a telephone line to Java, he draws the lake itself into a field of association with telecommunications technology, setting the two up in a mirror relation.

That technology, in turn, is bound up in European colonialism as a facet of first-wave globalization.[29] The empire functions here as Edward Said argues it does elsewhere in nineteenth-century European literature, as a "structure of attitude and reference," and "as a codified, if only marginally visible, presence in fiction."[30] Just as the lake connects to Java, the South Pacific having historically been a region of German imperial influence, the telegraph connects rural Brandenburg to China, another center of German colonialism. Dublsav remarks: "Schließlich ist es doch was Großes, diese Naturwissenschaften, dieser elektrische Strom, tipp, tipp, tipp, und wenn uns daran läge (aber uns liegt nichts daran), so könnten wir den Kaiser von China wissen lassen, daß wir hier versammelt sind und seiner gedacht haben" (When you get right down to it though, it really is a marvelous thing, this science business, this electric current. Tap, tap, tap and if we had a mind to (even though we don't), why we could let the Emperor of China know we've gotten together here and were thinking about him).[31] Germany, along with other European powers, had supported China against Japan during and after the First Sino-Japanese War (1894/95) with the aim of taking advantage of China's internal disarray to carve out a sphere of influence to compete with that of the United Kingdom.[32] In 1897 Germany occupied Qingdao and the Bay of Jiaozhou and began using the region as a naval base. The realities of the hydrocarbon economy were here too a motivating factor: the bay was supposed to serve as a station for replenishing coal supplies for German

---

28 Fontane, *GBA-EW*, I/17: 159; Fontane, *The Stechlin*, 111.

29 See also Marc Thuret, "Le charme discret de la mondialisation: Actualité du Stechlin," in *Identité(s) multiple(s)*, ed. Kerstin Hausbei and Alain Lattard (Paris: Presses Sorbonnes Nouvelle, 2008), 221–30.

30 Edward Said, *Culture and Imperialism* (New York: Vintage Books, 1994), 63.

31 Fontane, *GBA-EW*, I/17: 29; Fontane, *The Stechlin*, 18.

32 Thomas Nipperdey, *Deutsche Geschichte, 1866–1918*, 2 vols. (Munich: Beck, 2013), vol. 2, 654.

138 ♦ THE POETICS OF AN EMERGING ANTHROPOCENE

ships, and Germany hoped to assert its economic interests through mining and railway construction in the province of Shandong (ambitions that imperial competition and Chinese rebellions largely thwarted).[33]

What the mythic properties of the lake and the telegraph have in common, then, is that they function to collapse time and space. With the latter, nothing is distant, while the former shows that it never was. As Dubslav goes on to remark: "Und dabei diese merkwürdigen Verschiebungen in Zeit und Stunde. Beinahe komisch. Als Anno siebzig die Pariser Septemberrevolution ausbrach, wußte man's in Amerika drüben um ein paar Stunden früher, als die Revolution überhaupt da war" (And then all these odd mix-ups in time and hours. Almost comical. When the September Revolution broke out back in seventy in Paris, they knew about it over there in America a couple of hours before there even was a revolution).[34] He imagines the telegraph in a way that resembles a tachyonic antitelephone, a hypothetical device capable of sending information faster than light and thereby causing a paradox of causality, in this case that the knowledge that a revolution has happened comes before the revolution itself even breaks out. Joseph Vogl has argued that telegraphy in the novel transforms a world of historic depth into a universe of simultaneity, where the act of communicating, rather than the communication itself, becomes a historical event.[35] Vogl sees the lake in the novel as an emblem for Fontane's narration, one founded on a principle of correspondence where events manifest as reflexes of events, as when a seismic event elsewhere causes a disturbance on the lake, with the result that the broader world reaches into the world of the novel proportionally shrunk.[36] From this perspective, the telegraph represents a triumphalist strain of the Anthropocene thesis, breaking even such a seemingly intractable natural barrier as the speed of light. Of course, the fact that Dubslav is exaggerating also matters. As the sparrows perched on the telegraph wire remind us, it relies on a material network that functions within ecosystems constrained by the laws of physics.

Nor does the correspondence between the lake and the telegraph mean that the two simply collapse into each other. But then, they do not have to in order for us to glimpse within them an emerging Anthropocene reality. Dipesh Chakrabarty advances a notion of the Anthropocene that sees a doubling between the human of humanist histories and the human as geological agent. As a corollary, he distinguishes between "the globe"

33 Nipperdey, *Deutsche Geschichte, 1866–1918*, vol 2., 654–55.
34 Fontane, *GBA-EW*, I/17: 29; Fontane, *The Stechlin*, 18.
35 Joseph Vogl, "Telephon nach Java: Fontane," in *Realien des Realismus: Wissenschaft—Technik—Medien in Theodor Fontanes Erzählprosa*, ed. Stephan Braese and Anne-Kathrin Reulecke (Berlin: Vorwerk 8, 2010), 122.
36 Vogl, "Telephon nach Java," 119.

as a humanocentric construction, and "the planetary" in terms of earth systems, both of which are bound together by capitalism and technology.[37] If we see the lake as a planetary phenomenon and the telegraph as a global one, then their corresponding presence in the county of Ruppin makes the place a site where the emergence of an Anthropocene reality becomes surprisingly visible. Indeed, the entwinement of the planetary and the global shows up everywhere in the county's environs. The lightning rod on the Stechlin manor connects larger atmospheric forces to the grounds, and moreover it is as evocative of the potential for sudden violent historical shifts as the legendary red rooster at the bottom of Lake Stechlin. In the center of Dubslav's garden is a glass ball, product of the local glass industry that otherwise exports its goods elsewhere. Karla Müller reads it as an ironic object because while it stands in the nobleman's garden, the local glassworkers who made it are the novel's unseen agents of revolution.[38] But it is also an ironic thing by virtue of being an industrial commodity in a space of cultivated nature, the image of which it reflects.

Significantly, that same garden contains two aloe plants (more accurately, *Agave americana*), among other "exotic" flora. Inspired by a real aloe plant that once grew outside of the palace in Köpenick, now a district in Berlin, these aloe plants are there in the garden because of global trade and the accompanying history of European political hegemony over the Americas.[39] Compounding its significance as a symbol of the socioecological relations of an emerging Anthropocene is the fact that a flowering rush (*Butomus umbellatus*) became grafted onto one of the aloes when the wind carried over a seed from the swampy moat that surrounds the estate house. The narrator tells us that visitors tend to misrecognize the graft for the aloe's own blossom, meaning that a species from the swamp has an aesthetically higher status because it is a part of the more exotic plant. At the same time the aloe on which the rush grows is sickly, a circumstance that escapes the visitor intrigued by the plant's exoticism. If the difference between the healthy aloe and the sickly one is that the sickly one has the rush, that would suggest that the problem is not that the plants are out of place, but that the native rush has a parasitic relation to its non-native host. In a novel where characters like Adelheid appear as ridiculous because their conservative outlook is bound up in an insistence

37   Dipesh Chakrabarty, *The Climate of History in a Planetary Age* (Chicago, IL: University of Chicago Press, 2021), 3–4.

38   Karla Müller, *Schloßgeschichten: Eine Studie zum Romanwerk Theodor Fontanes* (Munich: Wilhelm Fink, 1986), 119.

39   For a history and interpretation of the plant's function in the novel, see Andreas Huck, "'Da ist nichts oberflächlich hingeworfen …': Zu Genese und Funktion des Aloe-Motivs im Stechlin," *Fontane-Blätter* 88 (2009): 154–59.

140 ♦ The Poetics of an Emerging Anthropocene

on place in the form of an extreme local patriotism, the native plant as parasitic is politically suggestive. We are also told, though, that the ones who do see the graft for what it is are the specialists who come to visit. In the case of the aloe, at least, the subjective aesthetic experience causes misapprehension where the objective scientific gaze recognizes the reality of the thing before it.

The network of correspondences that the novel constructs and that is central to its imagination of an emerging Anthropocene is also legible in one of its main human characters, the figure of Melusine von Barby. Melusine was briefly married to an Italian count named Ghiberti, but is now divorced and living in Berlin with her father and sister Armgard, Woldemar's future wife. The name Melusine is an allusion to the figure of the elemental water spirit, who, as mentioned in the previous chapter, Friedrich de la Motte Fouqué drew on for his novella *Undine* and Hans Christian Andersen reworked in his fairy tale "The Little Mermaid." Fontane's own fragmentary novel *Oceane von Parceval* also draws on the Melusine/Undine myth.[40] She is one of the more liberal characters, global in outlook and receptive to historical transformation. She articulates this liberal perspective in a key speech during a conversation with Pastor Lorenzen in chapter twenty-nine: "Alles Alte, so weit es Anspruch darauf hat, sollen wir lieben, aber für das Neue sollen wir recht eigentlich leben. Und vor allem sollen wir, wie der Stechlin uns lehrt, den großen Zusammenhang der Dinge nie vergessen. Sich abschließen, heißt sich einmauern, und sich einmauern ist Tod" (We should love everything that's old, as far as it has a claim to our respect, but it's for the new that we should really and truly live. And above all, as the Stechlin teaches us, never should we forget the great interrelatedness of things. To cut one's self off is to wall one's self in, and to wall one's self in is death).[41] The fact that the speech occurs in the middle of the novel is a sign of its significance, as does the fact that Melusine references it in her letter to Lorenzen at its close. The lake, viewed from this liberal perspective, represents a

---

40 On the Melusine motif see Fontane, *GBA*, I/17: 471–77. See also Jürgen Rothenberg, "Gräfin Melusine: Fontanes 'Stechlin' als politischer Roman," *Text & Kontext* 4, no. 3 (1976): 21–56; Hubert Ohl, "Melusine als Mythos bei Theodor Fontane," in *Mythos und Mythologie in der Literatur des 19. Jahrhunderts*, ed. Helmut Koopman (Frankfurt am Main: Vittorio Klostermann, 1979), 289–305; Klaus Briegleb, "Fontanes Elementargeist: Die Preußin Melusine. Eine Vorstudie zum *Stechlin*," in *Theodor Fontane am Ende des Jahrhunderts: Geschichte—Vergessen—Großstadt—Moderne*, ed. Hanna Delf von Wolzogen, Siegrid Thielking, Peter Pfeiffer, and Helmuth Nürnberger (Würzburg: Königshausen & Neumann, 2000), 109–22; Bettine Menke, "The Figure of Melusine in Fontane's Texts: Images, Digressions, and Lacunae," *The Germanic Review* 79, no. 1 (2004): 41–67, among others.

41 Fontane, *GBA-EW*, I/17: 320; Fontane, *The Stechlin*, 226.

THE POETICS OF AN EMERGING ANTHROPOCENE ♦ 141

"good" Anthropocene, one where the socio-ecological totality of "the great interrelatedness of things" coincides with what Lorenzen believes will be a more democratic, or at least more liberal, era. But Melusine's speech sees historical change in gradualist terms, where the old persists as long as it has a claim to legitimacy. Lake Stechlin, by contrast, with its red rooster, is not an image of gradualist change.[42] In that sense, Melusine's description of the conversation as a "revolutionär[er] Diskur[s]" (revolutionary discourse) is an exaggeration, if not outright misnomer.[43] Indeed, Melusine and Pastor Lorenzen make their pact to guide the younger aristocratic couple into the future because it is "the new" that is causing a crisis of legitimacy for the Junker class, a crisis produced specifically by financialization, industrialization, and urban expansion.[44]

Further belying the sunny vision of "the new" is the fact that Melusine's "great interrelatedness of things" speech is also meant to explain away an incident from the day before. Dubslav, Adelheid, Woldemar, Armgard, and Melusine had all taken a walk down to the lake that day. It being winter, the lake was covered in a layer of snow and ice, a view Melusine found disappointing. Dubslav responded that the reason for her disappointment is that the layer of ice prevents her from imagining the spout of water, and so he suggests that they break open the ice, "und der Hahn, wenn er nur sonst Lust hat, kommt aus seiner Tiefe herauf" (and the cock, if he were to feel like it, might come up from those depths of his).[45] Because the rooster also represents the possibility of revolutionary historical change, a possibility Dubslav remarks upon when he says "das Eis macht still und duckt das Revolutionäre" (the ice makes everything silent and represses the revolutionary element), his suggestion is a threatening one to the aristocratic characters, even the more liberal ones. Melusine responds to Dubslav's suggestion with genuine fear.[46] She admits to being superstitious and therefore not wanting to interfere in the elemental: "Die Natur hat jetzt den See überdeckt; da werd' ich mich also hüten, irgend was ändern zu wollen. Ich würde glauben, eine Hand führe heraus und packte mich" (Nature has covered over the lake for now and so I'll beware of wanting to change anything. I'd almost believe a hand

42   Hubert Ohl argues that in the drafts Fontane had assigned a more revolutionary position to Pastor Lorenzen, but even in the draft conversation Ohl cites, Lorenzen's position is about renewal of what is, "Dauer im Wechsel" (continuity in change) as Ohl himself characterizes it. Ohl, *Bild und Wirklichkeit*, 234–35.

43   Fontane, *GBA-EW*, I/17: 324; Fontane, *The Stechlin*, 229.

44   See Peter Uwe Hohendahl, "Theodor Fontane und der Standesroman: Konvention und Tendenz im Stechlin," in *Legitimationskrisen des deutschen Adels 1200–1900*, ed. Peter U. Hohendahl and Paul M. Lützeler (Stuttgart: Metzler, 1979), 266–71.

45   Fontane, *GBA-EW*, I/17: 316; Fontane, *The Stechlin*, 223.

46   Fontane, *GBA-EW*, I/17: 316; Fontane, *The Stechlin*, 222–23.

might reach out and take hold of me).[47] Not incidentally, Melusine's holy dread of breaking open the lake reflects Fontane's own fascination with the mythological and the elemental as rooted also in human psychology. Hubert Ohl makes this case when he argues that the female figure is a means of bringing forth the connection of human beings to mythic nature, and Renate Schäfer reads the fear as itself an indicator of her affinity for the elemental, being both the nymph's fear of being dragged down into her own realm, and at the same time the fear that the act of breaking the ice might also unsettle her uncanny non-human qualities.[48] The affinity Melusine has for mythic nature, furthermore, is yet another example of the trope of equating female to nature and, by contrast, male to culture. This trope has been the subject of debate in ecofeminist scholarship, inasmuch as it might seem to provide a basis for critiquing masculinist domination narratives on the one hand while also carrying with it the danger of devaluing both nature and women.[49]

Because Melusine has this affinity to the mythic and to the elemental, scholarship has sometimes seen in her an implicit threat to the bourgeois human order.[50] Amy Penrice, for instance, argues that as a divorced woman, Melusine occupies an extra-social position that ultimately grounds the association with the lake suggested by her name.[51] The fact that Melusine is not a nymph, though, but a human with mythic associations limits the extent to which we can read her and her reaction to breaking open the ice in mythic terms. Her fear of disturbing "the elemental" can cut two ways. Not wanting to break open the ice, and fearing an act of mythic violence, entails a respect for the integrity of nature as a realm in which humans had better not trespass. By the same token, it also reifies nature as an external force, an object to be dominated and conquered as much as it can threaten, and Melusine, in the final analysis, is very much on the side of the human and the social. She does not have the

---

47   Fontane, *GBA*, I/17: 316; Fontane, *The Stechlin*, 223.

48   Ohl, "Melusine als Mythos bei Theodor Fontane," 290, Renate Schäfer, "Fontanes Melusine-Motiv," *Euphorion: Zeitschrift für Literaturgeschichte* 56 (1962): 95.

49   See, for instance, Sherry Ortner, "Is Female to Male as Nature Is to Culture?," in *Women, Culture, and Society*, ed. Michelle Zimbalist Rosaldo and Louise Lamphere (Stanford, CA: Stanford University Press, 1974), 1–24; Carol MacCormack, "Nature, Culture and Gender: A Critique," in *Nature, Culture and Gender*, ed. MacCormack and Strathern, 1–24; Carolyn Merchant, "Reinventing Eden: Western Culture as a Recovery Narrative," in *Uncommon Ground*, ed. Cronon, 132–59; and Soper, *What Is Nature?*, 121–25, among others.

50   See Schäfer, "Fontanes Melusine-Motiv," 92; and Vincent Günther, *Das Symbol im erzählerischen Werk Fontanes* (Bonn: Bouvier, 1967), 64.

51   Amy Penrice, "Fractured Symbolism: Der Stechlin and The Golden Bowl," *Comparative Literature* 43, no. 4 (1991): 359–60.

connection to non-human beings that Wienke did in Theodor Storm's *Der Schimmelreiter*, nor do we see much evidence that she perceives herself as part of a continuum with planetary systems the way Ditha did in Adalbert Stifter's *Abdias*. And if we bring the realities of global capitalism back into the picture, then "the great interrelatedness of things" also looks deeply ambivalent, insofar as it is a condition brought about by extractivism.

The Great Interrelatedness of Things: Poetics and Politics of an Anthropocene Totality

The darker side of "the great interrelatedness of things," then, is that it also describes a reality of global extractivism in the pursuit of value production. We already saw how the subtext to the jocular suggestion of sending a telegram to the emperor of China includes the projection of military and economic power onto a region then destabilized by European imperialist activity. But the effects of capital extraction manifest themselves also in the Brandenburg landscape. The "new," for which Melusine says we should truly live, is not intrinsically a set of liberal democratic sensibilities that are increasingly defining the novel's present and implied better future, but rather can also designate political conflict that has environmental stakes.

The key agent of extractivism in the novel, the reactionary character Gundermann, is anything but a friend of democracy. Like Bertram Pfister in *Pfisters Mühle* he is in the milling business, but as owner of a chain of sawmills there is little in the way of *Mühlenromantik* about Gundermann. Where Pfister's mill was an anachronistic object that raised at most sentimental feelings in a narrator whose allegiances lay with the modern, Gundermann's chain of mills is as much a product of speculative capital as the factories Krickerode or Rhakopyrgos in Raabe's novel. Woldemar's friend Rex von Czako reports that Gundermann began with a single mill that grew to seven sawmills that now line the Rhin, a river in the Havel's watershed, and he has cornered the market on timber for Berlin's hardwood floors. Gundermann avidly supports the maintenance of current socio-economic hierarchies, in spite of his own social mobility, assuming a hardline stance against worker movements and anything that might hint of leftism or that might be, in his oddly self-referential signature expression, "Wasser auf die Mühlen der Sozialdemokratie" (water on the mills of the social democrats).[52] As an industrialist, Gundermann would seem to be the representative of the new, emerging Anthropocene reality, not the nobility who dominate the novel. In the conversation with Melusine

---

52   Fontane, *GBA-EW*, I/17: 28; Fontane, *The Stechlin*, 17.

144 ♦ The Poetics of an Emerging Anthropocene

in chapter twenty-nine, Lorenzen calls Werner Siemens and James Watt, industrialists like Gundermann, heroes of modernity and individuals who have taken the place of people like Friedrich II. But, in fact, Gundermann has recently been elevated to the nobility himself, marking the persistence of a feudal status quo not in spite of, but predicated on the ascendancy of the industrial bourgeoisie.[53] As much as *Der Stechlin* is about historical transitions, as Ernest Schonfield argues,[54] Gundermann casts into relief the reality that Melusine's position about respecting the old while living for the new by no means forecloses on reactionary, anti-democratic politics.

Gundermann is an Anthropocene figure not simply because he is an industrialist felling forests, but because he too is a node in a planet-wide network of socio-ecological relations. In his capacity as the owner of seven sawmills he is a mediator between the Brandenburg countryside and the city of Berlin, and so an agent for the commodification and consumption of the forest for the growing metropolis. The lumber industry in Fontane's works is, in general, a means by which the regional is bound up in translocal relations. Hankel's Stowage in *Irrungen, Wirrungen* (On Tangled Paths, 1888) is a notable example: even though Lene and Botho travel there because of its reputation for beauty and solitude, the stowage is the point through which local products pass into the wider world and vice versa.[55] In *Wanderungen durch die Brandenburg*, it turns out that the specific products exported through Hankel's Stowage are timber from local forests.[56] Another key sign of the interpenetration of global and local in the social (co-)production of nature is in the essay "Der Schwielow und seine Umgebungen" (The Schwielow and its Environs), where Fontane visits an acacia plantation. The acacia is a non-native species originally planted to decorate parks, only to prosper in the March, so that it is now cultivated for wood and traded in port cities like Hamburg, Stade, and Bremerhaven.[57]

---

53 See also Eda Sagarra, *Theodor Fontane: "Der Stechlin"* (Munich: Fink, 1986), 23. On Gundermann as an embodiment of social contradictions, see Walter Müller-Seidel, "Fontane: Der Stechlin," in *Der deutsche Roman: Vom Barock bis zur Gegenwart*, ed. Benno von Wiese, 2 vols. (Düsseldorf: August Bagel, 1963), vol. 2, 157–58.

54 Ernest Schonfield, "Wirtschaftlicher Strukturwandel in *Der Stechlin*," in *Theodor Fontane: Dichter des Übergangs*, ed. Patricia Howe (Würzburg: Königshausen & Neumann, 2013), 91–108.

55 Fontane, *GBA-EW*, I/10: 70, 79; Theodor Fontane, *On Tangled Paths*, trans. Peter James Bowman (London: Penguin, 2013), 66, 74. See also Lyon, *Out of Place*, 161–62.

56 Fontane, *GBA-WMB*, V/6: 557–58.

57 Fontane, *GBA-WMB*, V/3: 418–19.

In *Der Stechlin*, the global export of local products has a paradoxical effect for notions of place. On the one hand, it is a means by which the global reaches into the world of the novel, destabilizing notions of place. On the other hand, we see notions of place reified through commodity circulation. Beer is particularly emblematic of the latter dynamic. In the excursion to the beer garden Eierhäuschen (Egg Cottage), the party drinks the Munich brand Löwenbräu. The product and the brand name are not incidental. The late nineteenth century was the moment when beer became a mass-market commodity, and the production of beer increasingly industrialized and bound up in the system of financial capital. In 1872 Löwenbräu became the first Munich brewery to be publicly traded.[58] And on the more material front, beer spoils easily, and, being a landlocked city, Munich breweries could only compete globally once they had access to rail, as opposed to slower, unreliable networks of roads.[59] The party's drinks, in short, represent the spread of financial capital and the railway as a technology of the hydrocarbon economy. When Baronness Berchtesgaden, speaking with the authority of a Bavarian, raises her glass at the Eierhäuschen and states, "daß man nur ein echtes Münchener überhaupt nur noch in Berlin tränke" (one could drink a really genuine Munich beer only in Berlin), it reflects both the persistence of place in commodified form, inasmuch as the promotion of the site of beer production as a sign of quality is a marketing technique, as well as the corresponding dissolution of place, since a "genuine Munich beer" is only to be had in the Prussian capital.[60]

The party drinks their beer, meanwhile, in a landscape indelibly marked by the same socio-ecological realities that brought them their drinks in the first place. The expedition to the Eierhäuschen is ostensibly an escape from the city into "nature." For while the Barbys live in a house that is distinct because it has a garden, their house is adjacent to a rail line, and the evening sun slopes in through the smoke emitted by passing locomotives. The Spree river at the Reichstagsufer, that "echt berlinerisch-pittoresken Ecke" (genuinely Berlin-picturesque corner) is dominated by an advertisement featuring a twenty-foot girl holding a packet of Kneipp's malt coffee.[61] And in her letter inviting Woldemar along on the trip to the Eierhäuschen, Melusine echoes mid-nineteenth-century notions that "the poetic" was to be found at the margins of industrial society when

58 Christian Schäder, "Münchner Brauindustrie 1871–1945: Die wirtschafts-geschichtliche Entwicklung eines Industriezweiges" (PhD diss., Universität Regensburg, 1999), 76.

59 Schäder, "Münchner Brauindustrie 1871–1945," 164–73. For a broader history of the industrialization of beer production see Ian Hornsey, *A History of Beer and Brewing* (Cambridge: Royal Society of Chemistry, 2003), 365–484.

60 Fontane, *GBA-EW*, I/17: 176; Fontane, *The Stechlin*, 123.

61 Fontane, *GBA-EW*, I/17: 147; Fontane, *The Stechlin*, 102.

she says: "In unserer sogenannten großen Welt giebt es so wenig, was sich zu sehen und zu hören verlohnt; das meiste hat sich in die stillen Winkel der Erde zurückgezogen" (In this so called "great" world of ours there is so little worth hearing or seeing. Almost everything has withdrawn to the quiet corners of the earth).[62] The Eierhäuschen is presumably one of those "quiet corners," but the trip itself turns out to be a prolonged glimpse of the effects that urban and industrial sprawl have had on the landscape around Berlin. To get to the Eierhäuschen, the party takes a steamboat up the Spree, and the conversation gives way to one of the novel's more extended landscape descriptions. From the boat they see the arches of the rail track, behind which they can glimpse gardens and various constructions. Eventually the elevated railway retreats from the riverbanks, giving way instead to a landscape of fields and poplar trees, but also a steam shovel loading grit and sand from lime pits of the Berlin Mortarworks, "die hier die Herrschaft behaupteten und das Uferbild bestimmten" (held sway here, determining the look of the river's edge).[63] The German "Herrschaft," better translated as "domination," evokes the rhetoric of the conquest of nature.

Because of the prominence of the social character of the banks of the Spree, it might be tempting to see the gardens glimpsed through the arches as "mere pieces of greenery, [since] the fruit and flowers they provide are few in number and late survivors; they are anomalies," as Michael James White puts it.[64] To be sure, the environment throughout is thoroughly subjugated, and the novel sets the garden up as a poetic leftover when the narrator contrasts it with "aller dieser bei Alltäglichkeit und der Arbeit dienenden Dinge" (objects meant to serve the realms of the commonplace and labor).[65] The problem is that viewing the gardens and the patches of green as anomalies within an environment otherwise dominated by human construction ignores the unity of the image and opts instead for a segregation between the nature that continues as patches and the human trappings of modernity. The gardens themselves are obviously examples of nature as a social product; to regard them as spaces not yet touched by prosaic modernity is to understand them through a reified concept of nature that obscures the fact that whatever aesthetic character they might have arises because they stand in a dialectical relationship with "the realms of the commonplace and labor." And while the gardens may not be as obviously environmentally deleterious as the railway or the mortar works, they still belong

---

62 Fontane, *GBA-EW*, I/17: 159–60; Fontane, *The Stechlin*, 111.

63 Fontane, *GBA-EW*, I/17: 164; Fontane, *The Stechlin*, 114.

64 Michael James White, *Space in Theodor Fontane's Works: Theme and Poetic Function* (London: Modern Humanities Research Association, 2012), 141.

65 Fontane, *GBA-EW*, I/17: 164; Fontane, *The Stechlin*, 114.

to a landscape featuring "significant anthropogenic deposits,"[66] novel phenomena that spread across a large area and will leave a layer in the lithosphere that a future geologist could conceivably identify. They are, in short, a local image of an Anthropocene reality.

Nor is the Eierhäuschen itself an escape from industrial modernity into some "quiet corner," as Melusine puts it. The party has headed there to escape the city, but the day trip does not even offer the possibility of an escape from the "everyday" to the "Sunday," to borrow Karl Krumhardt's phrasing from *Die Akten des Vogelsangs*. After arriving at the Eierhäuschen the party decides to take a walk before settling in, "weil die wundervolle Frische dazu einlud" (since the wonderful fresh air was so inviting).[67] The choice to put off the drink for the sake of a walk is a matter of taking the opportunity for a kind of aesthetic experience inherent to that particular environment. The party walks up to the Spindlersfeld factory, a massive industrial laundry facility in what is now Berlin-Köpenick (and, as we saw in the previous chapter, the inspiration for Adam Asche and Rhakopyrgos in *Pfisters Mühle*). The smokestacks rise before them, and they see the smoke slowly drifting into what they took to be fresh air.[68] The reaction of the party is markedly different to Ebert's reaction to the factory at the end of *Pfisters Mühle*. There Ebert registered the slow-motion ecological catastrophe coming out of the factory, but, like everyone else in the scene, continued to enjoy tea on the veranda as if the very environmental destruction he was describing were not taking place. For the party in *Der Stechlin*, the appearance of the factory ends the expedition for fresh air. It is the furthest point of their walk, but it also prompts a discussion about industry as such. In some respects the scene resembles the "pastoral design" that, Leo Marx argues, American authors inherit and develop from classical pastoral literature, a design that consists of an industrial "counterforce" that disrupts the bucolic and introduces into the text a "larger, more complicated order of experience."[69] Marx's example is the train whistle in Nathaniel Hawthorne's "The Legend of Sleepy Hollow," where the train is part of a pattern of "crude, masculine aggressiveness in contrast with the tender, feminine, and submissive attitudes traditionally attached to the landscape."[70] The opposite is the case with the appearance of Spindlersfeld. Possible phallic connotations of the chimneys notwithstanding, the factory does not make a hypermasculine intrusion like the train in Leo Marx's

66 Jan Zalasiewicz et al., "Stratigraphy of the Anthropocene," *Philosophical Transactions: Mathematical, Physical and Engineering Sciences* 369, no. 1938 (2011): 1039–40.

67 Fontane, *GBA-EW*, I/17: 166; Fontane, *The Stechlin*, 116.

68 Fontane, *GBA-EW*, I/17: 167; Fontane, *The Stechlin*, 116.

69 Leo Marx, *The Machine in the Garden: Technology and the Pastoral Ideal in America* (Oxford: Oxford University Press, 2000), 25.

70 Marx, *The Machine in the Garden*, 29.

148 ♦ The Poetics of an Emerging Anthropocene

example. Instead it simply materializes on the horizon. Its appearance is disruptive, but without inducing the kind of shock that even Ebert had when he approached Krickerode for the first time.

Since production and consumption under the sign of industrialism also constitute the "great interrelatedness of things," environmental degradation is constitutive of that totality. In the conversation between Melusine and Lorenzen in chapter twenty-nine, Lorenzen claims that this new era may not necessarily be a happier era, but "so doch mindestens eine Zeit mit mehr Sauerstoff in der Luft, eine Zeit, in der wir besser atmen können" (at least it's an age with more oxygen in the air, an age where we can breathe better).[71] Of course, the images of smog at Spindlersfeld and after Dubslav's funeral suggest that, if anything, even if the breathing is getting better in a metaphorical sense, it is getting worse in a material sense.[72]

Against the "good" Anthropocene of a shift towards a more liberal society, there remains the "bad" Anthropocene of environmental degradation and general political conflict. Both strands come together most clearly in the way the aristocratic characters view the local glass industry. On the sunnier side, Woldemar sees glass production as a good thing precisely because it forges a connection to the world with economic benefits for local people. Woldemar makes this point to his father, who is suspicious of the local glass industry because he believes it to be out of place. But even in his rosy view of the glass industry, Woldemar points to its more repressive side when he observes vaguely that labor strikes do not happen in their area. Dubslav's disdain for the local glass industry, by contrast, is rooted in his own conservatism. He claims: "Aber so viel noch von guter alter Zeit zu finden ist, so viel findet sich hier, in unsrer lieben alten Grafschaft. Und in dies Bild richtiger Gliederung, oder meinetwegen auch richtiger Unterordnung (denn ich erschrecke vor solchem Worte nicht), in dieses Bild des Friedens paßt mir diese ganze Globsower Retortenbläserei nicht hinein" (But as much of the good old days as can still be found in this world, can be found right here, right here in our dear old county. And as far as I go, into this picture of the right kind of organization, or if you like the right kind of subordination—I don't shy away from that sort of word either—into this picture of tranquility, this whole Globsow retort-blowing factory doesn't fit).[73] The conservative sentiment about order, subordination, and what does and does not belong is connected to a normative notion of nature. Dubslav justified his removal of the colored glass windows from the viewing tower on the estate grounds because, "Ich empfand es aber wie 'ne Naturbeleidigung. Grün

71 Fontane, *GBA-EW*, I/17: 324; Fontane, *The Stechlin*, 229.
72 See also Zemanek, "(Bad) Air and (Faulty) Inspiration," 133.
73 Fontane, *GBA-EW*, I/17: 78; Fontane, *The Stechlin*, 52.

ist grün und Wald ist Wald" (Seemed to me sort of an insult to nature though. Green is green and woods are woods).[74] Remove the products of the local industry, in other words, and enjoy a more unmediated access to nature, never mind that the viewing tower and the remaining window frames mediate the outside world in their own right. And there are the aforementioned glass balls in his garden, reflecting the images of the non-native aloes growing there, undercutting the fantasy of a static nature where green is just green and woods are just woods. [75]

If Dubslav's discontent with the local glass industry were only a matter of conservative wistfulness, then his stance would be one of mere nostalgia for a pre-industrial past, the low political stakes of which he himself is conscious enough of to regard with his signature humor. As much as he dislikes glass production, for instance, he admits that he can make an exception if that glass happens to contain wine. But it turns out over the course of the conversation about glass production that Dubslav's real concern is the extent to which the global industrial supply chain that connects the region to the wider world is creating the conditions for both social and ecological destabilization. Imagining the vast quantity of glassware that has gone from the region into the world, Dubslav shifts from his more humorous tone into a full-throated jeremiad.

> Die schicken sie zunächst in andre Fabriken, und da destillieren sie flott drauf los und zwar allerhand schreckliches Zeug in diese grünen Ballons hinein: Salzsäure, Schwefelsäure, rauchende Salpetersäure. Das ist das schlimmste, die hat immer einen rotgelben Rauch, der einem gleich die Lunge anfrißt. Aber wenn einen der Rauch auch zufrieden läßt, jeder Tropfen brennt ein Loch, in Leinwand oder in Tuch, oder in Leder, überhaupt in alles; alles wird angebrannt und angeätzt. Das ist das Zeichen unsrer Zeit jetzt, "angebrannt und angeätzt." Und wenn ich dann bedenke, daß meine Globsower da mitthun und ganz gemütlich die Werkzeuge liefern für die große Generalweltanbrennung, ja, hören Sie, meine Herren, das giebt mir einen Stich.

> [First off they send them to other factories and there they just go ahead as fast as they can distilling things right into these green balloons, all kinds of awful stuff as a matter of fact: hydrochloric acid, sulfuric acid, smoking nitrate acid. That's the worst one of all. It always has a reddish yellow smoke that eats right into your lungs.
> But even if that smoke leaves you in peace, every drop of it burns a hole, in linen, in cloth, in leather, anything at all. Everything gets scorched and corroded. That's the sign of our times these days.

---

74 Fontane, *GBA-EW*, I/17: 63; Fontane, *The Stechlin*, 41.
75 Fontane, *GBA-EW*, I/17: 7; Fontane, *The Stechlin*, 3.

Scorched or corroded. And so when I consider that my Globsowers are going along with it, and as cheerfully as can be, providing the tools for the great universal world scorching, well then, let me tell you, gentlemen, that gives me a stitch of pain right here in my heart.[76]]

Dubslav's speech gives another glimpse into the darker side of Melusine's "great interrelatedness of things." The problem with glass balloons is first a matter of toxicity: they are receptacles for dangerous chemicals whose fumes damage the body and burn whatever materials they come into contact with, so that their relation in the "interrelatedness of things" is one of destruction. But "Generalweltanbrennung" (the great universal world scorching), is in equal measure a complaint about the real corrosive effects dangerous chemicals have as well as another metaphor for revolution, implicit in the image of the red rooster. The circulation of the glass balloons to other sites of production, then, also creates the interrelatedness, even as the chemicals destroy. Dubslav thereby links a critique of the physical effect that chemicals have on people and the world to a conservative social critique of the process of industrialization, with the workers as co-conspirators in the damage.

Read as a metaphor for revolution, Dubslav's worry that the proletariat will be unified through the centralization of capital on a trans-regional scale is a conservative reformulation of Karl Marx's prediction of the end of capitalism. For Marx, writing at the end of volume one of *Capital,* "capitalist production begets, with the inexorability of a natural process, its own negation. This is the negation of the negation."[77] In *Der Stechlin* glass production brings together the processes of environmental destruction on the one hand with the possibility of proletarian revolution on the other. Natural and human histories merge here because human economic activity is affecting the planet at a physical level and correspond to transformations in the political and economic spheres. Dubslav can only witness this process, the pain in his heart over the socio-ecological processes to which "his" Globsowers contribute an indicator that anxieties about waning status and impotency are the real feelings beneath his seeming openness and tolerance.[78] For all of the conversation around the subject of historical change, the red rooster never rises, and the revolution does not come. On the contrary, the novel ends with what appears to be restoration: Woldemar grows weary of careerism, Armgard loses interest in

---

76   Fontane, *GBA-EW, I/17:* 79–80; Fontane, *The Stechlin,* 53.

77   Marx and Engels, *Capital,* 929.

78   On Dubslav's own sense of waning status, see Ervin Malakaj, "Senescence and Fontane's *Der Stechlin,*" in *Fontane in the Twenty-First Century,* ed. John B. Lyon and Brian Tucker (Rochester, NY: Camden House, 2019), 232–33.

urban life, and as summer turns to fall the couple leaves Berlin and takes up residence at the estate in Stechlin.

At the level of its environmental thematic, the novel does not explicitly decry environmental degradation; in fact, nineteenth-century notions of progress find a greater embrace with Fontane than they do with any of the other authors included in this study. Part of the reason for this cautiously affirmative stance towards industrial modernity and the project of poeticizing the emerging Anthropocene reality is that the collapse of a distinction between human and natural histories does not result in an "end of nature" story. The history of the Menzer Forest Fontane relates in *Wanderungen durch die Mark Brandenburg* encapsulates the twin narratives of the Anthropocene reality that is core to the realism of *Der Stechlin*. The forest grows back after the Berliners switch to heating their homes with peat, and while the history of exploitation remains forever part of its character, social intervention is ultimately subsumed into longer natural histories. *Der Stechlin* ends on a similar note with Melusine's letter to Lorenzen. She concludes her letter with the words: "es ist nicht nötig, daß die Stechline weiterleben, aber es lebe *der Stechlin*" (It is not necessary that the Stechlins live on forever, but long live *the Stechlin*).[79] Instead of the continuity of the family Stechlin, Melusine affirms the continuity of *the* Stechlin, that is, the lake as a natural form and all it signifies. The human traces left on the planet likewise determine what we call the Anthropocene, constituting a set of historical circumstances wherein the social is not so much relativized against the broader scale of natural history, but rather becomes elevated into the longer history of the earth.

79 Fontane, *GBA-EW*, I/17: 462; Fontane, *The Stechlin*, 329.

Conclusion: The Nature of Realism

FIVE YEARS AFTER the publication of *Der Stechlin* and an ocean away, naturalist John Burroughs kicked off what came to be known as the "Nature Fakers" controversy with his essay "Real and Sham Natural History" in the March 1903 issue of *The Atlantic Monthly*. Burroughs's essay was an attack on authors like Ernest Thompson Seton and William J. Long, who depicted non-human life in an allegedly sentimentalized and anthropomorphized way, while boldly asserting the truth of their depictions, profiting, so Burroughs's allegation goes, off of a public taste for non-realism, "the popular love for the sensational and improbable."[1] Burroughs's objection is that the sensational and improbable are signs that the Nature Fakers are, in fact, attempting to pass off fictional accounts as non-fictional "nature writing," the "sham natural history" of the essay's title. Seton and Long, of course, understood themselves to be appealing to something else in their intended audiences, namely a desire to overcome a sense of disenchantment and alienation from nature that industrial and scientific culture had brought about. Long makes the connection explicit in the opening chapter of *A Little Brother to the Bear* when he says that the theories of evolution and of gravity occupy "the same comfortable category" as such phenomena of industrial culture as the telegraph and the steam engine.[2] Not incidentally, the "conquest of nature" in this instance is not simply a question of the proliferation of the trappings of industrial technology or the demythologizing effects of modern science, but in Long's American context is directly connected to the history of displacement and attempted extermination of Native American peoples. That fact means that the sentimental descriptions and kitschy nature illustrations that make up Long's and Seton's books have to be understood

---

1   Burroughs, "Real and Sham Natural History," 298. The opening of Seton's book is representative, making an explicit truth claim for both the content and the manner in which animals are depicted. "These stories are true. Although I have left the strict line of historical truth in many places, the animals in this book were all real characters. They lived the lives I have depicted, and showed the stamp of heroism and personality more strongly by far than it has been in the power of my pen to tell." Ernest Seton Thompson, *Wild Animals I Have Known* (New York: Charles Scribner & Sons, 1898), 9.

2   William J Long, *A Little Brother to the Bear* (Cambridge: Ginn & Company, 1903), 5.

in the context of the twin forces of political and economic consolidation, forces that create a world of human and non-human winners and losers.

The back-to-nature impulse, though, raises for Long the same problems that it did for the German realists. The fundamental problem of realist aesthetics, that is, truth and the reality of the realism, is still the pressing question in the Nature Fakers controversy. In "The Point of View," the opening chapter of *Little Brother to the Bear*, Long stakes a truth claim of his own. The modern nature writer, Long claims, must both collect and interpret the facts, "at first hand if possible."[3] "Interpretation" in the realm of non-fiction serves for Long a parallel function as does aestheticization, poeticization, or transfiguration (*Verklärung*) of the experiential world in the theory of German realism, because it is the instance through which mere mimesis becomes meaningful within the overall composition of the text. Long's justification for interpretation is very close to the argument Stifter makes in the preface to *Bunte Steine*, that the small reveals the truly large. Long writes: "For every fact is also a revelation, and is chiefly interesting, not for itself, but for the law or the life which lies behind it and which it in some way expresses. An apple falling to the ground was a common enough fact,—so common that it had no interest until some one thought about it and found the great law that grips alike the falling apple and the falling star."[4] Long was a preacher, and the claim that every fact is a "revelation" suggests a divine force behind perceptible reality in a rhetoric that is more unambiguously Christian than Stifter's deistic-sounding "sanftes Gesez."

The controversy received enough attention in the United States in the first decade of the twentieth century that President Theodor Roosevelt, who is remembered as a conservationist to this day, chose to weigh in (the very term "nature faker" is his coinage). The debate may seem largely like a historical curiosity, but it hinged on the same questions of realism relative to the representation of nature while also anticipating ecocritical debates on environmental representation arising at the end of the twentieth. Ninety years after the Nature Faker debate had subsided, problems of material factuality and representation, realist or otherwise, would play out again with the advent of ecocriticism as a subfield of academic literary criticism. The institutionalization of ecocriticism in the 1990s, complete with the founding of the Association for the Study of Literature and Environment (ASLE), the establishment of academic journals of ecocriticism, and the hiring of professors to teach ecocriticism in literature departments, occurred against a paradigm of poststructuralist literary theory that many ecocritics of the "first wave" felt dissolved and denied the

---

3   Long, *A Little Brother to the Bear*, 4.
4   Long, *A Little Brother to the Bear*, 4.

154 ♦ Conclusion

material reality of the worlds that texts represent.[5] Tempting though it might be to regard ecocritical debates as "academic" in a pejorative sense, these arguments are, like the Nature Fakers debate, noteworthy insofar as they mark the persistence of the same problems of truth and representation. In his 1995 book *The Environmental Imagination*, for instance, Lawrence Buell argues that "as we congratulate ourselves on outgrowing the mimetic illusion by making it the playful instrument of our will," literary critics, specifically "professionalized" literary critics employed in academic departments and schooled in literary theory, can never really escape the responsiveness of texts to the physical world.[6] To that end, a key dimension of Buell's project is about negotiating the claims of realism, particularly in the genre of nature writing, against (post-)modernist claims to discourse overriding mimesis: "Clearly the claims of realism merit reviving not in negation of these myths [that discourse overrides mimesis] but in counterpoise, so as to enable one to reimagine textual representation as having a dual accountability to matter and to discursive mentation."[7]

"Dual accountability" effectively splits the difference between an emphasis on nature as real-existing materiality and the broadly (and often hazily) defined postmodern paradigm that the realist-materialist strain of ecocriticism sought to correct. Glen Love's 2003 book *Practical Ecocriticism*, for instance, calls for a literary criticism that turns towards the natural sciences.[8] As late as 2009, S. K. Robisch argued for a more materialist criticism in his polemical essay "The Woodshed." While seeming to be at first blush an "anti-theory" polemic, Robisch's real target is a poststructuralism he characterizes as "neo-romanticism in piebald."[9] Against poststructuralism as a latter-day idealism, Robisch, akin to Buell and Love, argues for an (eco-)criticism that recognizes thought's conditionality on the reality of the material world.[10] This framing has strong resemblance to Marx and Engels's intervention against German Idealism and Young Hegelianism when they contrasts their own historical materialism with a "German philosophy which descends from heaven to earth, here we ascend from earth to heaven."[11] The mid-nineteenth-century theorists of German realism conceived of the process of aesthetic formation in similar terms, where realism begins with mimetic representation that is then rendered aesthetic.

5   On the "waves" of the environmental turn, see Buell, *The Future of Environmental Criticism*, 17–22.
6   Buell, *The Environmental Imagination*, 89–90.
7   Buell, *The Environmental Imagination*, 92.
8   Love, *Practical Ecocriticism*, 11.
9   Robisch, "The Woodshed," 703.
10   Robisch, "The Woodshed," 702.
11   Marx and Engels, *The German Ideology*, 47.

CONCLUSION ♦ 155

For the stories examined in this book, nature is not simply a set of realia to which the imperatives of realist representation apply. As the works of Stifter, Raabe, Storm, and Fontane demonstrate, nature and its condition determine realist aesthetics in a variety of ways. In the case of Adalbert Stifter, what counts as normative nature is a fundamental question to his realism. If we follow the theoretical argument he lays out in the preface to *Bunte Steine*, nature is its most natural where and when its workings are regular and gradualist. From that perspective, the moments of disruption and catastrophe, such as the wolf attack in *Brigitta* or the lightning strike that kills Ditha in *Abdias*, serve only to cast regular and gradualist nature in starker relief once order has been reinstated. But if that is the function of disorderly nature, then that nature has a higher status than Stifter admits by dismissing it as the truly small. It is a tacit admission that, at the very least, orderly, gradualist nature is unthinkable without disorderly, chaotic nature, meaning that the latter is ultimately just as normative and natural as the former. The relation of Stifter's fiction to the environmental depredations of industrial modernity works in similar terms. The goal of the social production of nature in his fiction, of course, is to a large extent to reinforce the regular workings of a harmonious nature. In that sense the remote places where *Brigitta*, *Abdias*, and *Der Nachsommer* are set contrast explicitly with places where industrial capitalism is most concentrated, places that appear often fleetingly, and then in disparaging terms, such as the poor air and water quality that Risach says already blights the lives of city dwellers. But those places only serve as contrasts because they are just as much sites of the domination of nature, created as they are through the banishment of all that disrupts the order, be it wolves or redstarts.

But environmental conditions also resist realist representation, as when the extermination of wild animals coupled with noise and light pollution undermine Karl Krumhardt's attempt to depict the forest as a peaceful place of nature in Wilhelm Raabe's *Die Akten des Vogelsangs*. The reflections on the poetic possibilities of the present in that novel and in *Pfisters Mühle* have a strong historical orientation: both narratives look back at the years surrounding German unification as the completion of a project of subsuming nature into an industrial mode of production. In spite of his narrators' inclination towards a nostalgia for a pre-industrial reality, the catastrophe had happened long before the past moments for which they harbor such nostalgia. Pfister's mill was already in decline, surviving more as a beer garden for urban daytrippers than from whatever was left of the milling business, and the Vogelsang neighborhood always anticipated its own industrial makeover, where the older green hedges were but embryonic forms of the later brick walls. Even to the extent that these novels can be seen as enacting a realist program of locating the "poetic" outside of industrial modernity, manifested as a highly subjective

156 ♦ CONCLUSION

sense of nostalgia, they remind that even the poetic project arises out of the conditions of the present. "Der Menschheit Dasein auf der Erde baut sich immer von neuem auf, doch nicht von demäußersten Umkreis her, sondern stets aus der Mitte" (Humanity's existence on earth rebuilds itself time and again, but not from the outermost circle inward, rather always from the center outward), as Karl Krumhardt writes towards the end of *Die Akten des Vogelsangs*. The comment is a reference to his papers, which for him are not separate from his home and modern existence, but integral to it.[12] When both Karl Krumhardt and Eberhard Pfister put down their pens, they return to the urban and industrial lives they live as confirmed members of the late nineteenth-century German bourgeoisie.

Raabe's novels stand at the end of a historical process that Theodor Storm's *Der Schimmelreiter* constructs in looking back to a fictional moment in eighteenth-century environmental history. Where Stifter's realism hinges on the question of which nature is the most normative nature, in *Der Schimmelreiter* nature defies human assumptions about reality most where humans dominate it the least. Storm's novella looks to the Enlightenment past as a political and aesthetic watershed emerging out of a more aggressive stance towards non-human nature. The dike as a technology of separation seeks to dominate non-human nature by excluding the forces of the ocean to create arable land, and in so doing excludes also the fantastic while effecting a shift from a more feudalistic to a more bourgeois socio-economic order. The novella's realism is born out of this nexus, but the fantastic and non-human forces persist through subsequent history in the figure of the ghost who rides when storms threaten the community of the polders.

Where Storm looks back to an originary moment of later environmental history and Raabe a present one, Fontane's *Der Stechlin* gestures again towards the future, specifically the future of an emerging Anthropocene. Here the aesthetic status of nature is now problematized at a global and planetary scale. The global socio-ecological reality resolves the problem of the supposed lack of poetic potential in the March Brandenburg, a lack that was thought to be intrinsic to the environment even without the smog from glass industries or the history of exploiting the forest for timber. The presence of those industries are the direct signs of an Anthropocene reality crystallizing in the novel, one that relocates the possibility of poesy away from the small scale and the local to the global. The novel's eponymous lake is, among other things, a symbol for a revolution that never arrives but that the novel implies will be an outcome of the historical shifts it depicts. By projecting revolutionary meaning onto a feature of the topography, one that has planet-wide connections, the

---

12   Raabe, *BA*, 19: 404; Raabe, *The Birdsong Papers*, 121.

possibility of a historical turning point in human timescales is situated over and against longer geological timescales.

Such a congealment of human and Earth histories is what presents itself to the tourist who makes their way to the viewing platform on the Drachenfels today, be it by the Drachenfels Railway, the construction of which Ernst Rudorff once so vociferously decried, or simply by foot. The railway has since been electrified, such that what appeared to Rudorff as an instance of wanton disregard for nature in the service of tourist pleasure in the nineteenth century can now be seen as a part of Germany's much vaunted *Energiewende*, or "Energy Turn," the program of phasing out both carbon-intensive as well as nuclear power production, in the twenty-first.

But in addition to the deep time of the not-entirely-extinct Laach Lake volcano to the southwest, the barges plying their way up and down the "corrected" Rhine below, the romantic medieval castle ruins above, or the adjacent neogothic Drachenburg Castle (itself as much the product of modern capital as the urban sprawl visible along the riverbanks beyond), the contemporary tourist might look towards the northwest. Beyond the horizon, about seventy kilometers as the crow flies, is the former site of the village of Lützerath. There in 2023 environmental activists faced off against police and the machines of the energy company RWE in an attempt to stop the demolition of the village for the expansion of the massive open pit coal mine Garzweiler II, a project endorsed, not incidentally, by Germany's Green Party. The diminutive "Lützi," by which activists affectionately referred to the village, suggests something small and precious, but the fight has a place within the larger political struggle to limit global warming and ensure a livable planet for those of us alive today as much as those yet to be born. Eckardt Heukamp, "the last farmer of Lützerath," had hung a banner reading "1,5° heißt: Lützerath bleibt!" (1.5 degrees means: Lützerath stays!) over the wall enclosing his farm's courtyard, itself a protected monument constructed in 1763.[13] The lignite to be mined from the spot where Lützerath once stood is the most inefficient grade of coal with the highest CO_2 output, and the more of it that is burned, the further the goal of limiting global warming to 1.5°C will be put out of reach. In other words, Heukamp's banner was a reminder that with the global climate and the habitability of the planet at stake, we misapprehend the ultimate destruction of "Lützi" if we read it as the loss of an old wall and a quaint agricultural village, just another provincial idyll fallen to the forces of industrial capital. What is true for Lützerath is also true for the villages, gardens, and seemingly

---

13 Barbara Schnell, "RWE versucht, die Leute zu brechen," *Frankfurter Rundschau*, September 5, 2022, https://www.fr.de/wirtschaft/rwe-versucht-die-leute-zu-brechen-91768865.html.

picturesque countrysides that make up the landscapes of German realism. German critics in the 1850s believed realism to be an aesthetic of the future. Looking back from the future now, that future orientation lies less in realism's strategies of rendering experiential and everyday life "poetic," and more in its imagination of an unfolding environmental history.

Bibliography

Abbey, Edward. *Desert Solitaire: A Season in the Wilderness*. New York: Ballantine Books, 1971.

Adorno, Theodor W. *Aesthetic Theory*. Translated by Robert Hullot-Kentor. Minneapolis: University of Minnesota Press, 1997.

Arndt, Christiane. *Abschied von der Wirklichkeit: Probleme bei der Darstellung von Realität im deutschsprachigen literarischen Realismus*. Freiburg im Breisgau: Rombach, 2009.

Attanucci, Timothy. *The Restorative Poetics of a Geological Age: Stifter, Viollet-Le-Duc, and the Aesthetic Practices of Geohistoricism*. Berlin: Walter de Gruyter, 2020.

Auerbach, Erich. *Mimesis: The Representation of Reality in Western Literature*. Translated by Willard Trask. Princeton, NJ: Princeton University Press, 2003.

B., A. "Review of *Der Stechlin* and *Zwischen zwanzig und dreißig*." *Literarisches Centralblatt für Deutschland*, December 12, 1898.

Bayerl, Günter. "Herrn Pfisters und anderer Leute Mühlen: Das Verhältnis von Mensch, Technik und Umwelt im Spiegel eines literarischen Topos." In *Technik in der Literatur: Ein Forschungsüberblick in zwölf Aufsätzen*, edited by Harro Segeberg, 51–101. Frankfurt am Main: Suhrkamp, 1987.

Bayerl, Günter, and Ulrich Troitzsch, eds. "Der 'Wasserprozeß' gegen Hoffmanns Stärkefabriken (1890)." In *Quellentexte zur Geschichte der Umwelt von der Antike bis heute*, 356–59. Göttingen: Muster-Schmidt, 1998.

Becker, Sabina. *Bürgerlicher Realismus: Literatur und Kultur im bürgerlichen Zeitalter 1848–1900*. Tübingen: A. Francke, 2003.

Begemann, Christian. "Figuren der Wiederkehr: Erinnerung, Tradition, Vererbung und andere Gespenster der Vergangenheit bei Theodor Storm." In *Wirklichkeit und Wahrnehmung: Neue Perspektiven auf Theodor Storm*, edited by Elisabeth Strowick and Ulrike Vedder, 13–37. Bern: Peter Lang, 2013.

———. *Die Welt der Zeichen: Stifter-Lektüren*. Weimar: J. B. Metzler, 1995.

Behrens, Christian. *Die Wassergesetzgebung im Herzogtum Braunschweig nach Bauernbefreiung und industrieller Revolution: Zur Genese des Wasserrechts im bürgerlichen Rechtsstaat*. Hamburg: Verlag Dr. Kovač, 2009.

Berendes, Jochen. *Ironie—Komik—Skepsis: Studien zum Werk Adalbert Stifters*. Tübingen: Niemeyer, 2009.

160 ♦ Bibliography

Berman, Russell. *The Rise of the Modern German Novel: Crisis and Charisma.* Cambridge, MA: Harvard University Press, 1986.

Berressem, Hanjo. "Ecology and Immanence." In *Handbook of Ecocriticism and Cultural Ecology,* edited by Hubert Zapf, 84–104. Berlin: Walter de Gruyter, 2016.

Blackbourn, David. *The Conquest of Nature: Water, Landscape, and the Making of Modern Germany.* New York: Norton, 2006.

Blasius, Rudolf, and Heinrich Beckurts. "Verunreinigung und Reinigung der Flüsse nach Untersuchungen des Wassers der Oker." *Deutsche Vierteljahrsschrift für öffentliche Gesundheitspflege* 27, no. 2 (1895): 337–60.

Block, Richard. "Stone Deaf: The Gentleness of Law in Stifter's *Brigitta.*" *Monatshefte* 90, no. 1 (1998): 17–33.

Blödorn, Andreas. "Doppelgänger, Geisterseher: Figuren der Spiegelung und der Wiederkehr bei Theodor Storm." *Schriften der Theodor-Storm-Gesellschaft* 66 (2017): 9–27.

Blumenberg, Hans. "Wirklichkeitsbegriff und Möglichkeit des Romans." In *Ästhetische und metaphorologische Schriften,* edited by Anselm Haverkamp, 47–73. Frankfurt am Main: Suhrkamp, 2001.

Böhme, Gernot. "Die Natur im Zeitalter ihrer technischen Reproduzierbarkeit." In *Natürlich Natur: Über Natur im Zeitalter ihrer technischen Reproduzierbarkeit,* 107–24. Frankfurt am Main: Suhrkamp, 1992.

Böse, Margot, Jürgen Ehlers, and Frank Lehmkuhl. *Deutschlands Norden: Vom Erdaltertum zur Gegenwart.* Berlin: Springer, 2018.

Brecht, Bertolt. *Werke. Große kommentierte Berliner und Frankfurter Ausgabe.* Edited by Werner Hecht. Frankfurt am Main: Suhrkamp, 1988–2000.

Briegleb, Klaus. "Fontanes Elementargeist: Die Preußin Melusine. Eine Vorstudie zum *Stechlin.*" In *Theodor Fontane am Ende des Jahrhunderts,* 109–22. Würzburg: Königshausen & Neumann, 2000.

Brinkmann, Richard. *Theodor Fontane: Über die Verbindlichkeit des Unverbindlichen.* Munich: R. Piper, 1967.

Brude-Firnau, Gisela. "Beredtes Schweigen: Nichtverbalisierte Obrigkeitskritik in Theodor Fontanes *Stechlin.*" *Monatshefte* 77, no. 4 (1985): 460–68.

Brüggemeier, Franz-Josef. *Das unendliche Meer der Lüfte: Luftverschmutzung, Industrialisierung und Risikodebatten im 19. Jahrhundert.* Essen: Klartext, 1996.

———. *Schranken der Natur: Umwelt, Gesellschaft, Experimente 1750 bis heute.* Essen: Klartext, 2014.

Brüggemeier, Franz-Josef, Mark Cioc, and Thomas Zeller. "Introduction." In *How Green Were the Nazis? Nature, Environment, and Nation in the Third Reich,* 1–17. Athens: Ohio University Press, 2005.

Brümmer, Franz. "Schnezler, August." In *Allgemeine Deutsche Biographie,* vol. 32, 173–74. Leipzig: Duncker und Humblot, 1891.

Buell, Lawrence. *The Environmental Imagination: Thoreau, Nature Writing, and the Formation of American Culture*. Cambridge, MA: Belknap Press of Harvard University Press, 1995.

————. *The Future of Environmental Criticism: Environmental Crisis and Literary Imagination*. Malden, MA: Blackwell, 2005.

————. *Writing for an Endangered World: Literature, Culture, and Environment in the U.S. and Beyond*. Cambridge, MA: Belknap Press of Harvard University Press, 2001.

Burroughs, John. "Real and Sham Natural History." *The Atlantic Monthly*, March 1903.

Castree, Noel. "Socializing Nature: Theory, Practice, and Politics." In *Social Nature: Theory, Practice, and Politics*, edited by Noel Castree and Bruce Braun, 1–21. Malden, MA: Blackwell, 2001.

Chakrabarty, Dipesh. *The Climate of History in a Planetary Age*. Chicago, IL: University of Chicago Press, 2021.

Crist, Eileen. "On the Poverty of Our Nomenclature." In *Anthropocene or Capitalocene?: Nature, History, and the Crisis of Capitalism*, edited by Jason Moore, 14–33. Oakland, CA: PM Press, 2016.

Cronon, William. "Foreword to the Paperback Edition." In *Uncommon Ground: Rethinking the Human Place in Nature*, 19–22. New York: W. W. Norton & Co, 1996.

————. "The Trouble with Wilderness, or, Getting Back to the Wrong Nature." In *Uncommon Ground: Rethinking the Human Place in Nature*, 69–90. New York: W. W. Norton & Co, 1996.

Crutzen, Paul J., and Eugene F Stoermer. "The 'Anthropocene.'" *IGBP Newsletter* 41 (2000): 17–18.

Darwin, Charles. *On the Origin of Species by Means of Natural Selection, or, The Preservation of Favoured Races in the Struggle for Life*. London: Penguin, 2009.

Demandt, Christian, and Philipp Theisohn, eds. *Storm-Handbuch: Leben—Werk—Wirkung*. Stuttgart: J. B. Metzler, 2017.

Demeritt, David. "Being Constructive About Nature." In *Social Nature: Theory, Practice, and Politics*, edited by Noel Castree and Bruce Braun, 22–40. Malden, MA: Blackwell, 2001.

Demetz, Peter. *Formen des Realismus: Theodor Fontane*. Munich: Carl Hanser, 1964.

Denkler, Horst. "Die Antwort literarischer Phantasie auf eine der 'größeren Fragen der Zeit': Zu Wilhelm Raabes 'Sommerferienheft' Pfisters Mühle." In *Neues über Wilhelm Raabe: Zehn Annäherungsversuche an einen verkannten Schriftsteller*, 81–102. Tübingen: Max Niemeyer, 1988.

Der Drachenfels: Ein Sagenhafter Ort. "Drachenfels." Accessed December 23, 2020. https://www.der-drachenfels.de/der-drachenfels.

Detering, Heinrich. "Ökologische Krise und ästhetische Innovation im Werk Wilhelm Raabes." *Jahrbuch der Raabe-Gesellschaft* 33 (1992): 1–27.

Dillard, Annie. *Pilgrim at Tinker Creek*. New York: HarperCollins, 2007.

162 ♦ BIBLIOGRAPHY

Dittmann, Ulrich. "Brigitta und kein Ende. Kommentierte Randbemerkungen." *Jahrbuch des Adalbert-Stifter-Instituts* 3 (1996): 24–28.

Doppler, Alfred. "Schrecklich schöne Welt? Stifters fragwürdige Analogie von Natur- und Sittengesetz." In *Adalbert Stifters schrecklich schöne Welt (Eine Koproduktion von Germanistische Mitteilungen und Jahrbuch des Adalbert-Stifter Instituts)*, 9–15. Linz: Adalbert-Stifter-Institut, 1994.

Douglas, Mary. *Purity and Danger: An Analysis of the Concepts of Pollution and Taboo*. London and New York: Routledge, 1992.

Downing, Eric. *Double Exposures: Repetition and Realism in Nineteenth-Century German Fiction*. Stanford, CA: Stanford University Press, 2000.

Drachenfelsbahn Königswinter. "Geschichte: Die lange Historie der ältesten Zahnradbahn Deutschlands—der Drachenfelsbahn." Accessed September 9, 2024. https://www.drachenfelsbahn.de/bahngeschichte.

Eisele, Ulf. *Realismus und Ideologie: Zur Kritik der literarischen Theorie nach 1848 am Beispiel des "Deutschen Museums."* Stuttgart: J. B. Metzler, 1976.

Fairley, Barker. *Wilhelm Raabe: An Introduction to His Novels*. Oxford: Clarendon Press, 1961.

Fehse, Wilhelm. *Wilhelm Raabe: Sein Leben und seine Werke*. Braunschweig: Vieweg, 1937.

Fontane, Theodor. *Große Brandenburger Ausgabe*. Edited by Gotthard Erler, Gabriele Radecke, and Heinrich Detering. 44 vols. in 12 parts. Berlin: Aufbau Verlag, 1994–.

———. *On Tangled Paths*. Translated by Peter James Bowman. London: Penguin, 2013.

———. *Sämtliche Werke*. Edited by Edgar Groß. 30 vols. Munich: Nymphenburger Verlagshandlung, 1963.

———. *The Stechlin*. Rochester, NY: Camden House, 1995.

———. *Werke, Schriften und Briefe*. Edited by Walter Keitel and Helmuth Nürnberger. 22 vols. in 4 parts. Munich: Carl Hanser, 1975.

Freud, Sigmund. "Das Unheimliche." In *Gesammelte Werke*, edited by Anna Freud, vol. 12, 227–68. London: Imago, 1947.

Freytag, Gustav. *Soll und Haben*. 37th ed. Leipzig: S. Hirzel, 1891.

Furst, Lilian R. *All Is True: The Claims and Strategies of Realist Fiction*. Durham, NC: Duke University Press, 1995.

Garrard, Greg. *Ecocriticism*. 2nd ed. Abingdon: Routledge, 2012.

Geisler, Eberhard. "Abschied vom Herzensmuseum: Die Auflösung des poetischen Realismus in Wilhelm Raabes 'Die Akten des Vogelsangs.'" In *Wilhelm Raabe: Studien zu seinem Leben und Werk; Aus Anlaß des 150. Geburtstages (1831–1981)*, edited by Leo A. Lensing and Hans-Werner Peter, 365–80. Braunschweig: pp-Verlag, 1981.

Gelderloos, Carl. *Biological Modernism: The New Human in Weimar Culture*. Evanston, IL: Northwestern University Press, 2020.

Ghosh, Amitav. *The Great Derangement: Climate Change and the Unthinkable*. Gurgaon: Penguin, 2016.

BIBLIOGRAPHY ♦ 163

Glaser, Horst Albert. *Die Restauration des Schönen: Stifters "Nachsommer."* Stuttgart: J. B. Metzler, 1965.

Glotfelty, Cheryll. "Introduction: Literary Studies in an Age of Environmental Crisis." In *The Ecocriticism Reader: Landmarks in Literary Ecology*, xv–xxxvii. Athens: University of Georgia Press, 1996.

Goethe, Johann Wolfgang von. *Werke*. Edited by Erich Trunz. 14 vols. Hamburg: Christian Wegner, 1964.

Göttsche, Dirk, Axel Dunker, and Gabriele Dürbeck, eds. *Handbuch Postkolonialismus und Literatur*. Stuttgart: J. B. Metzler, 2017.

Gottwald, Herwig. "Natur und Kultur: Wildnis, Wald und Park in Stifters *Mappe*-Dichtungen." In *Waldbilder: Beiträge zum interdisziplinären Kolloquium "Da ist Wald und Wald und Wald" (Adalbert Stifter)*, edited by Walter Hettche and Hubert Merkel, 90–107. Munich: Iudicum, 2000.

Grell, Erik J. "Homoerotic Travel, Classical Bildung, and Liberal Allegory in Adalbert Stifter's *Brigitta* (1844–47)." *The German Quarterly* 88, no. 4 (2015): 514–35.

Groves, Jason. "Stifter's Stones." In *A Companion to the Works of Adalbert Stifter*, edited by Sean Ireton, 227–49. Rochester, NY: Camden House, 2025.

———. *The Geological Unconscious: German Literature and the Mineral Imaginary*. New York: Fordham University Press, 2020.

Günther, Vincent. *Das Symbol im erzählerischen Werk Fontanes*. Bonn: Bouvier, 1967.

Hahn, Hans-Werner. *Die industrielle Revolution in Deutschland*. 3rd ed. Munich: Oldenbourg Wissenschaftsverlag, 2011.

Hahn, Walther. "Zu Stifters Konzept der Schönheit: 'Brigitta.'" *VASILO* 19, no. 3/4 (1970): 149–59.

Hamilton, Clive. "The Theodicy of the 'Good Anthropocene.'" *Environmental Humanities* 7 (2015): 233–38.

Harnischfeger, Johannes. "Modernisierung und Teufelspakt: Die Funktion des Dämonischen in Theodor Storms 'Schimmelreiter.'" *Schriften der Theodor-Storm-Gesellschaft* 49 (2000): 23–44.

Harvey, David. *Justice, Nature, and the Geography of Difference*. Cambridge, MA: Blackwell, 1996.

Haußmann, Walter. "Adalbert Stifter, Brigitta." *Der Deutschunterricht: Beiträge zu seiner Praxis und wissenschaftlicher Grundlegung* 3, no. 2 (1951): 30–48.

Heidegger, Martin. "The Question Concerning Technology." In *Basic Writings*, edited by David Krell, translated by William Lovitt, 2nd ed., 307–41. New York: HarperCollins, 1993.

Heimreich, M. Anton. *Nordfresische Chronik: Zum dritten Male mit den Zugaben des Verfassers und der Fortsetzung seines Sohnes, Heinrich Heimreich, auch einigen andern zur nordfresischen Geschichte gehörigen Nachrichten vermehrt*. Edited by Niels Falck. Tondern: Forchhammer, 1819.

164 ♦ Bibliography

Heise, Ursula K. *Sense of Place and Sense of Planet: The Environmental Imagination of the Global.* Oxford: Oxford University Press, 2008.

Helfer, Martha. "Natural Anti-Semitism: Stifter's Abdias." *Deutsche Vierteljahrsschrift Für Literaturwissenschaft und Geistesgeschichte* 78, no. 2 (2004): 261–86.

Helmers, Hermann. "Raabe als Kritiker von Umweltzerstörung. Das Gedicht 'Einst kommt die Stunde' in der Novelle 'Pfisters Mühle.'" *Literatur für Leser* 87, no. 3 (1987): 199–211.

Henning, Friedrich-Wilhelm. *Die Industrialisierung in Deutschland 1800–1914.* Paderborn: Ferdinand Schöningh, 1973.

Hermand, Jost. "Hauke Haien: Kritik oder Ideal des gründerzeitlichen Übermenschen." *Wirkendes Wort* 15 (1965): 40–50.

Hertling, Gunter. "Der Mensch und 'seine' Tiere: Versäumte Symbiose, versäumte Bildung. Zu Adalbert Stifters Abdias." *Modern Austrian Literature: Journal of the International Arthur Schnitzler Research Association* 18, no. 1 (1985): 1–26.

Hippe. "Letter to Käthe Fehse," November 19, 1948. G IX 32 : 36 # 14. Stadtarchiv Braunschweig.

Hofman, Alois. "Die Tierseele bei Adalbert Stifter." *VASILO* 13, no. 1/2 (1964): 6–15.

Hohendahl, Peter Uwe. *Literarische Kultur im Zeitalter des Liberalismus 1830–1870.* Munich: C. H. Beck, 1985.

———. "Theodor Fontane und der Standesroman: Konvention und Tendenz im Stechlin." In *Legitimationskrisen des deutschen Adels 1200–1900,* edited by Peter U. Hohendahl and Paul M. Lützeler, 263–83. Stuttgart: J. B. Metzler, 1979.

Holub, Robert C. *Reflections of Realism: Paradox, Norm, and Ideology in Nineteenth-Century German Prose.* Detroit, MI: Wayne State University Press, 1991.

Horkheimer, Max, and Theodor W. Adorno. *Dialectic of Enlightenment: Philosophical Fragments.* Translated by Edmund Jephcott. Stanford, CA: Stanford University Press, 2002.

Hornsey, Ian. *A History of Beer and Brewing.* Cambridge: Royal Society of Chemistry, 2003.

Howe, Patricia. "Faces and Fortunes: Ugly Heroines in Stifter's *Brigitta,* Fontane's *Schach von Wuthenow* and Saar's *Sappho.*" *German Life and Letters* 44, no. 5 (1991): 426–42.

Huck, Andreas. "'Da ist nichts oberflächlich hingeworfen …': Zu Genese und Funktion des Aloe-Motivs im Stechlin." *Fontane-Blätter* 88 (2009): 154–59.

Hunter-Lougheed, Rosemarie. "Adalbert Stifter: Brigitta (1844/47)." In *Romane und Erzählungen zwischen Romantik und Realismus: Neue Interpretationen,* edited by Paul M. Lützeler, 354–85. Stuttgart: Philipp Reclam jun., 1983.

Ireton, Sean. "Between Dirty and Disruptive Nature: Adalbert Stifter in the Context of Nineteenth-Century American Environmental Literature." *Colloquia Germanica* 44, no. 2 (2011): 149–71.

—————. "Geology, Mountaineering, and Self-Formation in Adalbert Stifter's *Der Nachsommer.*" In *Heights of Reflection: Mountains in the German Imagination from the Middle Ages to the Twenty-First Century*, 193–209. Rochester, NY: Camden House, 2013.

Irmscher, Hans Dietrich. *Adalbert Stifter: Wirklichkeitserfahrung und gegenständliche Darstellung.* Munich: Wilhelm Fink, 1971.

Jackson, David. "'Sie können Ihren eigenen Augen doch nicht mißtrauen': Noch einmal zum zweiten Rahmenerzähler in Theodor Storms *Der Schimmelreiter.*" *Schriften der Theodor-Storm-Gesellschaft* 64 (2015): 53–73.

Jolles, Charlotte. "Weltstadt—Verlorene Nachbarschaft: Berlin-Bilder Raabes und Fontanes." *Jahrbuch der Raabe-Gesellschaft* 29 (1988): 52–75.

Jurisch, Konrad. *Die Verunreinigung der Gewässer: Eine Denkschrift.* Berlin: R. Gaertner's Verlagsbuchhandlung, 1890.

Kaiser, Gerhard. "Der Totenfluß als Industriekloake: Über den Zusammenhang von Ökologie, Ökonomie und Phantasie in 'Pfisters Mühle' von Wilhelm Raabe." In *Mutter Natur und die Dampfmaschine: Ein literarischer Mythos im Rückbezug auf Antike und Christentum*, 81–107. Freiburg im Breisgau: Rombach, 1991.

Kaiser, Nancy. "Reading Raabe's Realism: *Die Akten des Vogelsangs.*" *Germanic Review* 59, no. 1 (1984): 2–9.

Keller, Gottfried. *Sämtliche Werke und Ausgewählte Briefe.* Edited by Clemens Heselhaus. 3 vols. Munich: Hanser, 1958.

Kern, Robert. "Ecocriticism: What Is It Good For?" *ISLE* 7, no. 1 (2000): 9–32.

Kluge, Thomas, and Engelbert Schramm. *Wassernöte: Umwelt- und Sozialgeschichte des Trinkwassers.* Aachen: Alano, 1986.

Koschorke, Albrecht. *Die Geschichte des Horizonts: Grenze und Grenzüberschreitung in literarischen Landschaftsbildern.* Frankfurt am Main: Suhrkamp, 1990.

Kristeva, Julia. *Powers of Horror: An Essay on Abjection.* Translated by Leon S. Roudiez. New York: Columbia University Press, 1982.

Krobb, Florian. *Erkundungen im Überseeischen: Wilhelm Raabe und die Füllung der Welt.* Würzburg: Königshausen & Neumann, 2009.

Laage, Karl E., ed. *Theodor Storm—Gottfried Keller: Briefwechsel.* Berlin: Erich Schmidt, 1992.

Lachinger, Johann. "Adalbert Stifters 'Abdias': Eine Interpretation." *VASILO* 18, no. 3/4 (1969): 97–114.

"leben." *Deutsches Wörterbuch von Jacob Grimm und Wilhelm Grimm*, 33 vols. (Leipzig: Hirzel, 1853–1971), vol. 12, www.woerterbuchnetz.de/DWB/leben.

Lee, Robert. "'Relative Backwardness' and Long-Run Development: Economic, Demographic and Social Changes." In *Nineteenth-Century Germany: Politics, Culture and Society 1780–1918*, edited by John Breuilly, 66–95. London: Edward Arnold, 2001.

Lefebvre, Henri. *The Production of Space.* Translated by Donald Nicholson-Smith. Malden, MA: Blackwell, 1991.

166 ♦ BIBLIOGRAPHY

Leopold, Aldo. *A Sand County Almanac, and Sketches from Here and There.* Oxford: Oxford UP, 1968.

Leucht, Robert. "Ordnung, Bildung, Kunsthandwerk. Die Pluralität utopischer Modelle in Adalbert Stifters *Der Nachsommer.*" In *Figuren der Übertragung: Adalbert Stifter und das Wissen seiner Zeit,* edited by Michael Gamper and Karl Wagner, 289–306. Zürich: Chronos, 2009.

Lindow, John. *Norse Mythology: A Guide to the Gods, Heroes, Rituals, and Beliefs.* Oxford: Oxford University Press, 2002.

Long, William J. *A Little Brother to the Bear.* Cambridge: Ginn & Company, 1903.

Love, Glen. *Practical Ecocriticism: Literature, Biology, and the Environment.* Charlottesville: University of Virginia Press, 2003.

Lukács, Georg. *German Realists in the Nineteenth Century.* Translated by Jeremy Gaines and Paul Keast. Cambridge, MA: The MIT Press, 1993.

Lyon, John B. *Out of Place: German Realism, Displacement, and Modernity.* New York: Bloomsbury Academic, 2013.

MacCormack, Carol. "Nature, Culture and Gender: A Critique." In *Nature, Culture and Gender,* edited by Carol MacCormack and Marilyn Strathern, 1–24. Cambridge: Cambridge University Press, 1980.

Mackenzie, Louisa, and Stephanie Posthumus. "Reading Latour Outside: A Response to the Estok–Robisch Controversy." *ISLE* 20, no. 4 (2013): 757–77.

Macleod, Catriona. *Fugitive Objects: Sculpture and Literature in the German Nineteenth Century.* Evanston, IL: Northwestern University Press, 2014.

Malakaj, Ervin. "Senescence and Fontane's *Der Stechlin.*" In *Fontane in the Twenty-First Century,* edited by John B. Lyon and Brian Tucker, 232–45. Rochester, NY: Camden House, 2019.

Marchesi, Greta. "Justus von Liebig Makes the World: Soil Properties and Social Change in the Nineteenth Century." *Environmental Humanities* 12, no. 1 (2020): 205–26.

Martini, Fritz. *Deutsche Literatur im bürgerlichen Realismus, 1848–1898.* 4th ed. Stuttgart: Metzler, 1981.

Marx, Karl, and Friedrich Engels. *Capital: A Critique of Political Economy.* New York: Penguin, 1990.

———. *The German Ideology.* Edited by C. J. Arthur. London: Lawrence and Wishart, 1974.

Marx, Leo. *The Machine in the Garden: Technology and the Pastoral Ideal in America.* Oxford: Oxford University Press, 2000.

McKibben, Bill. *The End of Nature.* 2nd ed. London: Bloomsbury, 2003.

Melville, Herman. *Moby-Dick.* New York: W. W. Norton & Co., 2002.

Menke, Bettine. "The Figure of Melusine in Fontane's Texts: Images, Digressions, and Lacunae." *The Germanic Review* 79, no. 1 (2004): 41–67.

Merchant, Carolyn. "Reinventing Eden: Western Culture as a Recovery Narrative." In *Uncommon Ground: Rethinking the Human Place in Nature,* edited by William Cronon, 2nd ed., 132–59. New York: W. W. Norton & Co., 1996.

Meyer, Kelly Middleton. "'Sohn, Abdias, gehe nun in die Welt ...': Oedipalization, Gender Construction, and the Desire to Accumulate in Adalbert Stifter's 'Abdias.'" *Modern Austrian Literature: Journal of the Modern Austrian Literature and Culture Association* 35, no. 1/2 (2002): 1–21.

Minden, Michael. "Stifter and the Postmodern Sublime." In *History, Value, Text: Essays on Adalbert Stifter; Londoner Symposium 2003*, 9–21. Linz: Adalbert-Stifter-Institut, 2006.

Moore, Jason W. *Capitalism in the Web of Life: Ecology and the Accumulation of Capital*. London: Verso, 2015.

Morton, Timothy. *The Ecological Thought*. Cambridge, MA: Harvard University Press, 2010.

———. *Ecology Without Nature: Rethinking Environmental Aesthetics*. Cambridge, MA: Harvard University Press, 2007.

Müller, Karla. *Schloßgeschichten: Eine Studie zum Romanwerk Theodor Fontanes*. Munich: Wilhelm Fink, 1986.

Müller-Seidel, Walter. "Fontane: Der Stechlin." In *Der deutsche Roman: Vom Barock bis zur Gegenwart*, edited by Benno von Wiese, 2 vols., vol. 2, 146–89. Düsseldorf: August Bagel, 1963.

Murphy, Patrick D. *Ecocritical Explorations in Literary and Cultural Studies: Fences, Boundaries, and Fields*. Lanham, MD: Lexington Books, 2009.

Nash, Roderick Frazier. *Wilderness and the American Mind*. 5th ed. New Haven, CT: Yale University Press, 2014.

Nipperdey, Thomas. *Deutsche Geschichte, 1800–1866: Bürgerwelt und starker Staat*. Munich: C. H. Beck, 2013.

———. *Deutsche Geschichte, 1866–1918*. 2 vols. Munich: C. H. Beck, 2013.

O'Connor, James. *Natural Causes: Essays in Ecological Marxism*. New York: The Guilford Press, 1998.

Ohl, Hubert. *Bild und Wirklichkeit: Studien zur Romankunst Raabes und Fontanes*. Heidelberg: Lothar Stiehm, 1968.

———. "Melusine als Mythos bei Theodor Fontane." In *Mythos und Mythologie in der Literatur des 19. Jahrhunderts*, edited by Helmut Koopman, 289–305. Frankfurt am Main: Vittorio Klostermann, 1979.

Ort, Claus-Michael. "Was ist Realismus?" In *Realismus: Epoche—Autoren—Werke*, edited by Christian Begemann, 11–26. Darmstadt: Wissenschaftliche Buchgesellschaft, 2007.

Ortner, Sherry. "Is Female to Male as Nature Is to Culture?" In *Women, Culture, and Society*, edited by Michelle Zimbalist Rosaldo and Louise Lamphere, 1–24. Stanford, CA: Stanford University Press, 1974.

Osterkamp, Barbara. *Arbeit und Identität: Studien zur Erzählkunst des bürgerlichen Realismus*. Würzburg: Königshausen & Neumann, 1983.

Penrice, Amy. "Fractured Symbolism: Der Stechlin and The Golden Bowl." *Comparative Literature* 43, no. 4 (1991): 346–69.

Phillips, Alexander Robert. "Adalbert Stifter's Alternative Anthropocene: Reimagining Social Nature in *Brigitta* and *Abdias*." In *German Ecocriticism in the Anthropocene*, edited by Caroline Schaumann and Heather Sullivan, 65–85. New York: Palgrave Macmillan, 2017.

168 ♦ BIBLIOGRAPHY

———. "Cheerful Terror: Stifter and the Aesthetics of Atmosphere." In *A Companion to the Works of Adalbert Stifter*, edited by Sean Ireton, 273–93. Rochester, NY: Camden House, 2025.

Plumpe, Gerhard. "Einleitung." In *Bürgerlicher Realismus und Gründerzeit: 1848–1890*, vol. 6, edited by Edward McInnes and Gerhard Plumpe, 17–83. Munich: Carl Hanser, 1996.

Plumwood, Val. *Feminism and the Mastery of Nature*. London: Routledge, 1993.

Pongs, Hermann. *Wilhelm Raabe: Leben und Werk*. Heidelberg: Quelle & Meyer, 1958.

Popp, Ludwig. "'Pfisters Mühle.' Schlüsselroman zu einem Abwasserprozeß." *Städtehygiene* 2 (1959): 21–25.

Prutz, Robert. *Die deutsche Literatur der Gegenwart. 1848 bis 1858*. 2nd ed. Leipzig: Ernst Julius Günther, 1870.

Raabe, Wilhelm. "Der Altstadtmarkt zu Braunschweig." *Freya: Illustrirte Blätter für die gebildete Welt* 6 (1866): 149.

———. "Die Akten des Vogelsangs," 1895 1893. Nachlass Wilhelm Raabe, Schriftsteller (1831–1910), H III 10 : 10. Stadtarchiv Braunschweig.

———. "Letter to Margarethe Raabe," January 17, 1891. Nachlass Wilhelm Raabe, Schriftsteller (1831–1910). H III 10 : 2. Stadtarchiv Braunschweig.

———. *Novels*. Edited by Volkmar Sander. New York: Continuum, 1983.

———. *Sämtliche Werke: Braunschweiger Ausgabe*. Edited by Karl Hoppe. 26 vols. Göttingen: Vandenhoek und Ruprecht, 1966–94.

———. *The Birdsong Papers*. Translated by Michael Ritterson. London: Modern Humanities Research Association, 2013.

Renz, Christine. *Geglückte Rede: Zu Erzählstrukturen in Theodor Fontanes "Effi Briest," "Frau Jenny Treibel" und "Der Stechlin."* Munich: Wilhelm Fink, 1999.

Rigby, Kate. *Dancing with Disaster: Environmental Histories, Narratives, and Ethics for Perilous Times*. Charlottesville: University of Virginia Press, 2015.

Rigby, Kate, and Axel Goodbody. "Introduction." In *Ecocritical Theory: New European Approaches*, 1–14. Charlottesville: University of Virginia Press, 2011.

Rindisbacher, Hans. *The Smell of Books: A Cultural-Historical Study of Olfactory Perception in Literature*. Ann Arbor: The University of Michigan Press, 1992.

Riordan, Colin. "German Literature, Nature and Modernity before 1914." In *Nature in Literary and Cultural Studies: Transatlantic Conversations on Ecocriticism*, edited by Catrin Gersdorf and Sylvia Mayer, 313–30. Amsterdam: Rodopi, 2006.

Robisch, S. K. "Ecological Narrative and Nature Writing." In *A Companion to American Fiction, 1865–1914*, edited by Robert Paul Lamb and G.R. Thompson, 187–200. Malden, MA: Blackwell, 2005.

———. "The Woodshed: A Response to 'Ecocriticism and Ecophobia.'" *ISLE* 16, no. 4 (2009): 697–708.

Roebling, Irmgard. "'Von Menschentragik und wildem Naturgeheimnis': Die Thematisierung von Natur und Weiblichkeit in 'Der Schimmelreiter.'" In *Stormlektüren: Festschrift für Karl Ernst Laage zum 80. Geburtstag*, edited by Gerd Eversberg, David Jackson, and Eckart Pastor, 183–214. Würzburg: Königshausen & Neumann, 2000.

Roebling, Irmgard. *Wilhelm Raabes doppelte Buchführung: Paradigma einer Spaltung*. Tübingen: Max Niemeyer, 1988.

Rohse, Eberhard. "'Transzendentale Menschenkunde' im Zeichen des Affen: Raabes literarische Antwort auf die Darwinismusdebatte des 19. Jahrhunderts." *Jahrbuch der Raabe-Gesellschaft* 29 (1988), 168–210.

Rollins, William. *A Greener Vision of Home: Cultural Politics and Environmental Reform in the German Heimatschutz Movement, 1904–1918*. Ann Arbor: University of Michigan Press, 1997.

Rosenbaum, Lars. "Absence and Omnipresence: On the Significance of Waste in Stifter's *Der Nachsommer*." Translated by Sean Ireton. In *A Companion to the Works of Adalbert Stifter*, edited by Sean Ireton, 200–224. Rochester, NY: Camden House, 2025.

Rothenberg, Jürgen. "Gräfin Melusine: Fontanes 'Stechlin' als politischer Roman." *Text & Kontext* 4, no. 3 (1976): 21–56.

Rudorff, Ernst. "Über das Verhältnis des modernen Lebens zur Natur." *Preußische Jahrbücher* 45 (1880): 261–76.

Sagarra, Eda. *Theodor Fontane: "Der Stechlin."* Munich: Wilhelm Fink, 1986.

Said, Edward. *Culture and Imperialism*. New York: Vintage Books, 1994.

Sammons, Jeffrey. *The Shifting Fortunes of Wilhelm Raabe: A History of Criticism as a Cautionary Tale*. Columbia, SC: Camden House, 1992.

———. *Wilhelm Raabe: The Fiction of the Alternative Community*. Princeton, NJ: Princeton University Press, 1987.

Schäder, Christian. "Münchner Brauindustrie 1871–1945: Die wirtschaftsge-schichtliche Entwicklung eines Industriezweiges." PhD diss., Universität Regensburg, 1999.

Schäfer, Renate. "Fontanes Melusine-Motiv." *Euphorion: Zeitschrift für Literaturgeschichte* 56 (1962): 69–104.

Schaumann, Caroline. *Peak Pursuits: The Emergence of Mountaineering in the Nineteenth Century*. New Haven, CT: Yale University Press, 2020.

Scherpe, Klaus. "Rettung der Kunst im Widerspruch von bürgerlicher Humanität und bourgeoiser Wirklichkeit: Theodor Fontanes vier-facher Roman 'Der Stechlin.'" In *Poesie der Demokratie: Literarische Widersprüche zur deutschen Wirklichkeit vom 18. zum 20. Jahrhundert*, 227–67. Cologne: Pahl Rugenstein, 1980.

Scheuren, Elmar. "The Rhine as a Symbol: Aspects, Meanings and Functionalization of a Memory Landscape." In *The Rhine: National Tensions, Romantic Visions*, edited by Manfred Beller and Joep Leerssen, 133–67. Leiden: Brill, 2017.

Schmidt, Julian. "Neue Romane." *Die Grenzboten: Zeitschrift für Politik und Literatur* 19, no. 4 (1860): 481–92.

Schnell, Barbara. "RWE versucht, die Leute zu brechen." *Frankfurter Rundschau*, September 5, 2022. https://www.fr.de/wirtschaft/rwe-versucht-die-leute-zu-brechen-91768865.html.

Schonfield, Ernest. "Wirtschaftlicher Strukturwandel in *Der Stechlin*." In *Theodor Fontane: Dichter des Übergangs*, edited by Patricia Howe, 91–108. Würzburg: Königshausen & Neumann, 2013.

Schwarz, Anette. "Social Subjects and Tragic Legacies: The Uncanny in Theodor Storm's *Der Schimmelreiter*." *The Germanic Review* 73, no. 3 (1998): 251–66.

Scott, James. *Against the Grain: A Deep History of the Earliest States*. New Haven, CT: Yale University Press, 2017.

Sessions, George. "Reinventing Nature, …? A Response to Cronon's *Uncommon Ground*." *The Trumpeter* 13, no. 1 (1996): n.p.

Soper, Kate. *What Is Nature?: Culture, Politics and the Non-Human*. Oxford: Blackwell, 1995.

Sporn, Thomas. "Wilhelm Raabe: Ökologisch?" *Diskussion Deutsch* 12, no. 57 (1981): 56–63.

Stifter, Adalbert. *Brigitta: With Abdias, Limestone, and The Forest Path*. London and Chester Springs, PA: Angel Books; Dufour Editions, 1990.

———. *Gesammelte Werke*. Edited by Max Stefl. 6 vols. Frankfurt am Main: Insel, 1959.

———. *Indian Summer*. Translated by Wendell W. Frye. 3rd ed. Bern and New York: Lang, 2006.

———. *Motley Stones*. Translated by Isabel Fargo Cole. New York: New York Review of Books, 2021.

———. *Sämmtliche Werke*. Edited by August Sauer, Franz Hüller, Kamill Eben, Gustav Wilhelm, et al. 19 vols. Prague: Calve; Reichenberg: Kraus, 1901–40; Graz: Stiasny, 1958–60.

———. *Werke und Briefe: Historisch-Kritische Gesamtausgabe*. Edited by Alfred Doppler, Wolfgang Frühwald, Hartmut Laufhütte, et al. 40 vols. in 10 parts. Stuttgart: Kohlhammer, 1978–.

Storm, Theodor. *Sämtliche Werke in vier Bänden*. Edited by Karl E. Laage. Frankfurt am Main: Deutscher Klassiker Verlag, 1988.

———. *The Rider on the White Horse and Selected Stories*. Translated by James Wright. New York: New York Review of Books, 2009.

Strowick, Elisabeth. *Gespenster des Realismus: Zur literarischen Wahrnehmung von Wirklichkeit*. Paderborn: Wilhelm Fink, 2019.

Sullivan, Heather. "Dirt Theory and Material Ecocriticism." *ISLE* 19, no. 3 (2012): 515–31.

———. "Dirty Traffic and the Dark Pastoral in the Anthropocene: Narrating Refugees, Deforestation, and Melting Ice." *Literatur für Leser* 37, no. 2 (2014): 83–97.

Sumner, David Thomas. "'That Could Happen': Nature Writing, the Nature Fakers, and a Rhetoric of Assent." *ISLE* 12, no. 2 (Summer 2005): 31–53.

Swales, Martin. *Epochenbuch Realismus: Romane und Erzählungen*. Berlin: Erich Schmidt, 1997.

Swales, Martin, and Erika Swales. *Adalbert Stifter: A Critical Study.* Cambridge: Cambridge University Press, 1984.

Tau, Max. *Landschafts- und Ortsdarstellung Theodor Fontanes.* Oldenburg: Schulzesche Hofbuchdruckerei, 1928.

Tausch, Harald. "Wasser auf Pfisters Mühle. Zu Raabes humoristischem Erinnern der Dinge." In *Die Dinge und die Zeichen: Dimensionen des Realistischen in der Erzählliteratur des 19. Jahrhunderts*, edited by Sabine Schneider and Barbara Hunfeld, 175–211. Würzburg: Königshausen & Neumann, 2008.

"The Anthropocene." International Union of Geological Sciences, March 20, 2024. https://www.iugs.org/_files/ugd/f1fc07_40d1a7ed58de458c9f 8f24de5e739663.pdf?index=true.

The Bible: Authorized King James Version. Oxford: Oxford University Press, 2008.

Thienemann, August. "'Pfisters Mühle.' Ein Kapitel aus der Geschichte der biologischen Wasseranalyse." *Verhandlungen des Naturhistorischen Vereins der preußischen Rheinlande und Westfalens* 82 (1925): 315–29.

———. "Wilhelm Raabe und die Abwasserbiologie." *Mitteilungen für die Gesellschaft der Freunde Wilhelm Raabes* 15 (1925): 124–31.

Thompson, Ernest Seton. *Wild Animals I Have Known.* New York: Charles Scribner & Sons, 1898.

Thums, Barbara. "Vom Umgang mit Abfällen, Resten, und lebendingen Dingen in Erzählungen Wilhelm Raabes." *Jahrbuch der Raabe-Gesellschaft* 48 (2007): 66–84.

Thuret, Marc. "Le charme discret de la mondialisation: Actualité du Stechlin." In *Identité(s) multiple(s)*, edited by Kerstin Hausbei and Alain Lattard, 221–30. Paris: Presses Sorbonnes Nouvelle, 2008.

Vaupel, Elisabeth. "Gewässerverschmutzung im Spiegel der schönen Literatur." *Chemie in unserer Zeit* 19 (1985): 77–85.

"verklettern." *Deutsches Wörterbuch von Jacob Grimm und Wilhelm Grimm*, 33 vols. (Leipzig: Hirzel, 1853–1971), vol. 25, www.woerterbuchnetz. de/DWB/verklettern.

Vischer, Friedrich Theodor. *Aesthetik, oder Wissenschaft des Schönen.* Stuttgart: Carl Mäckes, 1846.

Vogl, Joseph. "Telephon nach Java: Fontane." In *Realien des Realismus: Wissenschaft—Technik—Medien in Theodor Fontanes Erzählprosa*, edited by Stephan Braese and Anne-Kathrin Reulecke, 117–28. Berlin: Vorwerk 8, 2010.

Walker, John. *The Truth of Realism: A Reassessment of the German Novel 1830–1900.* London: Legenda, 2011.

Wanning, Berbeli. *Die Fiktionalität der Natur: Studien zum Naturbegriff in Erzähltexten der Romantik und des Realismus.* Berlin: Weidler, 2005.

Weber, Kurt. "'Au fond sind Bäume besser als Häuser.' Über Theodor Fontanes Naturdarstellung." *Fontane-Blätter* 64 (1997): 134–57.

White, Lynn. "The Historical Roots of Our Ecologic Crisis." In *The Ecocriticism Reader: Landmarks in Literary Ecology*, edited by Cheryll

172 ♦ Bibliography

Glotfelty and Harold Fromm, 3–14. Athens: University of Georgia Press, 1996.

White, Michael James. *Space in Theodor Fontane's Works: Theme and Poetic Function.* London: Modern Humanities Research Association, 2012.

White, Richard. "'Are You an Environmentalist or Do You Work for a Living?': Work and Nature." In *Uncommon Ground: Rethinking the Human Place in Nature,* edited by William Cronon, 2nd ed., 171–85. New York: W. W. Norton & Co., 1996.

Wiese, Benno von. "Adalbert Stifter: Brigitta." In *Die deutsche Novelle von Goethe bis Kafka: Interpretationen,* vol. 2, 127–48. Düsseldorf: August Bagel, 1956.

"Wildnis." In *Deutsches Wörterbuch von Jacob Grimm und Wilhelm Grimm,* 33 vols. (Leipzig: Hirzel, 1853–1971), vol. 30, www.woerterbuchnetz. de/DWB/wildnis.

Wilke, Sabine. "Pollution as Poetic Practice: Glimpses of Modernism in Wilhelm Raabe's *Pfisters Mühle.*" *Colloquia Germanica* 44, no. 2 (2011): 195–214.

Williams, Raymond. "Ideas of Nature." In *Culture and Materialism: Selected Essays,* 67–85. London: Verso, 1980.

———. *The Country and the City.* New York: Oxford University Press, 1973.

Winkler, Markus. "Die Ästhetik des Nützlichen in 'Pfisters Mühle': Problemgeschichtliche Überlegungen zu Wilhelm Raabes Erzählung." *Jahrbuch der Raabe-Gesellschaft* 38 (1997): 18–39.

Yusoff, Kathryn. *A Billion Black Anthropocenes or None.* Minneapolis: University of Minnesota Press, 2018.

Zalasiewicz, Jan, Mark Williams, Richard Fortey, Alan Smith, Tiffany L. Barry, Angela L. Coe, Paul R. Bown, et al. "Stratigraphy of the Anthropocene." *Philosophical Transactions: Mathematical, Physical and Engineering Sciences* 369, no. 1938 (2011): 1036–55.

Zemanek, Evi. "(Bad) Air and (Faulty) Inspiration: Elemental and Environmental Influences on Fontane." In *German Ecocriticism in the Anthropocene,* edited by Caroline Schaumann and Heather Sullivan, 129–45. New York: Palgrave Macmillan, 2017.

Zimmermann, Hans Dieter. "Was der Erzähler verschweigt: Zur politischen Konzeption von Der Stechlin." In *Theodor Fontane am Ende des Jahrhunderts: Internationales Symposium des Theodor-Fontane-Archivs zum 100. Todestag Theodor Fontanes, 13.-17. September 1998 in Potsdam,* edited by Hanna D. von Wolzogen, 129–42. Würzburg: Königshausen & Neumann, 2000.

Index

Abbey, Edward, 26, 42
Adorno, Theodor W., 64, 81–82,
  112–13
Allgemeines Landrecht (Prussia,
  1794), 11–12
Andersen, Hans Christian, 113, 140
Anthropocene, 31–32, 71, 129–30,
  133–34, 136, 138–41, 143–44,
  148, 151, 156–57
antisemitism, 29, 52–53
Arndt, Christiane, 85–86
Arrhenius, Svante, 11
Association for the Study of Literature
  and Environment (ASLE), 153–54
Atlantic Monthly (magazine), see
  Nature Fakers Debate
Attanucci, Timothy, 70
Auerbach, Erich, 7–8
Augsburger Allgemeine Zeitung, 48

Battle of Schleswig (1848), 115
Becker, Sabine, 5n10
beer brewing, 145
beet sugar industry, 29, 72–74, 75–76,
  79
Begemann, Christian, 61, 109
Berman, Russell, 45, 48
Blackbourn, David, 4–5, 117
Brecht, Bertolt, 10
Brinkmann, Richard, 132–33
Buddeus, Aurelius, 48
Buell, Lawrence, 53, 74, 79, 154
Bund Heimatschutz, 2–3. *See also*
  Rudorff, Ernst
Burroughs, John, *see* Nature Fakers
  Debate
Byron, George Gordon, Lord, 1

Canova, Antonio, 98

Chakrabarty, Dipesh, 138–39
climate change, *see* global warming
coal (fossil fuel), 67, 116, 129, 137–
  38, 157
Cronon, William, 43
Crutzen, Paul, 129
Customs Union, *see* Zollverein

Dampfkessel-Verordnung (1831),
  12
Danube River, 33–34, 48, 50, 135
Darwin, Charles, 99
Denkler, Horst, 73, 82n37
Detering, Heinrich, 89
Dickens, Charles, 7
Dillard, Annie, 26
Dittmann, Ulrich, 50
Doestoevsky, Fyodor, 9
Doppler, Alfred, 36–37
Douglas, Mary, 6
Downing, Eric, 7
Drachenfels, 1–2, 157

ecocriticism, 9, 26–28, 73–74, 153–54
Edict of Nantes (1685), 95
Eichendorff, Joseph von, 3
Eisele, Ulf, 22–23
Energiewende (Energy Turn), 157
environmentalism, 3, 5, 11, 17–20,
  28, 36, 42, 67, 74
Eurasian Steppe, 50–51. *See also*
  puszta

Fairley, Barker, 76–77, 82n37
Fehrbellin, Battle of, 135–36
Fehse, Wilhelm, 76, 87
Feuerbach, Ludwig, 15–16
Flaubert, Gustave, 9

174 ♦ INDEX

Fontane, Theodor, 4, 5–6, 7, 8n21, 11, 22, 28, 129; works by, *Irrungen, Wirrungen* (On Tangled Paths), 144; *Oceane von Parceval*, 140; *Stechlin, Der*, 4, 10, 24–25, 31–32, 65, 113, 129, 130–33, 134–35, 136–51, 156–57; "Unsere lyrische und epische Poesie seit 1848" (Our Lyric and Epic Poetry since 1848), 21, 23–24; *Wanderungen durch die Mark Brandenburg* (Wanderings through the March Brandenburg), 128–30, 135–36, 144, 151
Fouqué, Friedrich de la Motte, 113, 140
Freud, Sigmund, 33–34
Freytag, Gustav, 28–29
Friedrich II (Prussia), 129, 144
Friedrich, Caspar David, 33, 67
Furst, Lilian, 6

Gelderloos, Carl, 32n89
Ghosh, Amitav, 107, 119
global warming, 18, 22, 157
Glotfelty, Cheryll, 27
Goethe, Johann Wolfgang von; works by, *Faust* 106; "Prometheus," 61
Grenzboten, Die (journal), 22, 28
Groves, Jason, 53, 70

Haeckel, Ernst, 11, 99
Hamilton, Clive, 134
Harnischfeger, Johannes, 126
Harvey, David, 53–54
Hawthorne, Nathaniel, 147
Hegel, Georg Wilhelm Friedrich, 5, 22–23, 95
Heidegger, Martin, 16–17
Heimrich, M. Antoni, 103
Helfer, Martha, 53
Hermand, Jost, 105
Heukamp, Eckardt, 157
Heym, Georg, 32
Hoddis, Jakob van, 32
Holub, Robert, 6–7
Horkheimer, Max, 112–13

Humboldt, Alexander von, 60
Hunter-Lougheed, Rosemarie, 49

imperialism, 8–9, 29, 31–32, 64, 137–38, 143
Ireton, Sean, 50, 67, 70

Jade Bay, 107
Jurisch, Konrad, 19–20, 21

Kaiser, Gerhard, 80
Kaiser, Nancy, 94
Keller, Gottfried, 108, 124; works by, *Der grüne Heinrich* (Green Henry), 25
Kern, Robert, 74
Klopstock, Friedrich Gottlieb, 114
Klüger, Ruth, 52–53
Koschorke, Albrecht, 85
Kristeva, Julia, 109–10

Laach Lake, 1, 157
Leitha (river), 50
Leucht, Robert, 61n102
Leopold, Aldo, 25–26, 63
Liebig, Justus von, 48
Linum (Brandenburg), 129
Lisbon Earthquake (1755), 107, 131
Long, William J, *see* Nature Fakers Debate
Love, Glen, 18–19, 27, 154
Lukács, Georg, 30, 90, 102
Lunden (North Frisia), 103
Lützerath (North Rhine-Westphalia), 157–58
Lyon, John, 9, 92n63

Marchesi, Greta, 48
Martini, Fritz, 132
Marx, Karl, 9, 15–16, 67, 150, 154
Marx, Leo, 147–48
McKibben, Bill, 17–18
Melville, Herman, 25
Menzer Forest, 128–30, 151
Merchant, Carolyn, 46–47
Meyer, Kelly Middleton, 56
Moore, Jason, 4n8, 10

INDEX ♦ 175

Morton, Timothy, 58, 119
Müller, Karla, 139
Müller, Wilhelm, 3, 32
Murphy, Patrick, 27

Nash, Roderick, 42, 48–49
nature writing, 11, 25–27, 34, 152,
154. *See also* Nature Fakers Debate
National Socialism, 3, 77n12
Nature Fakers Debate, 25, 152–54

Ohl, Hubert, 133, 141n42, 142
Oker River, 72, 76
Osterkamp, Barbara, 45

pastoral, 16, 45–46, 147
peat (fuel), 116–17, 129, 151
Penrice, Amy, 142
Plauen Valley, 3, 21, 32
Pleistocene, 2, 135
Plumwood, Val, 56
pollution, 3, 4, 6–7, 19–20, 21, 30,
33–34, 73–77, 80, 81, 83, 89–91,
129, 130, 149–50, 155
Pongs, Hermann, 76–77
Popp, Ludwig, 77
puszta (Hungary), 37–38, 40–41,
42, 46, 48, 50–51. *See also* Great
Eurasian Steppe

Raabe, Gertrud, 76
Raabe, Margarethe, 72
Raabe, Wilhelm, 4, 5, 6, 7, 10–11,
12, 28, 31, 32, 71, 75–76,
95, 130, 136, 148, 155, 156;
environmentalist reception of,
73–74, 76–77, 90–91, 102; works
by, *Abu Telfan*, 79; *Akten des
Vogelsangs, Die* (The Birdsong
Papers), 30, 74–75, 91–102,
147, 155–56; *Altershausen*, 73;
Chronik der Sperlingsgasse, Die (The
Chronicle of Sparrow Lane), 73;
Pfisters Mühle (Pfister's Mill), 7, 10,
12, 30, 72–73, 74, 75–91, 101–2,
130, 143, 147, 155; *Stopfkuchen*
(Stuffcake / Tubby Schaumann), 94

railroads, 2, 4, 7, 15, 78, 97–98, 138,
145, 146–47, 157
"relative backwardness" (thesis), 8–9,
11
Revolution of 1848, 21–22, 24, 28,
63,
Rhine River, 1–2, 12–15, 17, 47,
157
Rigby, Kate, 106, 121, 125
Rindisbacher, Hans, 91
Riordan, Colin, 90–91
Robisch, S.K., 18n50, 154
Romanticism, 1, 22, 30, 39–40, 42,
45, 57, 87, 95, 154
Roosevelt, Theodor, 153
Rosenbaum, Lars, 63–64
Rudorff, Ernst, 2–6, 19, 21, 28, 32,
157

Said, Edward, 137
Sammons, Jeffrey, 7n19, 73–74,
83n37
Schäfer, Renate, 142
Schiller, Friedrich, 95
Schmidt, Julian, 22, 23, 28–29
Schnezler, Ferdinand Alexander,
86–88
Schonfield, Ernest, 144
Schwartz, Charles (illustrator), 26
Schwarz, Anette, 105, 107
Scott, James, 125
Seton, Ernest Thompson, *see* Nature
Fakers Debate
skyglow, 97. *See also* pollution
Siemens, Werner von, 143–44
smog, *see* pollution
Spindler, Johan Julius, 75n9. *See also*
Spindlersfeld
Spindlersfeld (factory), 147–48
Sporn, Thomas, 73
sprawl, urban and industrial, 3, 4, 6, 7,
16, 30, 32, 66, 71, 74, 91–92, 97,
100, 130, 146, 157
Stadler, Ernst, 32
Stechlin (lake), 4, 10, 31, 128, 130–
31, 134, 136–39, 140–42, 151,
156

176 ♦ INDEX

Stifter, Adalbert, 4, 5–6, 7, 8n21, 10–11, 23, 24, 28, 29–30, 32, 33–37, 70–71, 155, 156; works by, *Abdias*, 29, 34, 35, 36, 51–59, 71, 121, 143, 155; *Bunte Steine* (Motley Stones), 35–36, 39, 71, 133, 153, 155; *Brigitta*, 10, 29, 34, 36, 37–51, 52, 54, 55, 59, 61, 71, 155; *Nachsommer, Der* (Indian Summer), 24, 29, 34, 36, 45, 51, 59–71, 79, 112, 118, 155; "Staat, Der" (The State), 63; "Über Stand und Würde des Schriftstellers" ("On the Status and Worth of the Writer"), 24; "Winterbriefe aus Kirchschlag" (Winter Letters from Kirchschlag), 33–34; "Zur Psichologie der Tiere" (On the Psychology of Animals), 55

Stoermer, Eugene, 129

Storm, Theodor, 4, 5–6, 7, 10–11, 28, 32, 103, 105, 107, 108; works by, "Ostern" (poem), 114–15; *Schimmelreiter, Der* (The Rider on the White Horse) 4, 10, 30–31, 103–14, 115–27

Strowick, Elisabeth, 119–20

Sullivan, Heather, 6, 105

Tau, Max, 132

Tausch, Harald, 83n37

Tears of St. Lawrence (Perseid meteor shower), 96

telegraph, 4, 7, 31, 78, 130, 135–39, 152

Thienemann, August, 77

Torgau (POW Camp), 77n12

Turner, J.M.W., 1

Undine (mythical character), 113, 140

Vaupel, Elisabeth, 77

Vesuvius, 44, 49

Virchow, Rudolf, 99

Vischer, Friedrich Theodor, 5, 95

Walker, John, 9

Wasserprozesse (water trials), 12, 76

Watanabe-O'Kelly, Helen, 39, 58

Watt, James, 129, 143–44

Wattenmeer (Wadden Sea), 106–7, 117, 118, 123–24

Wenden, 76

White, Lynn, 16

White, Michael James, 146

White, Stewart Edward, 26

Wieland, Christoph Martin, 7, 78

Wiese, Benno von, 38n18, 49

Williams, Raymond, 9–10, 15

Winkler, Markus, 83n37

Wright, James, 124n50

Zollverein (German Customs Union), 8

Printed in the United States
by Baker & Taylor Publisher Services